IT HAPPENED TO ME

Series Editor: Arlene Hirschfelder

Books in the It Happened to Me series are designed for inquisitive teens digging for answers about certain illnesses, social issues, or lifestyle interests. Whether you are deep into your teen years or just entering them, these books are gold mines of up-to-date information, riveting teen views, and great visuals to help you figure out stuff. Besides special boxes highlighting singular facts, each book is enhanced with the latest reading lists, websites, and an index. Perfect for browsing, there are loads of expert information by acclaimed writers to help parents, guardians, and librarians understand teen illness, tough situations, and lifestyle choices.

1. *Epilepsy: The Ultimate Teen Guide,* by Kathlyn Gay and Sean McGarrahan, 2002.
2. *Stress Relief: The Ultimate Teen Guide,* by Mark Powell, 2002.
3. *Learning Disabilities: The Ultimate Teen Guide,* by Penny Hutchins Paquette and Cheryl Gerson Tuttle, 2003.
4. *Making Sexual Decisions: The Ultimate Teen Guide,* by L. Kris Gowen, 2003.
5. *Asthma: The Ultimate Teen Guide,* by Penny Hutchins Paquette, 2003.
6. *Cultural Diversity—Conflicts and Challenges: The Ultimate Teen Guide,* by Kathlyn Gay, 2003.
7. *Diabetes: The Ultimate Teen Guide,* by Katherine J. Moran, 2004.
8. *When Will I Stop Hurting? Teens, Loss, and Grief: The Ultimate Teen Guide to Dealing with Grief,* by Ed Myers, 2004.
9. *Volunteering: The Ultimate Teen Guide,* by Kathlyn Gay, 2004.
10. *Organ Transplants—A Survival Guide for the Entire Family: The Ultimate Teen Guide,* by Tina P. Schwartz, 2005.
11. *Medications: The Ultimate Teen Guide,* by Cheryl Gerson Tuttle, 2005.
12. *Image and Identity—Becoming the Person You Are: The Ultimate Teen Guide,* by L. Kris Gowen and Molly C. McKenna, 2005.
13. *Apprenticeship: The Ultimate Teen Guide,* by Penny Hutchins Paquette, 2005.
14. *Cystic Fibrosis: The Ultimate Teen Guide,* by Melanie Ann Apel, 2006.
15. *Religion and Spirituality in America: The Ultimate Teen Guide,* by Kathlyn Gay, 2006.
16. *Gender Identity: The Ultimate Teen Guide,* by Cynthia L. Winfield, 2007.

BULLYING

THE ULTIMATE TEEN GUIDE

MATHANGI SUBRAMANIAN

IT HAPPENED TO ME, NO. 38

ROWMAN & LITTLEFIELD
Lanham • Boulder • New York • Toronto • Plymouth, UK

Published by Rowman & Littlefield
4501 Forbes Boulevard, Suite 200, Lanham, Maryland 20706
www.rowman.com

10 Thornbury Road, Plymouth PL6 7PP, United Kingdom

British Library Cataloguing in Publication Information Available

Library of Congress Cataloging-in-Publication Data

Subramanian, Mathangi, 1980–
  Bullying : the ultimate teen guide / Mathangi Subramanian.
    pages cm. — (It happened to me ; No. 38)
  Includes bibliographical references and index.
  ISBN 978-0-8108-9054-1 (cloth : alk. paper) — ISBN 978-0-8108-9055-8 (ebook)
  1. Bullying—Juvenile literature. 2. Cyberbullying—Juvenile literature. I. Title.
  BF637.B85S83 2014
  302.34'3—dc 3   2013044839

♾™ The paper used in this publication meets the minimum requirements of American
National Standard for Information Sciences—Permanence of Paper for Printed Library
Materials, ANSI/NISO Z39.48-1992. Printed in the United States of America

For Santhosh Ramdoss

Contents

Acknowledgments

This book would not have been possible without the support of many. Thanks to Tatyana Kleyn for putting me in touch with Scarecrow Press, encouraging me to join the Ultimate Teen Guide club, and being a mentor and friend. Thanks to Monisha Bajaj, who provided me with source material, including her excellent co-authored curriculum, "In the Face of Xenophobia"; who constantly pushes me toward new opportunities; and who has cheered me on through thick and thin. Thanks to Maria Hantzopolous for connecting me with sources, reading a sample chapter, and generally being amazingly encouraging, warm, and welcoming. Thanks to Ali Michael for her insightful comments—without you, chapter 5 would have been a mess! Thanks to Tejpreet Kaur and Christine Highet for connecting me with teens who provided their stories. Thanks to Namit Singh who was a contributor and an editor—your comments on chapter 10 made this a better book. Thanks to Tali Horowitz for connecting me with Courtney Stein at Radio Rookies, who not only introduced me to Temitayo Fagbenle, but also read a chapter and provided comments. Thanks to Rohini Mohan for being my writing partner and making the process so much fun. Thanks to Jan Atwell, Carlos Menchaca, Margaret Nelson, Regina Poreda-Ryan, Nick Rolf, and Aysha Schomburg for guiding me through the anti-bullying policy process while I was at city council: I wrote chapters 10 and 11 with you in my mind.

Thanks to the Fulbright Foundation for funding a year without an office job, which gave me the time and space to work on this manuscript.

Thanks to my editor, Arlene Hirschfelder, whose insight and encouragement made this manuscript possible. The article clippings and advice she sent me across the ocean were essential for finding my words.

Thanks to my family for cheering me on and always believing that one day I would be an author—even when I didn't believe it myself. Thanks especially to my mom, who served as my mail depot and go-between while I lived in Bangalore and worked with an American press.

Thanks to my husband, Santhosh Ramdoss, for being by my side throughout this, my first book, and who I hope will be by my side through many others. You make me believe in the possibility of a better world.

Introduction

Lady Gaga, a famous musician, who was overweight as a child.

Tyra Banks, African American model and host of *America's Next Top Model*, who was taller and skinnier than her classmates.

Sherman Alexie, prize-winning author of *The Absolutely True Diary of a Part-Time Indian*, who was the only Native American student at his school.

Me, a writer and educator, who was one of a handful of Indian Americans in my town.

And quite possibly you, your siblings, cousins, aunts, uncles, teachers, parents, and friends.

What could such a diverse group of people have in common? We, along with about half of all high school students in the United States, have experienced bullying.[1]

Recent research indicates that 47 percent of American high school students claim that they have been bullied, and 50 percent say that they have bullied others.[2] Each day, six out of every ten young people witness some kind of bullying.[3] Whether you are the victim of bullying, witness bullying, or are a bully yourself, you—like me—have probably been affected by bullying multiple times in your life.

Bullying is defined as a series of "negative actions" targeted at one or more individuals repeatedly over time.[4] Some negative actions are verbal, like calling someone names, sending someone insulting text messages, or using words to make someone feel small. Others are physical, like pinching, pushing, or hitting. Others are social, like excluding someone from a group, or spreading rumors about a person. Usually, the bully acts this way because he or she has more power than the victim.[5] Maybe the bully has more friends, money, physical strength, or connections in the community. Bullying happens when individuals abuse their power, which is one reason why bullying can make us feel so unsafe and out of control.

Adults may tell you that bullying is a rite of passage, or something everyone goes through in the process of becoming an adult. They may tell you that they were bullied, but they turned out fine and so it's nothing to worry about, really. They may even tell you that being bullied makes you stronger.

Just because bullying happens so often to so many teens does not mean that it is okay. Regardless of how common it is, bullying is a form of violence, and violence should never be considered a normal part of anyone's life. Victims of bullying can suffer emotional damage in the form of anxiety, depression, and, in extreme cases, suicide.[6] They also are at risk of becoming bullies themselves: for example, in a recent study about one-third of victims of sexual harassment said that after they were bullied, they began sexually harassing their peers.[7] While many people believe that bullies should be punished for their actions, others believe that what bullies really need is counseling. In fact, bullies are just as much at risk as victims: teens who act like bullies are more likely to skip school, use drugs, and go to jail later in life.[8] Bystanders or witnesses—individuals who watch bullying happen from the sidelines—also face emotional consequences. They can become desensitized to violence, can get drawn into bullying behaviors, or can be bullied themselves if they decide to stand up for the victim.[9] If they decide not to stand up for the targets of bullying, they may feel guilty, powerless, or hopeless.

I still remember the first time I was bullied. I was in preschool finishing an art project when one of my classmates suggested that we play blocks. I was getting up to join them when this same girl—who could not have been older than four—told me firmly that I could not play with them because I was a "darky." The other kids, all of whom were White, nodded in agreement. They left me alone at the art table in my smock, my black bangs falling into my eyes, my brown-skinned hands spotted with finger paint.

Although it was decades ago, and although I was bullied many times after that for many different reasons, my memory of that early moment is still clear. I remember what I was wearing, the creamy smell of the finger paint, and the sound of plastic building blocks tumbling onto a carpet where I was forbidden. Most of all, I remember the way it made me feel.

I felt scared and alone, like I had no one to turn to for help. I felt like no one in the world understood what I was going through. Watching the other children play, I felt like I would never have friends again. Worst of all, I felt like the bullying was my fault. I was sure I deserved to be excluded because I was different—even though I had no control over the color of my skin, and never would.

Before I was bullied, I hadn't thought much about my brown skin and black hair, features I inherited from my Indian parents. I knew that being the child of immigrants meant my home was a bit different from my friends' homes. For example, I knew that not everyone spoke two languages with their parents, or ate dinner with their hands, or wrote blue aerogramme letters to their grandparents every weekend. Before I was bullied, I thought all of these differences made me special. After I was bullied, I felt like being different made me a target. Suddenly, all I wanted to do was blend in and hide the fact that I was Indian—something that was impossible to do. Now, remembering that feeling makes me sad. I am proud of who I am and what I look like. What right does anyone have to take that pride away from me?

As an adult, I have spent a lot of time talking to teens who have been affected by bullying. Many of them feel as I did—that the bullying was their fault, that they were alone and that they should try to blend in and cover up their differences. Now I know that bullying doesn't happen because the victim deserves it. Bullying happens because the bully wants power. This might happen because the bully has social or emotional issues. It could also happen because our society rewards aggressive behavior. While it isn't easy to be compassionate for your bully when you are the victim, understanding their motivations can help you make the bullying stop.

Many people are bullied for being different than everyone else. Some, like me, are a different racial or ethnic background from their classmates. Others have disabilities. Others have physical differences that make them stand out—they may be tall, overweight, skinny, have curly hair, or wear glasses. Still others identify as transgender, lesbian, or gay. One of these people is a writer named Dan Savage, who identifies as gay. Savage started a YouTube channel called *It Gets Better* where kids and adults who were bullied can tell their stories. For more on the *It Gets Better* campaign, see below.

The *It Gets Better* Campaign

When writer Dan Savage was a teenager, life was tough.[a] Both he and his brother were bullied. Savage's brother felt comfortable asking their parents for help. Savage did not. The reason was that Savage's classmates were bullying him about something he hadn't told his parents about: his sexual orientation. At a young age, Savage knew he was gay and was afraid that his parents would not understand. In fact, when he was eighteen and came out to his mother, she became upset and was unsupportive.

In 2005, Savage married a man named Terry Miller. They adopted a son named D.J. Savage became a successful and popular writer and radio personality, and his mother came to accept and love both him and his husband. His memories of being a teenager are painful and sad. But his life got better.

In 2010, Savage realized that teens needed to hear this message of hope—especially when he heard about a series of LGBTQ (lesbian, gay, bisexual, transgender, and queer) young people who committed suicide because they were afraid of whether others would accept their sexual orientation. After a little bit of research, Savage learned that teens who identify as gay are about four times more likely to attempt suicide than their straight peers.[b] He wanted to help—but how?

Savage realized that when he was growing up he had no adult role models who had been through what he had been through. He wished he had known that bullying doesn't last forever, that men who love other men can have happy and fulfilling lives, and that love and community are possibilities, no matter who you are. Knowing that, he felt, would have given him hope.

So in the fall of 2010, Savage and his husband recorded a YouTube video sending this important message: it gets better. They called their website the It Gets Better Project (www.itgetsbetter.org) and invited others to post messages of comfort for students who identify as LGBTQ. After just two years, the site had over a thousand videos featuring everyday people as well as celebrities such as Colin Farrell, Anne Hathaway, Ke$ha, and President Barack Obama.

To participate in the project, go to www.itgetsbetter.org. You can learn more about Dan Savage, LGBTQ youth, and preventing bullying. Best of all, you can upload a video telling your story, spreading optimism. Who knows—maybe your video will change a teen's life.

No one should ever be ashamed of who they are. Differences are what make life worth living—people with different perspectives and backgrounds create unique art work, generate innovative ideas, and make the world a more interesting place. By making people afraid of being who they are, bullying negatively affects our families, our homes, our communities, and our schools. By forcing people to conform, bullying makes the world a little less safe and a little less interesting. By standing up to bullies, we affect more than just individuals. We question widespread assumptions about what is cool and what is not, what is normal and what is abnormal, and who is powerful and who is powerless. Addressing bullying also addresses social structures that make us afraid to be who we are, or keep us from achieving our potential. That's why standing up to bullying is so important: standing up to bullies means standing up to damaging assumptions about identities, behaviors, and everything we take for granted about who we are and how we act. And that, truly, is a powerful thing.

The purpose of this book is not only to help you understand bullying from multiple perspectives—bullies, teens who are bullied, witnesses, teachers, parents, and policy makers—but also to give you tools to make your community bully-free. With a little bit of knowledge and a lot of hard work and cooperation, we can end bullying.

Notes

1. Bryan Goodwin, "Bullying Is Common—and Subtle," *Educational Leadership* 69, no. 3 (2011): 82.
2. Goodwin, "Bullying Is Common," 82.
3. National Crime Prevention Council, "Bullying: Information and Resources to Help Prevent the Serious Problem of Bullying," *National Crime Prevention Council: Topics*, 2013, http://www.ncpc.org/topics/bullying (accessed July 20, 2013).
4. Dan Olweus, *Bullying at School* (Malden, MA: Blackwell Publishing, 1993), 9.
5. Olweus, *Bullying at School*, 9.
6. Nancy M. Bowllan, "Implementation and Evaluation of a Comprehensive, School-Wide Bullying Prevention Program in an Urban/Suburban Middle School," *Journal of School Health* 81, no. 4 (April 2011): 167–173.
7. Hill and Kearl, *Crossing the Line: Sexual Harrassment at School*, 3.
8. Bowllan, "Implementation and Evaluation," 167.
9. Barbara Coloroso, *The Bully, the Bullied, and the Bystander: From Preschool to High School—How Parents and Teachers Can Help Break the Cycle of Violence* (New York: HarperResource, 2003), 63.

a. National Public Radio, "Dan Savage: For Gay Teens, Life 'Gets Better,'" *National Public Radio*, March 23, 2011, http://www.npr.org/2011/03/23/134628750/dan-savage-for-gay-teens-life-gets-better (accessed July 20, 2013).
b. L. Kann, E. Olsen, T. McManus, S. Kinchen, D. Chyen, W. Harris, and H. Wechsler. "Sexual Identity, Sex of Sexual Contacts, and Health-Risk Behaviors among Students in Grades 9–12—Youth Risk Behavior Surveillance, Selected Sites, United States, 2001–2009," *Morbidity and Mortality Weekly* 60, no. 2207 (2011): 43.

THE FUNDAMENTALS

∙∙

This book is all about bullying: why it happens, when it happens, where it happens, who it happens to, and how it affects us all. In this chapter, we'll begin our study of bullying by discussing basic terms and concepts that are repeated throughout this volume.

Violence

When we hear the word *violence*, many of us think of bodily assault. In reality, violence is not just physical; it is also verbal, emotional, psychological, cultural, and structural. It takes many forms and can be found in many places.

You are probably familiar with direct violence, defined as harmful behavior that prevents us from being who we are and living our lives in the way we choose.[1] It can be physical, verbal, psychological, sexual, or emotional. Just as a violent action can break our bones, it can also humiliate us, erase us, frighten us, or threaten us.[2] Direct violence is sometimes called visible violence because we can see it happening.

Bullying is a form of direct violence many of us witness from a young age. Any repeated negative action that makes a person feel diminished, inadequate, or unsafe is a type of bullying. Physical bullying includes pinching, spitting, hitting, kicking, pushing, punching, or otherwise physically hurting victims, as well as damaging or destroying personal property. Verbal bullying includes intense and repeated teasing, calling someone names, or threatening to hurt someone or his or her loved ones. Psychological bullying includes humiliation or social exclusion, such as denying someone an invitation to social events, keeping someone from sitting at a lunch table, or convincing others to ostracize someone.

Two less visible categories of violence make this overtly destructive behavior possible: cultural and structural. Cultural violence is any idea, belief, or attitude that creates an atmosphere where hurtful actions become socially acceptable.[3] Cultural violence is found in religion, pop culture, art, music, books, or beliefs and traditions. Media that treat women as sex objects promote cultural violence by supporting the idea that women are commodities, rather than people. Teens who bully others by calling them "gay" promote cultural violence by sending the message that it is not safe to be lesbian, gay, bisexual, transgender, or queer (LG-BTQ). The effects of this bullying extend beyond the victim, affecting witnesses who may hide their identities or beliefs out of fear of being targeted.

Structural violence is the process by which groups of individuals who have power grant themselves access to more resources than those who have less power.[4] Examples of structural violence include disproportionately suspending or otherwise disciplining teens who are Black or Latino, or refusing to build infrastructure that could allow physically disabled students to fully participate in school activities.

Both of these invisible forms of violence influence the way we think and act, as well as the spaces that fill our daily lives, like hospitals, workplaces, and—most relevant for teens—schools. The patterns and ideas that emerge from cultural and structural violence are manifested as humiliation, teasing, exclusion, or even physical assault. For example, structural violence creates an imbalance of resources that make some neighborhoods wealthy and others impoverished. Bullies who make fun of their peers for being unable to afford the latest fashions are responding to cultural violence.

Ending bullying means embracing peace and promoting a culture of caring for, rather than harming, others. Teen Wilson To, a high school student in Nevada, used social media to change the culture at his school. In 2012, he created a

Wilson To and the Atech Compliments Page

Like many American high schools, Atech High School in Las Vegas, Nevada, had a problem with bullying. High school senior Wilson To wanted to do something to change this. In 2012, he started a movement in the space where teens hang out the most: online.

To created a Facebook page where students could anonymously post compliments about each other. His reasoning was, "A lot of quiet individuals don't think much of what they do, but when they get compliments for things they didn't realize about themselves, it helps to build self-esteem."[a]

The page took off beyond To's imagination. As of September 2013, it had over six hundred likes and thousands of posts. Students praised everything from their friends' senses of humor to their work ethic to their talents.

For example, on September 12, 2013, a student wrote, "Talibah Abdul-Wahid is a hard worker and an outstanding co-officer. She puts forth so much time and effort into school, clubs, her jobs and cupcakes. Talibah is one of the most sincere and sweetest people I've ever met, and I am extremely grateful to have another year with her. You're the best Talibah!"[b]

On May 3, 2013, another student wrote, "Keirvy Lipa is actually really nice and caring. He is always the first one to help anyone with whatever they need. I admire how much of his time he gives to helping others."[c]

One of the best things about the page is that once a compliment is displayed, students can post their positive comments. Some posts have over twenty-five comments, all adding onto the original statement. This creates a cycle of positivity that makes both those receiving and giving the compliment happy.

To remained anonymous until the end of the year, when he passed on the site's administration to another student, whose identity is also unknown. Together, though, Atech teens are committed to maintaining the site, and the culture of acceptance, love, and nonviolence that it embraces.

Before he left, To got one special gift: an anonymous compliment of his own. It read, "At the end of the day, we all want someone to recognize and acknowledge us for our greatness, even through our flaws, to know in our hearts that someone truly does care about us even when we are far away from each other. Wilson To, thank you for establishing Atech Compliments; you were the catalyst who helped people to express and experience this kind of love for each other."[d]

Facebook page where students could anonymously post compliments about each other. To read more about how this simple act changed To's school, see page 2.

Ending bullying also requires us to stop excusing violence in multiple forms by calling it simply "boys being boys" or "rites of passage." To understand violence, we must understand another fundamental: power.

Power

At its base, bullying is about power. Bullies want power, victims feel powerless, and witnesses react to bullying based on how much power they lack, want, or have. Throughout this book, you will learn how power affects the decisions individuals make about how they treat others and themselves.

Bullies may act destructively in reaction to a lack of power in some area of their life. For example, in this volume, you'll read the stories of bullies who developed anger issues because they grew up in abusive households. Bullying someone may give teens a sense of power and control over their lives that they feel nowhere else. In fact, one recurring theme in this book is that many bullies are or have been victims of bullying themselves—either at the hands of other teens or at the hands of adults. This is why one of the most successful ways to combat bullying is to integrate bullies into communities, giving them a sense of safety and inclusion, and helping them rely on friends, rather than violence, to cope.[5]

Just as feeling out of control makes some teens act like bullies, it can plunge others into depression. One of the worst consequences of being bullied is feeling helpless, alone, and powerless. This points to another recurring theme in this book: the need for free and available mental health services. Not only can mental health professionals help teens develop coping skills, they can also serve as nonjudgmental listeners and advisers. For some, accessing services like these can literally be the difference between life and death.

During adolescence, many of us measure our success based on the number of friends we have. Consequently, for teens, one of the greatest forms of power is popularity.[6] Bullying is intimately tied to popularity. Think about it: bullies are often popular, while victims are not. Witnesses will sometimes calculate how they respond to bullying based on whether their actions will help them gain or lose friends. Plus, even though none of us want to be bullied, the traits we associate with bullies are positive: bullies are seen as strong, confident, and even clever or funny, while victims are seen as weak, isolated, and weird. Even though most people would say they believe bullying is bad, when it actually happens, they give bullies positive attention and power.

There are specific reasons why this happens. For one thing, American society values masculinity, which is a word to describe anything male. For boys in particular, aggressive behavior is both encouraged and expected.[7] In fact, some boys bully others because they feel insecure about their masculinity. Later in this book, you'll read stories of boys who became bullies to cover up their sexuality or other traits that are not considered masculine. You'll also read about the other side of valuing masculinity, which is devaluing femininity or anything female. This is one reason experts believe that sexual harassment, which usually involves boys bullying girls, is so prevalent: from a young age, boys learn that treating women as sexual objects is not only acceptable, but positive, since it makes others think they are manly.[8]

Gender—or being male or female—is an example of an identity category. Identity is another recurring concept in this book that is intimately connected with power and with bullying.

Identity

Identity is a word that describes personal characteristics that affect the way people treat us and how much power we have in society. Examples of identity are race, ethnicity, gender, sexual orientation, class, and faith. Each of us has multiple identities that influence both who we are and how society perceives us.

If you have an identity that does not traditionally have power within our social structure and that has suffered a history of discrimination, you probably belong to an oppressed group. In the United States, African Americans and women are both oppressed groups who have been denied their rights in the past. African Americans experienced slavery, after which they spent years fighting for the end of segregation. They still experience direct, cultural, and structural violence in the form of racism. Women were not allowed to vote until the 1920s, and even today they are often paid lower wages than men for the same jobs, or are treated as sex objects. Both of these groups must struggle for power in our society.

Since every person has multiple identities, some of your identities might make you privileged, while others might make you oppressed. For example, I (the author) am a straight, middle class, woman of color. As a woman and a person of color, I fit into an oppressed group. But as straight and middle class, I am privileged. To think more about your own identity, try filling out the Power Matrix on page 6.

Although teens who identify with oppressed groups may not be viewed as powerful, this does not make them powerless. In fact, oppressed groups have been responsible for major cultural and political changes throughout history. For example, in the 1960s, African American teens helped outlaw segregation by participating in nonviolent protests at high schools and universities. These teens were members of oppressed groups, but they changed the world. Today, teens from oppressed groups around the country fight for protection against being bullied because of who they are.

Just as our identities can expose us to bullying, they can also make us powerful. This is another theme in this book: recognizing the power that you have to change bullying in your school. All of us have the power to be allies to others, regardless of our identity, popularity, or past. Throughout this book, you will read about teens who have made a difference in their schools and communities by standing up to bullying. Sometimes this comes at great personal cost. Other times, it involves the simple choice to avoid abusing power. This leads us to another theme in this book: we all play multiple roles in bullying, sometimes all at once. The question is how we can use our roles for promoting nonviolence.

? Power Matrix Activity

You have multiple identities that make you who you are. Some of these identities might give you power, while others might expose you to oppression. To think about your own multiple identities, copy the power matrix (table 1.1) onto a separate piece of paper and try filling it in for yourself.

Table 1.1 Power Matrix

	Gender	Race	Religion	Class	Sexuality	Weight	Disability Status
Your Identity							
Privileged?							
Oppressed?							

My matrix is included in table 1.2 as an example.

Table 1.2 The Author's Matrix

	Gender	Race	Religion	Class	Sexuality	Weight	Disability Status
Your Identity	Female	Asian American	Hindu	Middle	Straight	Average	Fully Able
Privileged?				X	X	X	X
Oppressed?	X	X	X				

Here are some follow-up questions to think about or discuss with your friends:

1. Which of your identities give you power and which of your identities do not?
2. What other categories could you add to this chart?
3. In the categories where you are oppressed, what do you think needs to happen to help give you more power?
4. In the categories where you are privileged, how can you use your power to help support individuals who are not privileged?

Roles in Bullying

Throughout this book, you will read about bullies, victims, and witnesses. These are terms that are used both in this volume and in many other books about bullying. *Bullies* are individuals who repeatedly abuse others physically, verbally, or emotionally. *Victims* are individuals who are the targets of bullies. *Witnesses* or *bystanders* are individuals who watch bullying happen and choose to abuse the victim along with the bully, defend the victim against the bully, or remain silent.

These terms are shorthand for complex concepts—in fact, the concepts are so complex that each one has a dedicated chapter in this book. They can be problematic because they oversimplify the roles of the actors in any bullying situation. For one thing, the terms seem to mark out distinct categories. For example, if you are a bully, according to these terms, you are always the person who uses your power to hurt others. In reality, many bullies start out as victims. Similarly, some victims can bully others because they are frustrated about being bullied themselves. And witnesses may also sometimes be victims and bullies depending on how they choose to use their role as witnesses. The idea that teens can fit one category only is false and misleading.

Similarly, using the terms *bully*, *victim*, and *witness* can make it seem like these words summarize a teen's total experience and personality. In fact, all of us have multiple dimensions to our lives. A bully might also be an artist or an athlete. A victim might also be a sibling and a best friend. A witness might be an aspiring lawyer or engineer or musician. And a bully, victim, or witness might be a survivor of dating violence, domestic abuse, or other trauma that could influence the way he or she chooses to behave. In other words, all of us lead complicated lives that cannot be reduced to any one role.

Finally—and perhaps most importantly—bullying is a behavior, not a person. This means that everyone who is affected by bullying—including bullies themselves—can change. This may be difficult to believe if you are trapped in a cycle of abuse. On the other hand, knowing change is possible can also make bullying more bearable. Bullies are, in fact, people who choose to engage in negative behavior. Witnesses can make a choice about how they act as witnesses. Sometimes our choices are restricted by our power in a given situation (especially when we are victims of bullying) but the fact remains that being a bully, victim, or witness is not a fixed identity. A bully does not have to be a bully forever, just as a victim does not have to be a victim forever.

This potential for change is a major theme in this book. So is understanding why people act the way they do. For each of these roles, life circumstances and contexts influence whether individuals are at risk of acting like bullies or becoming victims. In this book, you will look carefully at the risk factors behind each of these roles. For example, you will find that many times individuals engage in negative behavior because they do not fully realize it is negative: based on what they see on television or in their homes or neighborhoods, they may believe that they are acting completely normally. Helping these individuals understand different perspectives and giving them the tools they need to approach human interactions—and, in particular, conflict—nonviolently can make them change. Similarly, making them feel safe, secure, and included can reduce their reliance on abusing power as a way of reacting to insecurity.

Addressing Bullying in the Moment

One of the trickiest things about combating bullying is that it requires both short- and long-term solutions. Although the ideal tactic for stopping bullying is taking time to change the climate of a school, teens also need strategies for dealing with bullying the moment that it happens. In this book, you will hopefully gain these strategies—or, at the very least, some ways to brainstorm strategies with your friends.

Standing up to bullies can be scary, particularly if there is a threat that doing so will expose you to violence. Throughout the book, we emphasize the fact that teens should make decisions about addressing bullying based on how safe they feel. If you feel reacting to a bully is going to put you at risk, you should not feel guilty for staying out of it. Sometimes the best way to support a friend being bullied or to cope with being bullied yourself is to do so after the incident has occurred. However, if the risk of standing up to a bully feels severe, it is probably a good idea to alert an adult that you trust. No one should have to live in constant fear, and if a bully is so dangerous as to be threatening within the moment, it is wise to get help.

This book also has a set of strategies for dealing with a friend you care about who is acting like a bully. This goes back to another theme we discussed: the fact that everyone is capable of changing. Just as it is painful to watch bullies targeting your friends, it is also painful to watch your friends make hurtful choices, particularly when you know those friends can treat you with respect, love, and care. Your friend may be frustrated or angry about his or her behavior, but be unsure how to stop. Showing your support could help this friend change, benefiting not just the friend but also everyone he or she has bullied. This is another recurring theme in this book: bullies may be powerful, but nothing is more powerful than genuine friendship and support.

Let's Get Started!

Now that you've learned about some of the main ideas in this book, it's time to explore these themes in greater depth. This book has numerous stories from teen likes you. It also has activities for self-reflection designed to help you recognize patterns in your life, talk about what you are seeing, and find avenues for creating change. Remember that you are powerful and that even small steps toward nonviolence make a big difference.

Notes

1. Johan Galtung, "Cultural Violence," *Journal of Peace Research* 27, no. 3 (1990): 292.
2. Galtung, "Cultural Violence," 292.
3. Galtung, "Cultural Violence," 291–305.
4. Galtung, "Cultural Violence," 291.
5. Bob Costello, Joshua Wachtel, and Ted Wachtel, *The Restorative Practices Handbook for Teachers, Disciplinarians, and Administrators* (Bethlehem, PA: International Institute for Restorative Practices, 2009), E-book.
6. Jessie Klein, *The Bully Society: School Shootings and the Crisis of Bullying in America's Schools* (New York: New York University Press, 2011), 12.
7. Klein, *The Bully Society*, 47.
8. Joanne N. Smith, Mandy Van Deven, and Meghan Huppuch, *Hey, Shorty! A Guide to Combating Sexual Harassment and Violence in Public Schools and on the Streets* (New York: Feminist Press at the City University of New York, 2011), 124.

---

a. Krystie Yandoli, "Wilson To, High School Senior, Created Facebook Compliments Page to Challenge Bullying, Spread Positivity (VIDEO)," *Huffington Post*, July 4, 2013, http://www

.huffingtonpost.com/2013/07/04/wilson-to-facebook-compli_n_3541453.html (accessed September 30, 2013).

b. Anonymous, "Atech Compliments," Facebook, https://www.facebook.com/atech .compliments?fref=ts (accessed September 30, 2013).

c. Anonymous, "Atech Compliments."

d. Anonymous, "Atech Compliments."

BULLIES

···

When we hear about bullying, we usually hear the victim's story: why he or she was bullied, how he or she is feeling, and what can be done to help him or her. We rarely hear the voices of bullies who are responsible for these incidents, and so we frequently do not know why they bully others, how they feel after they bully others, or what it would take to make them stop. To stop bullying, we must understand why bullies do what they do and address the causes of their destructive decisions. As we discussed in the first chapter, although we often refer to students who bully others as simply "bullies," it is important to remember that we are all complex individuals who are more than just our worst actions. Someone who acts like a bully may also be an athlete, an artist, a sibling, or a friend. The key question this chapter addresses is: How can we help potential bullies to choose compassion over violence?

In this chapter, you will learn about the ways that social structures and personal experiences influence whether teens become bullies. You will read about ways that teens like you are working with their schools and communities to introduce their peers to tools for coping with intense feelings like insecurity, anger, and grief in a healthy way. You will also learn the importance of having compassion for others even when they are behaving badly. In fact, as you will read in these pages, negative behavior is frequently a cry for help. Individuals who feel happy, safe, and loved do not become bullies: in fact, just like victims, bullies need our help to heal.

Why Teens Become Bullies

About half of teens who participated in a recent survey identified as bullies.[1] Maybe you are one of these teens. Or maybe you are friends with one of them— or used to be. If someone you know and care about makes a mistake like bullying others, you probably want him or her to change. Likewise, if you yourself act like a bully, you would most likely prefer different, more nonviolent ways to approach conflict, attain popularity, or gain a sense of security.

Researchers say that teens who act like bullies tend to fit into one of two categories: popular members of their community or outcasts who suffer from social anxiety.[2] These teens frequently exhibit risky behaviors like having trouble following rules, valuing aggression and violence, suffering from anxiety, or becoming frustrated easily.[3] But not all young people who have these characteristics become bullies. So why do some teens choose to become bullies while others do not?

Bullying happens because individuals make specific choices at key moments. However, these choices are not instantaneous and arbitrary. In fact, they come from a teen's history, family, culture, and ideals—a combination of factors that we refer to as the social context. Teens who consistently see adults solve problems peacefully learn by example how to navigate conflict nonviolently. Teens who grow up around abusive, violent adults do not. Similarly, some teens have support systems of peers and adults who can help them constructively address their mistakes or cope with trauma. Others feel that they have no one to turn to when they need support, and consequently feel insecure, powerless, and hopeless.

Our social contexts include more than just our personal lives and histories. We decide how to behave based on what we see around us, which includes much more than our family and friends: whenever we watch television or movies, listen to music, or read books, newspapers, and magazines, we receive messages about how we should look, what we should believe, and how we should act. Our communities absorb these messages as well and react to us based on the conclusions they draw. Some of our decisions are rewarded through praise or popularity, while others are punished by teasing, exclusion, or ostracism. The feedback we receive from the media and our personal experiences influences the choices that we make.

In this section, you will learn about both the individual and social contexts that make bullies who they are. Just like victims, bullies need help to cope with violence: the violence they experience and the violence they inflict on others.

Growing Up with Violence

Teens who are exposed to direct violence are at risk of becoming bullies. A study in Massachusetts found that 19 percent of middle school–aged bullies said a family member had hurt them in the past twelve months, compared to only 5 percent of middle school victims; similarly, 17 percent of bullies said they had recently seen a violent incident happen within their family, compared to only 6 percent of middle school victims.[4] The numbers rose even more for bully-victims, or individuals who reported that they had both been bullied and bullied others: almost one quarter of middle school–aged bully-victims grew up in households where they experienced violence regularly.[5]

As these statistics make clear, many bullies experience trauma and violence at home. They may grow up in households where family members abuse them, their siblings, or one of their parents. They may live in shelters or group homes where they routinely witness or experience crime. They may be part of gangs or peer groups who use violence to cope with conflict and change.

Experiences like these make teens think that violence is an acceptable tool for overcoming challenges, a belief that puts them at risk for becoming bullies. For

Miguel Ayala's Story

In *YCteen*, teenager Miguel Ayala says he tried to use fighting and bullying to control anger problems he developed because of childhood experiences with violence. Ayala's mother physically abused him and his siblings. Whenever she beat him, he felt afraid, powerless, and angry. He would cope with his intense emotions using violence. Ayala remembers, "I would curse at people in public and say obscene things to females. I was a terrible bully."[a]

Although Ayala knew his behavior was hurtful, it was the only tool he had for dealing with his pain. Ayala remembers, "It made me feel a little better to do those things. It made me feel like I had all the guts in the world, and it released my rage to make other people as mad as I felt."[b]

Ayala eventually learned to cope with his intense emotions when he started attending group therapy and a special high school that included regular meetings with a social worker. He continued to struggle with his emotions, but developed a strategy for dealing with them when he felt so depressed that he was suicidal. He says, "For now, I try to focus on the positives in my life and I try not to think about my problems too much. When that doesn't work, I tell myself that if I give in to the stupidity and really lose it, then I'm letting the bullies win."[c] By *bullies*, Ayala means his family members, peers who were in foster care with him, and even some of the adult staff at his group home.

It can be hard to be sympathetic to a bully when he or she is hurting you, but Ayala's example shows that not all bullies act the way they do because they are popular or powerful. In fact, Ayala became abusive because he was abused. Ayala's perspective shows that if we want to combat bullying, we have to address everyone involved—including the bully. Ayala's story also illustrates one of the greatest dangers of allowing violence to continue: in some cases, it can create more bullies.

example, bullying may be the only outlet they have to express anger, depression, or anxiety. Or, bullying may give them a sense of power in a world where they constantly feel out of control.

Not every young person who experiences instability or hardship becomes a bully. Some teens grow up in difficult circumstances but do not cope with their emotions by hurting others. Others get help by meeting regularly with social workers, getting therapy, or joining after-school programs that help them feel empowered by channeling their negative energy into more positive activities like sports or the arts.

No one—child, teen, or adult—should have to experience violence and abuse. If you know someone who may be experiencing serious issues in his or her home, talk to a trusted adult about how you might be able to help. See the list of resources on page 15.

Bullying and Popularity

Having personal problems is not the only reason that people become bullies. Some teens act like bullies because they believe it is a socially acceptable behavior. In American society, we constantly receive messages from the media and our peers that associate bullying with popularity and success. In movies and television shows about high school, the popular characters are aggressive, have sharp tongues, and, more often than not, bully the less popular characters. While the scripts may be written so that we have sympathy for the victims, it is clear which characters have the most power: the bullies. This does not mean that teens simply watch an episode of *Gossip Girl* or *The Real Housewives of New Jersey* and make a conscious decision to become bullies. Instead, they internalize these messages, often without even knowing it. When they are with a group of their peers, and they are presented with an opportunity to bully someone, they may associate this behavior with the glamorous characters on their favorite shows.

Or, they may crave popularity and acceptance, and they may notice that their peers who act like bullies get the most respect. Just like on television and in the movies, teens often find that the students who have the most power in schools are bullies. This often happens because both adults and peers in their schools and campuses do not hold them accountable for their actions. For example, when male athletes—especially the most talented ones—act violently or aggressively, parents, teachers, and administrators sometimes write off their behavior as a natural part of growing up.[6] When sports teams win games and championships, they create a positive image for the entire community. Consequently, the athletes are considered heroes who are capable of doing no wrong, and their bad behavior is excused, ignored, or unnoticed.

Resources for Teens Who Experience Violence

Sometimes teens become bullies because they are victims of violence. If you think someone you know needs help, first speak to an adult you trust. Together, you may consider calling one of the following organizations for resources for addressing the issues.

Administration for Children and Families
U.S. Department of Health and Human Services
http://www.childwelfare.gov/preventing/
This website has a link to a national network of partner organizations designed to help prevent the abuse of children and teens.

National Child Abuse Hotline
http://www.childhelp.org/
1-800-442-4453
This organization has a twenty-four-hour hotline that you can call to get immediate help, or to describe the case to see if the individual in question might be a victim of abuse.

The National Domestic Violence Hotline
www.thehotline.org
1-800-799-SAFE
This hotline is another emergency resource if you think that the individual in question experiences or witnesses violence regularly in his or her home.

Bullying comes not just from social messages about popularity, but also as a result of how much we value wealth. In many schools and in just about every television show or movie about adolescents, teens who can afford designer clothing, expensive sneakers, or fancy cars are considered the most popular and have the most power.[7] Students who may not be able to purchase these items are less popular and may be victimized by teens who have the resources to keep up

Bullies are often individuals who crave power—sometimes because they have it already and sometimes because they don't.

with the latest trends.[8] In the United States especially, being wealthy is a sign of success. Consequently, adults in schools may think that teens with money come from good homes with strong values—particularly if the teens are White—and may overlook their bullying behavior as silly mistakes rather than a recurring problem.[9] Poorer students may not stand up to these bullies because they believe that their poverty is a sign that their families are inferior. On some level, they may believe that they deserve to be bullied because they are unable to dress or behave like their rich peers, which—they believe—makes them inherently un-cool.

In both of these cases, bullies are teens whose identities make them powerful in society. Teens who have privileges may bully other students because, based on what they see, they know they can get away with it. They may become bullies because they believe it will help them climb the social ladder and gain even more power. Likewise, victims may choose not to stand up for themselves because they feel they will not be heard.

As we've discussed, teens make choices about their behavior based on what they see around them. Until we stop rewarding bullying with popularity and praise, teens will continue to think positively about this destructive behavior. There is another, larger social trend that many experts believe encourages teens to be bullies: the way we think about gender.

Masculinity and Bullying

Teens who are bullied sometimes believe that they will never escape the harassment because their bullies are popular students whose abusive behavior only seems to enhance their power and popularity. Some researchers think that this is because bullying is seen as masculine behavior. Since we, as a society, value masculine behavior more than feminine behavior, they argue, we put pressure on ourselves and others to act in specific, masculine ways that are not always healthy or positive.[10] For example, both boys and girls feel pressure to do things like hide their emotions, deal with conflict using physical aggression, and keep their problems to themselves, all of which are traditionally associated with men. On the other hand, both boys and girls try not to cry, express physical or emotional pain, or be overly sensitive, all of which are traditionally associated with women. In summary, feminine behaviors are mostly seen as weak and worthless, whereas masculine behaviors are promoted and encouraged.

Do you agree? Try the following self-reflection exercise to see what you think.

 Self-Reflecting on Masculinity

Some researchers think that one of the reasons bullying is so prevalent in our society is that it is associated with masculinity, which means anything to do with the male gender.

Since men tend to have more power than women, behavior associated with men tends to be valued more. Consequently, both men and women feel pressure to act in masculine ways. Many of these masculine habits are aggressive, violent, and associated with bullying.

Let's see if you agree. Copy the chart in table 2.1 onto a separate piece of paper and try to fill it out. In the first two columns, check off whether you think the behavior is masculine (associated with men) or feminine (associated with women). If you get stuck, think about how people you know react to these behaviors. Do they say things like, "Be a man," or "Don't act like a girl," or "Man up," when they see these behaviors? If so, check feminine. If not, check masculine.

Then check off whether you think the behavior is cool or uncool. Add up your responses and put your totals in table 2.2. When you are done, answer the self-reflection questions that follow. Ask your friends to do the same and compare your responses.

Table 2.1 Self-Reflecting on Masculinity

Behavior	Masculine?	Feminine?	Cool?	Uncool?
Crying				
Talking about emotions				
Being sensitive to teasing				
Being independent				
Being strong and/or athletic				
Being tough				
Being quiet				
Being submissive				
Being authoritative				
Being nurturing				
Getting into a physical fight and winning				
Getting into a physical fight and losing				
Feeling lonely				
Being catty or gossipy				
Being self-confident				
Being confrontational				

Behavior	Masculine?	Feminine?	Cool?	Uncool?
Being meek				
Being gentle				
Feeling uncertain				
Being vulnerable				
Being powerful				

Table 2.2 Totals

Masculine and Positive	Masculine and Negative	Feminine and Positive	Feminine and Negative

1. Look at your totals. How many masculine behaviors were positive? How many feminine behaviors were positive?
2. Which of these behaviors were difficult for you to categorize as masculine or feminine? Why were they difficult to categorize?
3. Which of these behaviors were difficult for you to categorize as cool or uncool? Why were they difficult to categorize?
4. How does labeling behavior as masculine or feminine affect men *and* women? What behaviors might men want to engage in that they can't because they will be called feminine? What behaviors might women want to engage in that they can't because they will be called masculine?
5. What can you do at your school to make it easier for people to behave the way that they would like to behave, regardless of their gender?

Many types of bullying are associated with masculinity. For example, it is often considered cool for men to aggressively pursue women. Consequently, some teen boys may engage in sexual harassment or dating violence because they think it proves to the world that they are heterosexual, dominant over women, and sexually successful, all of which are associated with masculinity and with being cool.[11] Yet, this behavior is demeaning to women and heterosexist, meaning that it is discriminatory against young people who may identify as lesbian, gay, bisexual, or queer. Furthermore, in the Girls for Gender Equity study of sexual harassment discussed in chapter 7, teen researchers found that many teen boys thought that young women found sexual harassment flattering, when in reality the women found it frightening and uncomfortable.[12] The attitude that the teen boys displayed is evidence of the prevailing opinion that to be a man, one should be openly and aggressively heterosexual. This thinking is not only sexist, it is heterosexist: it assumes that all boys are attracted to girls and all girls are attracted to boys, when in reality, some teens may not be romantically interested in the opposite sex.

Other examples of how perceptions of masculinity and femininity lead to violence are incidents of teen boys fighting other teen boys to protect "their" women.[13] A bully may pick on a boy by insulting his girlfriend. The boy may then feel that if he does not retaliate physically, he is not fulfilling his masculine role as the protector of his girlfriend, even if his girlfriend feels perfectly capable of sticking up for herself.[14] Even if he prefers not to fight, the boy may worry that his peers will consider him weak if he walks away.

Some teen boys bully others to prove that they are strong, dominating, and heterosexual.[15] They are afraid that if they do not act in masculine ways, they could be singled out for being too meek, gentle, or submissive. Consequently, they choose to engage in violent behavior like bullying in order to avoid being bullied themselves. Similarly, some teens bully others in order to hide an aspect of their identity that they fear will make them into victims of bullying themselves. Lance Bass, former member of the popular band 'N Sync, for example, says that he was a bully because he wanted to cover up the fact that he was gay. For more on his story, see page 21.

Sometimes teen girls act like bullies to prove that they, too, have masculine characteristics like being tough, strong, and independent. They may also support their male friends when they bully their female friends, thinking that their female friends should have been more careful and their male friends are just "boys being boys." But teen girls also react to pressures they feel to act feminine. For example, in many schools, it is not socially acceptable for girls to fight physically. Some researchers believe that this is why girls bully and intimidate each other verbally. You may have noticed this in popular culture as well: television shows and books

Lance Bass's Story

If you love popular music, you may know that Lance Bass used to be a member of the band 'N Sync. What you may not know is that Lance Bass used to be a bully. Bass says that although he never physically assaulted anyone, he routinely made homophobic comments, which means that he used words that insult individuals who identify as lesbian, gay, bisexual, transgender, or queer.[d] He says he acted like a bully to hide a secret: he was gay, something that was not acceptable according to the masculine, heterosexual world of high school. Bass says that he thought if he picked on others, he would draw attention away from himself. He said, "I was the typical teenager that just wanted to put it off of me and make someone else have that scarlet letter on them."[e]

Now, Bass is arguably one of the most famous people in the world. He feels comfortable enough about his sexuality to talk about it openly. If only he had been made to feel comfortable doing this as a teenager, perhaps he would not have been a bully.

In an interview with MTV, Bass said that when it comes to bullies, we should all remember, "There's always a bigger story than what you see."[f] Bass filmed the video to raise awareness about victims of bullying. However, his interview reminds us that teens who bully others also often require attention and care.

such as the *Gossip Girl* series or movies such as *Mean Girls* portray girl bullies using social hierarchies to exclude or harass each other. Compare this to the way you see media portray men fighting: while girls are called "catty" or worse, boys who fight are often called "tough" or "fearless." Again, masculinity affects the way we see the world and the behaviors of both genders.

If we change the way we think about gender, both men and women could benefit. For one thing, bullies would feel less pressure to prove their worth using violence and aggression—qualities that are negative even though they are associated with masculinity. Instead, they might feel that they could resolve conflicts or cope with their emotions peacefully without losing their social status. For another thing, fighting gender stereotypes helps us all be ourselves without worrying about what is cool or not. Men would be able to cry or express their emotions without feeling like they were making themselves vulnerable to bullying, while women would feel more comfortable standing up for themselves without worrying about not being ladylike. Finally, if we could stop seeing certain negative behaviors like bullying as masculine, teens might stop seeing bullying as a path to popularity and acceptance.

The Risks of Being a Bully

Being a bully can have immediate negative effects on teenagers. Studies show that teens who are bullies are more likely to engage in self-destructive behavior like taking drugs and skipping school.[16] They are more likely to become sexually active earlier than their peers and to engage in vandalism.[17] They are also more likely to drop out of school, a decision that can limit their ability to be economically secure as adults.[18]

Dropping out is not the only long-term effect of bullying. When bullies grow up, they have a greater risk of abusing drugs and alcohol and abusing their family members, including their future spouses and children.[19] Teens who end up in the criminal justice system are likely to have been bullies before they were incarcerated.[20] This may be because teens who are bullies grow up watching others use power and violence to hurt others, and therefore do not know of alternative, positive ways to behave when they feel anxious or insecure, or when they find themselves facing a personal conflict. The risks they face may not be specifically because they were bullies as teens, but instead may be because of the circumstances in their lives that made them act like bullies in the first place.

Bullies suffer from long-term consequences if they continue to practice these behaviors and rely on violence and aggression as a way to cope with their lives. In order to stop bullying, the bully needs support as well. In the next section, you will learn about effective ways to help bullies change.

Approaches to Helping Bullies Stop Bullying

In most schools and campuses, if a bully is caught, the administration reacts by punishing him or her for the negative behavior. Administrators choose this course of action because it sends a clear message that violence is unacceptable. Furthermore, it discourages other students from acting like bullies by illustrating the serious repercussions they may face if they choose to abuse others.

While it is important to ensure that bullies face the consequences of their actions, punishing them does not necessarily address the underlying problem that makes them resort to violence in the first place. In this section, you will learn about some alternative approaches designed to help bullies change their behavior permanently by helping them confront violence in their own worlds and by giving them tools to embrace nonviolence.

Mental Health Services

Students who act like bullies are twice as likely as their peers to have mental issues like anxiety, depression, and attention deficit disorder.[21] As discussed earlier in this section, many develop these symptoms as a result of past trauma. Others are born with these conditions and so have a harder time controlling their behavior than other teens.[22] In all of these cases, getting access to counseling, medication, or other help could be exactly what teens need to cope with their challenges and stop their negative behavior. Yet, when a bullying incident occurs, the mental health professionals usually focus on the victim, rather than screening the bully as well. In some cases, the bully may want to stop his or her behavior, but may be unable to do so without the assistance of a professional who can help the bully learn how to control his or her behavior.

Adults who provide mental health services are trained to give teens the tools to cope with trauma, manage illnesses like anxiety and depression, regulate behavior, and, when appropriate, use medication to regulate themselves. Some can also connect teens with people like social workers who can help them get out of abusive situations and into safe and loving homes. Mental health service providers include therapists, counselors, psychologists, psychiatrists, and social workers. As discussed earlier in this chapter, many teens become bullies because of problems they are facing in their personal lives. A professional counselor or therapist can help teens identify and cope with these underlying issues, which in turn will help them feel safer and more secure. These positive emotions can help bullies realize that the anger and lack of control they feel cannot be resolved through bullying, but through taking care of themselves. Furthermore, some teens who are bullies may have serious problems that they cannot handle alone, such as homelessness, addiction, or abuse. Mental health services create spaces where teens can not only talk about these serious worries, but also connect with resources that will help them resolve these needs once and for all.

Many schools do not have individuals like this on staff, either because they are not legally mandated to do so or because they do not have the funding or resources to hire someone. Other times schools do have adults available to talk to students but the adults' case loads are so large that it can be difficult to provide services consistently. Local hospitals and community-based organizations often have mental health staff who teens can speak to at low or no cost if schools are not equipped to serve them. If you have a friend who you believe would benefit from this type of care, talk to a teacher or trusted adult about options inside and outside of school.

Restorative Justice

An important part of growing up is building a community of people that you can trust. Studies show that teens who have strong friendships with peers and healthy relationships with adults (including teachers, counselors, administrators, and their own parents or their peers' parents) are more socially and academically successful, less likely to be bullied, and less likely to become bullies.[23] Bullies may not have adults in their lives that they can trust or friends who make them feel safe, accepted, and able to be themselves. In fact, some teens act like bullies simply because they mistakenly think it is the best way to become popular.[24] Yet, schools often punish bullies for their behavior by removing them from class, suspending them, or even expelling them. This has the potential to isolate bullies even further, making the underlying problem worse.

Furthermore, when teens act like bullies they sometimes find themselves caught in a pattern. They may not know why they made the decision to be a bully in the first place, or they may feel as though one initial bad decision has trapped them into being the type of person who intimidates and harasses others.[25] Or, they may have no one to turn to for help with their personal problems, and the anxiety and stress that they feel about these circumstances may be driving them to bad behavior.[26] Or, they may not know how serious their actions are, and how much damage they are inflicting on their victims.[27]

Bullies should face the consequences of their actions, and schools need to send a clear message that hurtful behavior is unacceptable. But what if the first step was to ask bullies to talk to their victims about their behavior? What if bullies had to face a punishment that actually involved repairing the damage that they caused? What if their peers got to help decide the punishment? And what if bullies got a chance to ask for help to address the reasons why they made the decision to be bullies in the first place?

Schools that believe in *restorative justice* use questions like these to structure their disciplinary system. The model looks different in schools across the country, but the fundamental tenets remain the same. The approach treats bullies as members of a community who have made a bad decision and are capable of change.[28] It requires teens who act like bullies to work with victims to figure out how to address the damage they have caused, and it gives everyone a chance to talk before a decision is made collectively.[29] Some say that the philosophy of restorative justice came from indigenous cultures in Australia, where it was important for everyone's grievances to be aired before a decision was made. This is the spirit that drives restorative justice projects around the world.

A school that uses restorative approaches addresses conflict in a number of different ways. After a first incident, a teacher or administrator may pull a teen aside and ask what he or she was doing, how he or she thinks his or her actions may have affected other students, and how he or she can repair any damage that may have been done. Each class might have regular circle time, where students all get the opportunity to talk about how a bullying incident affected them, and what they would like to see done about it. In some schools, circle time happens daily so that students get to know each other better, and talking about their lives becomes safe and routine. Serious, repeated incidents may be addressed through a conference with a facilitator who was not involved and students and/or adults who were involved. In the case of a bullying incident, it might include the bully, the victim, the families of the bully and the victim, witnesses or friends, teachers, or anyone else that either the bully or the victim thinks should be involved. At the end of the conference, everyone in the room agrees on a set of appropriate consequences, including the person accused of harming others.[30]

A bully may have to write a letter of apology to the student he or she victimized, or become part of a peer mediation program to learn about conflict resolution. The bully may have to spend time repairing the school through painting over graffiti or working in a community garden. All of these consequences hold bullies accountable for their actions and communicate that the school will not tolerate bullying behavior. However, they also help bullies feel included by making them active contributors to the community, putting them in situations where they may make friends or discover talents and interests they never knew they had, and teaching them nonviolent approaches to conflict resolution. Finally—and most importantly—they allow bullies to break unhealthy patterns and to establish a

All about Restorative Justice

When teens at Humanities Prep high school in New York City get in trouble, they appear before a Fairness Committee, a disciplinary body designed using the principles of restorative justice. The committee always has two students, one teacher, and an additional teacher to facilitate. The people on the committee differ depending on the case. During the committee meeting, the group hears all sides of the story and then works together to decide on the appropriate consequences.[9]

Teens at Humanities Prep value the Fairness Committee for a variety of reasons. Teen Luis, who is now an alumnus, says that unlike other types of discipline, the Fairness Committee helps teens feel like they were able to explain their actions and actually be heard. He says, "I especially loved the whole thing Fairness . . . because . . . usually people just get suspended. But Fairness allows people to speak both sides of their story . . . it's a good process to go through . . . for people to have their voice heard."[h]

At Humanities, the discipline code is based on certain core values, and students go before the Fairness Committee when they break one. Teens can take both peers and adults to the committee. Likewise, teachers can take their students before the committee.[i] Rebecca, another teen who went to Humanities, said the committee helped her remember these values, which represent the way she wants to act and the type of person she wants to be. She said, "Well, most of the time you don't even think about the core values until you've broken one, or you get pulled in to do a Fairness, and you're like, 'oh yeah, those are things we're supposed to be living by.' But core values are good, and we need to be reminded of them."[j] In Rebecca's case, getting "pulled into a Fairness" could mean going in front of the committee or being the other teen on the committee who has to help decide on consequences.

Diego, a teen who was having trouble with his behavior, says that the Fairness Committee helped him feel like he had adult allies at his school. He urges his teachers, "Please keep doing Fairness. I'm telling you, it works, even though I hated it at the time. When I was having some issues in [a teacher's] class, he took me to Fairness . . . it showed me that [they] cared, but even more it brought me closer to my teachers."[k] Diego's response reflects a goal of restorative justice that can be instrumental in changing the behavior of a bully: it brings individuals into the community and makes them feel secure in their relationships. As discussed, this can help teens realize that they do not have to act like bullies to feel safe, cared for, and popular.

If you feel that restorative justice could help you as an individual and your school as a whole, here are some groups that may be able to help you bring restorative justice practices to your school, campus, or community.

Center for Court Innovations
New York City, New York
http://www.courtinnovation.org/

Center for Restorative Justice and Peacemaking
St. Paul, Minnesota
http://www.cehd.umn.edu/ssw/RJP/

Communities for Restorative Justice
Boston, Massachusetts
http://www.c4rj.com

Chicago Area Project
Chicago, Illinois
http://www.chicagoareaproject.org/

The Dignity in Schools Campaign
New York City, New York
http://www.dignityinschools.org/

International Institute for Restorative Practices
Bethlehem, Pennsylvania
http://www.iirp.edu/

Restorative Resources
Sonoma, California
http://www.restorativeresources.org/

new identity based on nonviolence. This process ensures that one mistake does not define a teen for the rest of his or her life.

Making your school or campus a place where restorative justice is an option requires you to ally with other students and supportive teachers to make change. There may be students and adults who resist the idea, especially since most of us are used to relying on punishment to keep order in schools. However, the time and energy it takes can be worth it. In West Oakland, California, one troubled school used restorative justice to reduce suspensions by 87 percent and to eliminate all expulsions.[31] Internationally, restorative justice has been shown to reduce the rate of teens repeating their offenses (whether it was bullying or a criminal offense), decrease trauma and stress among victims (which is key to preventing victims from becoming bullies), and lower rates of violent crime.[32] Most importantly, restorative justice approaches create thoughtful, empathetic teens who will grow up into responsible adults. For some teen perspective on restorative justice, and to find out more about how you can bring it to your school, see All about Restorative Justice on page 25.

Changing the School Climate

Earlier in this chapter, we talked about how individuals sometimes become bullies because of personal issues, and they sometimes become bullies because of social pressures. From watching the ways in which other people react to their actions, teens may learn that being a bully leads to popularity, power, and prestige. One way to address this is to stop treating bullies as tough, popular leaders and stop treating victims as weak, powerless outsiders. Educators have a phrase for this: changing the school climate.

Restorative justice approaches and mental health services are both first steps to changing your school's climate. You've probably heard the word *climate* used to describe the way a place feels, especially in terms of the weather: does it feel hot, cold, wet, dry, windy, or sunny? Similarly, when we talk about school climate, we mean the way that a school feels when you are part of the community as a teen or as an adult. One of the most effective ways to combat bullying is to work with your community to create a climate where harassing, intimidating, and disrespecting others feels unacceptable. If bullies do not think that they will gain popularity, power, or emotional safety from bullying others, they will consider other options for dealing with their insecurities or personal problems.

The National School Climate Center is one of the leading authorities on preventing bullying. They've developed a series of surveys that can help students, parents, and teachers assess their school climate and how it can be improved. To see some questions from their assessment, see What's Your School's Climate? on page 29.

Changing school climate can be difficult. It requires changing the attitudes of students, teachers, parents, administrators, and other staff in your school building. Here are a few aspects of your school to keep in mind if you are interested in working with your community to improve the climate:

Learning

Think about what you learn at school. Does your school include students who have different abilities, backgrounds, strengths and challenges, or do these students feel excluded or ostracized? Do you learn about different historical ex-

What's Your School's Climate?

The National School Climate Center's main goal is to stop bullying before it starts. To help teens and adults think about how to improve the way their school feels, the organization has developed a number of surveys for parents, teachers, and students. Table 2.3 has some sample questions from the survey developed for middle and high school students.[1] Copy them onto another sheet of paper and write down your answers. Compare your answers with a friend's answers. Then think about the reflection questions that follow.

Table 2.3 Assessing Your School Climate

	Strongly Disagree	Disagree	Neither Agree nor Disagree (Neutral)	Agree	Strongly Agree
In my school, we talk about ways to help us control our emotions.					
In my school, we talk about the ways our actions will affect others.					
Many students at my school go out of their way to treat other students badly.					
Adults in my school seem to work well with one another.					

	Strongly Disagree	Disagree	Neither Agree nor Disagree (Neutral)	Agree	Strongly Agree
My school tries to get all families to be part of school activities.					
Adults in this school have high expectations for students' success.					

1. How do these questions help you think about your school's climate?
2. What are some areas of your school that could be improved? What's working well?
3. Who could help you address some of the problems you've identified?

To learn about the full school climate survey, check out the National School Climate Center at www.schoolclimate.org

periences from different racial and ethnic groups? Are you able to relate your experiences to the curriculum? Do you have opportunities to practice nonviolent conflict resolution through group work, class discussions, or other activities? In schools with excellent climates, students feel included in class and they feel that the adults in their building believe in their ability to succeed. They also get opportunities to work with diverse students and learn about cooperation, sharing, and conflict resolution.

You can improve your school climate by working with teachers to improve what you learn in class every day, also known as the curriculum. Perhaps you could try and read books in your English class that come from authors who are from your community, or learn more about the role of people in your community in history, or talk in science and math about diverse people who have contributed to the field. You might also ask adults if you could have time for dialogue every day to discuss issues that are affecting your life, and to get to know students and teachers better, perhaps during an advisory period or homeroom. This could even be as simple as doing a journal entry that someone in your school reads and responds to frequently. Think also about your talents and your friends' talents. Do the classroom and after-school activities at your school give you the opportunity to shine? You could think about starting groups at your school that give everyone a chance to show off what they do best.

Another way to think about learning is to closely watch your favorite teacher. What does he or she do to make you feel included, valued, and safe? What if every classroom at your school looked like this? Talk to this teacher about what he or she does to make the class feel fun and safe. Ask if he or she might be willing to work with you to ensure that other teachers do the same.

Discipline

In schools with excellent climates, learning is valued above everything else. Therefore the rules are there to remove barriers to learning, rather than to simply punish students or keep them in line or under control. This is one reason why restorative justice approaches can be effective: they help students clearly see why disciplinary actions are being taken, rather than feeling like punishment is just arbitrary.

You can change your school climate by changing the disciplinary system. Do you feel that students are given the tools they need to regulate their behavior? Do you feel that students are punished fairly and consistently, and that they learn from their mistakes? Do you feel that your school is strict about the right offenses, or do you feel that students are punished for the wrong behaviors? Do you feel that students have multiple chances to improve, or that they are trapped in patterns that they have trouble escaping? Talk to an adult about these questions, and together think about approaches—such as those in this chapter—that could help you improve the discipline system in your school.

Inclusion

In every school, teens and adults have different strengths and weaknesses. For students with disabilities, their physical or learning challenges are sometimes more obvious than those of students who are able-bodied. One way to improve inclusion at your school is to think about whether it is physically accessible to students who may be in wheelchairs. If it is not, what does it say about those students and their place in the community? If bullies are looking for someone to pick on, they often try and target students who are weak and unsupported. If the school is sending signs that certain students are more valuable than others, students may react to this by victimizing those who have no support.

This is true not just of the teens at your school but also adults. Think about which parents are made to feel welcome and how staff, such as cafeteria workers and janitors, are treated. Are richer parents treated better than poorer parents? Are all staff well paid and spoken to with respect? Your community can send the message that everyone is valuable and no one deserves to be bullied. Or it can send the message that some people have more power than others and social hierarchies will never be broken.

Beyond Bullies

One of the best ways to help teens who are acting like bullies is to be supportive friends to the bully or, in some cases, the victim. In the next chapter, you will read about the effects of bullying on teens who are targets of bullying and the relationship between them and bullies.

Notes

1. Bryan Goodwin, "Bullying Is Common—and Subtle," *Educational Leadership* 69, no. 3 (2011): 82–84.
2. U.S. Department of Health and Human Services, "Risk Factors," Stopbullying.gov, http://www.stopbullying.gov/at-risk/factors/index.html#morelikely (accessed December 29, 2012).
3. U.S. Department of Health and Human Services, "Risk Factors."
4. Center for Disease Control, "Bullying among Middle and High School Students—Massachusetts, 2009," *Morbidity and Mortality Weekly* 60, no. 15 (April 22, 2011): 467.
5. Center for Disease Control, "Bullying among Middle and High School Students," 467.
6. Jessie Klein, *The Bully Society: School Shootings and the Crisis of Bullying in America's Schools* (New York: New York University Press, 2011), 26.
7. Klein, *The Bully Society*, 23.
8. Klein, *The Bully Society*, 23.
9. Klein, *The Bully Society*, 24.
10. Klein, *The Bully Society*, 10.
11. Klein, *The Bully Society*, 62.
12. Joanne N. Smith, Mandy Van Deven, and Meghan Huppuch, *Hey, Shorty! A Guide to Combating Sexual Harassment and Violence in Public Schools and on the Streets* (New York: Feminist Press at the City University of New York, 2011), 121.
13. Klein, *The Bully Society*, 62.
14. Klein, *The Bully Society*, 62.
15. Klein, *The Bully Society*, 48.

16. Nancy M. Bowllan, "Implementation and Evaluation of a Comprehensive, School-wide Bullying Prevention Program in an Urban/Suburban Middle School," *Journal of School Health* 81, no. 4 (April 2011): 167.

17. U.S. Department of Health and Human Services, "Effects of Bullying," Stopbullying .gov, http://www.stopbullying.gov/at-risk/effects/index.html#bully (accessed December 29, 2012).

18. U.S. Department of Health and Human Services, "Effects of Bullying."

19. U.S. Department of Health and Human Services, "Effects of Bullying."

20. Bowllan, "Implementation and Evaluation,"167.

21. Lara Salahi, "Bullies Nearly Twice as Likely to Have a Mental Health Disorder," *ABC News*, October 22, 2012, http://abcnews.go.com/Health/Wellness/bullies-mental-health-disorder/ story?id=17518230#.UO0K8eSTxTI (accessed 9 January 2013).

22. Salahi, "Bullies Nearly Twice as Likely."

23. Centers for Disease Control and Prevention, *School Connectedness: Strategies for Increasing Protective Factors among Youth* (Atlanta, GA: U.S. Department of Health and Human Services, 2009), 3.

24. U.S. Department of Health and Human Services, "Support the Kids Involved," Stopbullying .gov, http://www.stopbullying.gov/respond/support-kids-involved/index.html#address (accessed December 29, 2012).

25. Bob Costello, Joshua Wachtel, and Ted Wachtel, *The Restorative Practices Handbook for Teachers, Disciplinarians, and Administrators* (Bethlehem, PA: International Institute for Restorative Practices, 2009), E-book.

26. Costello, Wachtel, and Wachtel, *The Restorative Practices Handbook*.

27. Costello, Wachtel, and Wachtel, *The Restorative Practices Handbook*.

28. Costello, Wachtel, and Wachtel, *The Restorative Practices Handbook*.

29. Costello, Wachtel, and Wachtel, *The Restorative Practices Handbook*.

30. Costello, Wachtel, and Wachtel, *The Restorative Practices Handbook*.

31. Michael D. Sumner, Carol J. Silverman, and Mary Louise Frampton, *School-Based Restorative Justice as an Alternative to Zero-Tolerance Policies: Lessons for West Oakland* (Berkeley: Thelton E. Henderson Center for Social Justice, University of California, 2010), 3.

32. Lawrence W. Sherman and Heather Strang, *Restorative Justice: The Evidence* (London: Smith Institute, 2007), 4.

a. Miguel Ayala, "Beating the Bullies," *YCteen*, 2002, http://www.ycteenmag.org/topics/bullying/Beating_the_Bullies.html?story_id=FCYU-2002-07-02 (accessed October 21, 2012).

b. Ayala, "Beating the Bullies."

c. Ayala, "Beating the Bullies."

d. John Stephens, "Lance Bass, Former 'N Sync Member: I Was Once a Bully," *Huffington Post*, January 9, 2013, http://www.huffingtonpost.com/2013/01/09/lance-bass-nsync-bullying_n _2442825.html (accessed January 29, 2013).

e. Stephens, "Lance Bass."

f. *Lance Bass Responds to Recent Suicides* (video), Reactions to Tyler Clementi's Death, MTV .com, October 1, 2010, http://www.mtv.com/videos/news/579128/lance-bass-responds-to -the-recent-suicides.jhtml#id=1649108 (accessed January 29, 2013).

g. Maria Hantzopolous, "The Fairness Committee: Restorative Justice in a Small Urban Public High School," *Prevention Researcher* 20, no. 1 (February 2013): 7–10.

h.   Hantzopolous, "The Fairness Committee," 9.

i.   Hantzopolous, "The Fairness Committee," 8.

j.   Hantzopolous, "The Fairness Committee," 9.

k.   Hantzopolous, "The Fairness Committee," 9.

l.   National School Climate Center, "Student Survey Form II: Middle / High School Students," *Comprehensive School Climate Inquiry: Measuring the Climate for Learning*, 2013, http://www .schoolclimate.org/programs/documents/Student-MS-HS-CSCI%20v-3.pdf (accessed February 13, 2013).

3

VICTIMS

In this chapter, you will learn about victims, or teens who are bullied. Just as bullies are more than their negative behavior, victims are more than just targets. They might also be athletes, writers, artists, musicians, or actors. They might love designing clothes or taking photographs, or they might have a talent for public speaking or student government. For many teens, the most painful aspect of being bullied is finding their identity reduced to that of a victim. Instead of being recognized for their interests, talents, and successes, attention becomes focused on the fact that they are experiencing repeated violence. This attention may come in the form of harassment from students who, after the bullying, see victims as vulnerable and needy, or pity from well-meaning friends and family. This treatment can make victims feel powerlessness and insecure, emotions that lead to the trauma that underpins some of most damaging consequences of being victimized, including contemplating or committing suicide.[1]

Victims do not need pity. They need our help, support, and respect. In this chapter, you will learn what it means to be a victim of bullying, an essential first step in understanding how you can help students who are targets of violence regain their confidence and self-respect. You will learn why some teens are more vulnerable to victimization than others, how bullying affects teens in the short and long term, and what you can do to support friends and peers who are bullied. Throughout, you will see examples of teens who treated their victimization as an opportunity to create change. Sadly, you will also see examples of teens who lacked the support they needed and took extreme measures such as becoming violent themselves or committing suicide. Victims of bullying are diverse, but they all have one thing in common: they want the violence to stop.

Who Gets Bullied

Over thirteen million young people are victims of bullying every single year.[2] Each day, about 160,000 of these students stay home from school because they are afraid of their bullies.[3] Most likely, you know one or more teens who have been bullied; you may even have been bullied yourself.

Since bullying is widespread, it is almost impossible to make generalizations about victims. Some studies suggest that young people who have low self-esteem, feel ashamed of themselves, or experience anxiety are at greater risk of being bullied than their peers, perhaps because they become quiet and removed or do not respond to violence, choices that their peers interpret as physical and emotional fragility.[4] Although no teen should be victimized for genuinely expressing emotion or choosing to deal with conflict peacefully, some bullies mistakenly take these behaviors as opportunities to continue their negative behavior.[5]

Researchers also say that before the bullying began, many victims suffered from social isolation; some may not be able to identify a single person who they

Teens who face social isolation are more likely to be victims of bullying.

consider a close and trusted friend.[6] Bullies see these teens as easy targets because they do not have a group of peers to support them.[7] Furthermore, teens who have few friends may feel ashamed, isolated, or worthless. Projecting these feelings also puts them at risk for victimization and begins a destructive cycle: once bullying starts, it becomes harder for victims to make friends. Other teens may fear that befriending the victim will make them targets as well. Or, worse, they may begin to see the victim as weak, worthless, and, in extreme cases, deserving of abuse.[8] This false and harmful assumption is based on social systems that reward violence, strength, and aggression, which in turn make teens see bullies as powerful and worthy of popularity and respect.

Teen Adam Kreitzman experienced bullying on his basketball team in sixth grade. He has since become involved in a club in his school that combats social isolation, or the practice of excluding teens from peer groups and friendships. Kreitzman feels that if more teens were self-reflective about why social isolation occurs, they could combat it. To read more about his story, see below.

Social Bullying: Adam Kreitzman's Story

When teen Adam Kreitzman was in sixth grade, some of his friends started talking about him behind his back. Kreitzman found the experience hurtful and did not understand why his friends would treat him this way. Here, he reflects on his experience, how he has changed his own behavior because of it, and the work he does with an organization with a teen board dedicated to combating social isolation.

The closest I have been to being bullied is when a student spread lies about me and complained that I was not fit for basketball when I happened to have a bad game once in 6th grade. The entire team had not been playing well but that day I missed two open shots while we were 20 points down anyway. I found it shocking that my teammate had told many classmates about a game "they lost because of Adam (me) who would not make the A team next year anyway." The coach was a player's dad and negative comments were made in front of him. That dad never taught us a lesson: that we are a team and should comfort one another in times of losses.

Kids often do not think about the consequences of simply talking "bad" about someone else. They don't understand the responsibility they have to be nice to others. I am surprised when I read about how mean some kids are to others; I don't understand how someone can be proud after bullying someone!

Perhaps because of my work with Beyond Differences [http://www.beyond differences.org/], an organization which combats social isolation and teaches everyone the importance of "simply reaching out to everyone," I have become more acutely aware of what is said around me. Whenever someone spreads lies or negative comments about someone else somehow I have my "antennas" out and I remember these events and I intervene by saying something positive to the person who has been bullied or criticized and I don't agree with the person who bullies or who is mean.

I don't think I was a bully ever but once I caught myself saying to my best friend who is a great baseball player and who never played basketball before "you suck at basketball" when he came to my home and we had a game where I scored 23–0. I saw how he was frustrated and I immediately apologized. I remembered the time when I was actually bullied in some ways when a kid spread lies about me and so I felt bad and apologized many times and then asked to have a baseball game with my friend because I knew I would suck at it anyway since baseball is not my thing.

I think kids who are busy volunteering for good causes and who want to be nice can make a huge difference. We can either be blind to those who are bullied or active in stopping it.[a]

Sometimes teens suffer from social isolation because of aspects of their identities. They may not be able to interact with peers because of a disability, language issue, or mental illness, or they may have an identity that makes them a part of an oppressed group. In the next section, you will learn about how power and popularity determine who is at risk of becoming a victim.

Bullying and Power

As we discussed in chapter 1, fundamentally, bullying is about power. Victims cannot avoid or escape bullying simply by changing the way they act, nor should they: none of us should have to change who we are out of fear.

Many teens are bullied because they have less power and privilege than the individual who is bullying them. Research suggests that often, this power difference is related to a victim's identity. In this section, you will learn to recognize patterns concerning why bullies sometimes—but not always—disproportionately target teens who belong to oppressed groups, a concept we discussed in chapter 1.

Teens who identify as LGBTQ (lesbian, gay, bisexual, transgender, or queer) or are perceived to be LGBTQ are frequent victims of bullying. Research repeatedly shows that LGBTQ teens experience more verbal and physical harassment than their peers who identify as straight.[9] This is particularly true of transgender teens who might be born male but identify as female, or born female but identify as male. Other transgender teens may be born without a clear sex, meaning that they are neither fully male nor fully female. According to a recent study, 82 percent of teens who identify as transgender feel unsafe at their schools because of bullying and harassment associated with the way they express their gender.[10]

Teens may victimize their LGBTQ peers because they believe that doing so will earn them popularity and status. Bullies sometimes feel that targeting those who do not conform to gender stereotypes reinforces their own masculinity, femininity, or heterosexuality.[11] Adults who witness bullying related to sexual orientation or gender expression may not see it as a serious issue, or may not know how to intervene. Transgender youth reported that adults and peers were much more likely to recognize and respond to sexist and racist remarks than homophobic remarks or remarks about gender expression.[12] This pattern not only points to the need for more awareness about how to respond to transphobic and homophobic bullying, it also reinforces the power of bullies who target LGBTQ teens, sending the message that being straight or masculine or feminine is normal and anything else is inferior.

In reality, our perceptions of gender and sexuality—just like our ideas about many kinds of identities—are the results of cultural violence derived from the idea that males and females must be punished, ridiculed, or humiliated if they do not behave, dress, and fall in love in specific ways. This cultural violence is not universal, though. The Navajo tradition, for example, values transgendered individuals.[13] In 2001, Navajo transgender teen Fred Martinez was murdered because of his gender identity, a tragedy that led members of his community to reflect on the sources and impact of cultural violence stemming from nonnative beliefs. Read more about Martinez and the documentary he inspired on page 40.

Teens who come from low-income backgrounds are also more likely to be victims of bullying.[14] Bullies may not specifically tease them for having less money, but rather for the choices that they make because they are not as wealthy as other students. For example, they may not be able to afford the latest clothes and may be harassed for wearing fashions that are out of date or worn out. They may not be able to take part in social activities like eating at expensive restaurants or attending pricey events because they do not have enough money, and so become isolated or excluded.

Fred Martinez: The Story of Two Spirits

In 2001, eighteen-year-old Shaun Murphy was convicted of killing sixteen-year-old Navajo Fred Martinez. After the investigation, officials concluded that the murder was motivated by Murphy's suspicion of Martinez's identity as "two-spirited," a Navajo word used to describe individuals who feel both male and female.[b] Consequently, the act was labeled a hate crime, or an illegal activity motivated by extreme prejudice and discrimination. Martinez is one of the youngest hate crime victims in history.

Although Martinez's community tried to ignore the murder at first, eventually, they could not ignore the press attention, and so they began a conversation.[c] Historically, the Navajo honor *nádleehí*, or those who identify as both male and female, just like Martinez.[d] After the teen's death, Navajos who identified as LGTBQ began to wonder when their community stopped embracing gender diversity and started persecuting it. They talked about how the Navajo have four different genders instead of two, and that some indigenous cultures recognize even more genders.[e] When, they wondered, did they start conforming to violent cultural beliefs that portrayed transgender peoples as abnormal, rather than celebrated, powerful, and balanced?[f]

This self-examination spurred change both within and outside of Martinez's community. The local high school established a strong Gay-Straight Alliance that remained active ten years later.[g] His story inspired a documentary that traveled the United States, educating and inspiring young people about global traditions that value transgender people, and challenging the perception that being either male or female is superior to other gender identities.[h] Although homophobia and transphobia persists throughout the Southwest, Martinez's death made people recognize that these beliefs were arbitrary and violent, rather than norms that they should simply embrace without questioning.

To learn more about Martinez's story, and to find out how to bring the film to your school, check out the *Two Spirits* film website at www.twospirits.org.

Another group of teens that may suffer from social isolation are teens with disabilities, whose differences may become their defining characteristics even though their personalities are shaped by much more than just one trait. Many differently abled teens may be great athletes, artists, comedians, or musicians. Unfortunately, they are also often targets of bullying because their peers do not bother to get to know them, or to understand their capabilities and interests.

Some teens with special needs have conditions that make it difficult for them to relate to people or register emotions in the same way as their peers. For example, teens with Asperger's syndrome have difficulty reacting appropriately to social cues, and may panic if they change daily routines.[15] However, they tend to be able to keep up or excel academically, so they are in classes with students who unfairly see them as strange, abnormal, or weak, and therefore potential targets for bullying.[16] In fact, a recent study shows that 46 percent of students with Asperger's experience bullying in the form of physical assault, verbal harassment, and social isolation, a percentage that is three times higher than their peers who are not affected by the disorder.[17] The risk rises when students have other issues as well, such as attention-deficit/hyperactivity disorder.[18]

Teens with physical disabilities may be excluded from opportunities to interact with peers informally and form friendships. For example, some may have a condition such as cerebral palsy that makes them frail, requiring them to avoid classes like gym or barring them from participation on sports teams. Others may have special diets that make it impossible for them to eat in the cafeteria. Still others may find their peers underestimating them, believing that because they are unable to perform certain tasks, they do not lead dynamic lives. In fact, disability is just one aspect of every differently abled teen's life. Eighteen-year-old Sawyer Rosenstein, for example, lost the use of his legs because he was punched in the knees by a bully. He is now wheelchair bound. He has become an outspoken advocate against bullying and violence, among his many other interests. To read more about Rosenstein, see page 42.

Certain identities and experiences may make teens more likely to be victims of specific kinds of bullying, particularly dating violence. For example, studies estimate that at least a quarter of teen mothers experience intimate partner violence; some studies say that the level could be as high as 50 to 80 percent.[19] Teens who witness domestic violence at home are more likely to be victims of domestic violence themselves.[20] Again, these teens do not automatically become victims because of their backgrounds, but they are at higher risk than their peers, perhaps because they have not had experience in a variety of relationships, and therefore are unable to recognize the warning signs of violent behavior. For more on dating violence, see chapter 8.

Sawyer Rosenstein's Story

When Sawyer Rosenstein was in middle school, he wanted to be an actor. He loved to talk, laugh, and fool around. He said that his theatricality made him "one of the odd ones out," and made him the target of bullying.[i] Although he reported the harassment to his school administration, Rosenstein said that staff did nothing, and the bullying continued. The school's choice to ignore the reporting had serious consequences: a bully punched Rosenstein in the knees, which led to an unusual condition called a spinal blood clot, paralyzing Rosenstein below the waist. Now, even after nineteen surgeries, he is in a wheelchair and unable to walk.

Rosenstein said that at first he was devastated. He says, "I'd ask, 'Why me?' I had fits of depression."[j] After this initial stage, he decided to use what had happened to him to try and create change. He has become an outspoken advocate for implementing effective bullying policies in schools, including creating improved reporting systems and more timely and useful responses. "I want kids to report what's going on. I want accountability," he says.[k]

Rosenstein has not let his physical challenges impair him from living an active life. In addition to working to prevent bullying, he has a wide variety of interests—most recently, he's started teaching classes at a space center for children and recording and broadcasting his own podcasts. He says, "I could feel sorry for myself, but I've got a life to live, and I'm happy."[l] Rosenstein's optimism and drive show the power teens have to overcome serious obstacles, and to change lives, regardless of their physical abilities.

Finally, bullying tends to decrease as teens get older. Consequently, more ninth grade students report seeing or experiencing bullying than twelfth grade students.[21] As teens mature, they begin to learn to value diversity. They also learn new ways to communicate and deal with conflict. This combination makes them less likely to both bully and be victims of bullying.

Bullying affects many different kinds of individuals, and everyone has his or her own story about what it was like to be a victim. Writers from diverse backgrounds are starting to tell more and more stories about experiencing bullying as a result of their identities. For some great reads about bullying from multiple perspectives, check out Being Bullied: Read All about It! on page 43.

Being Bullied: Read All about It!

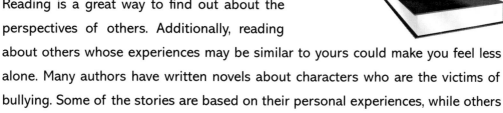

Reading is a great way to find out about the perspectives of others. Additionally, reading about others whose experiences may be similar to yours could make you feel less alone. Many authors have written novels about characters who are the victims of bullying. Some of the stories are based on their personal experiences, while others are entirely imagined. Here are some titles to check out.

The Absolutely True Story of a Part-Time Indian, by Sherman Alexie (2007, Little, Brown Books for Young Readers, 288 pages). Native American teen Junior is bullied by everyone from his best friend to his family to the students in his new school. He decides to change his life by enrolling in a high school that is miles away from the American Indian reservation where he lives. He soon makes friends at his new school and joins the basketball team, where he begins to learn who he is and how to cope with his life as a constant outsider. Alexie says this novel is based on his own experiences as a teen.

Blue Boy, by Rakesh Satyal (2009, Kensington, 352 pages). Kiran is an Indian American boy who prefers ballet and makeup to sports and trucks. His gender and racial identities make him an outcast and a victim of bullying. Suddenly, he has an idea: maybe his victim status is not because he is strange or defective. Maybe he is actually the reincarnation of the Hindu God Vishnu. In this hilarious and touching story, Kiran comes to terms with who he is and how to be proud of his identity.

Jumped, by Rita Williams-Garcia (2009, Amistad Press, 169 pages). Trina accidentally upsets the perpetually angry basketball player Dominique. Soon the rumor gets out that Dominique is going to jump her outside their inner-city high school. It seems like everyone at school knows what's about to happen—except for Trina. This book is told from the perspectives of the bully, the victim, and the witness.

Shine, Coconut Moon, by Neesha Meminger (2007, Margaret McElderry Books, 256 pages). Samar (Sam), who was raised by a single mother, had not thought much about her Sikh heritage until after September 11. This is the story of how Sam comes to terms with her identity while she remembers bullying she faced as a child, is forced to confront her boyfriend's abusive behavior, and struggles to protect her turban-wearing uncle and newfound Sikh community from hate crimes that have been plaguing the neighborhood.

Tell Us We're Home, by Marina Tamar Budhos (2011, Atheneum Books for Young Readers, 320 pages). Jaya, Maria, and Lola live in a wealthy suburb where they share a common identity: they are all the daughters of nannies. When Jaya's mother's employer accuses her of stealing, the three friends must fight the adults and teens who bully them and their mothers.

Twisted, by Laurie Halse Anderson (2007, Penguin Books, 272 pages). When Tyler is arrested for vandalizing his school, he goes from being the nerdy boy in the background to the feared bad boy. When Bethany, the sister of the boy who bullies Tyler, becomes interested in him, Tyler begins to wonder who he really is and what he cares about.

Wonder, by R. J. Palacio (2012, Knopf Books for Young Readers, 320 pages). August is born with a severe facial deformity that makes it difficult for him to do basic things like eating and smiling. In fifth grade, he decides to stop home schooling and join a regular school for the first time. Told from multiple viewpoints, this is the story of how he overcomes bullying with the help of his family and his friends.

Short- and Long-Term Effects of Bullying

Bullying is a public health issue that can have serious mental and physical health consequences. There is a growing body of research about the short- and long-term effects of being a victim of bullying. In the short term, victims are more likely than their peers to experience depression, insomnia, and a loss of appetite.[22] They may have trouble making friends, and they may struggle with anxiety.[23] These issues can make it difficult for them to concentrate, which in turn could make them lose interest in activities they enjoy.[24] Some of these patterns extend into adulthood. For example, compared to their peers, bullying victims have a greater probability of having anxiety problems, panic disorders, and depression when they are older.[25]

Victims also run a high risk of falling behind academically. Due to the aforementioned lack of concentration, they may not be able to study properly and maintain their grades.[26] Additionally, hundreds of thousands of bullying victims skip school to avoid being harassed or persecuted.[27] These teens may struggle to catch up with their peers when they return and may find the dual pressure of facing a bully and recovering lost time overwhelming. As a result, they may drop out of school. Recent research shows that avoiding bullying is a common reason why students do not complete their education.[28]

Perhaps the most serious potential consequence of bullying is suicide. Victims are at risk for ending their own lives both as teens and when they get older.[29] Not every victim of bullying feels suicidal. However, cases in which victims committed suicide have garnered national attention and have brought bullying into the spotlight as a serious threat to young people's well-being. Sometimes victims take their own lives because they have underlying mental health issues, such as depression, that make it difficult for them to cope with strong emotions. Other times victims commit suicide because they are tired of living in fear or of keeping secrets. This is one reason why suicide has become a serious concern in the LGBTQ community: in September 2010, for example, four teen boys in four different parts of the United States who identified as gay committed suicide within the space of just nineteen days.[30] One of these victims was Tyler Clementi, whose case you will read more about in chapter 6.

If you or a friend has suicidal thoughts, get help immediately. In the case of a peer, ask a trusted adult to alert a counselor or psychologist who can assess whether this individual is in danger of harming himself or herself. If you are feeling suicidal, speak to an adult immediately. You can also call suicide helplines that are staffed with operators that are trained to work with teens and maintain your confidentiality. The National Suicide Prevention Lifeline can be reached at 1-800-273-TALK (8255). (If you are hard of hearing, you can call 1-800-799-4889.) Your call will be connected to a crisis center in your area so you can get immediate, local help. To find out more, go to http://www.suicidepreventionlife line.org/.

Victims are not the only teens who have a higher risk of suicidal tendencies than their peers. In fact, this trend is also true of bullies. This is just one similarity: in fact, the line between bully and victim is much thinner than you might think.

Bully-Victims

Victims and bullies face many of the same issues. Just like victims, bullies are more likely than their peers to face depression, anxiety, and suicidal thoughts as adults.[31] Perhaps it is not surprising, then, that a sizeable percentage of victims become bullies. There is a term for individuals who go from being the target of harassment to the perpetrator of harassment: bully-victims.

Experts say that bully-victims are some of the most vulnerable students in school. They often have the fewest friends and the most trouble adjusting socially.[32] Many have short tempers that they are unable to control.[33] Many become frustrated easily, or unable to hide what they are feeling. Just like bullies, bully-victims experience violence from both adults and peers.[34] Just like victims, bully-victims are often socially isolated, with few peers that they can call close friends.

About a quarter of teens involved in online bullying—called cyberbullying and discussed in chapter 6—have both bullied others and been bullied themselves.[35] The possibility of anonymity may give teens who feel victimized by face-to-face bullying a sense of power that they would not have in the real world. Consequently, online platforms are the perfect places for teens who feel powerless and out of control to take revenge on their bullies without fear of physical reprisal. Although teen victims may gain temporary emotional relief from acting like bullies, violence can never be stopped using violence.

Another type of bullying in which bully-victims are commonly involved is sexual harassment. A recent study shows that 29 percent of students who sexually harass others were sexually harassed themselves.[36] Furthermore, 95 percent of students who told researchers that they had sexually harassed others said that they had previously been sexually harassed.[37] Almost a quarter of teens in the study who admitted to being harassers said that they did it to "get revenge," a reason that reflects the desires of a victim to gain power and control back from his or her harassers.[38] It is notable that about one-third of the students surveyed said that they thought their actions as harassers "were stupid," indicating that they recognized that their behavior is unacceptable and should be changed.[39]

The risk of becoming a bully is one of the many reasons why it is important to provide victims of bullying with the services and support they need to heal. In the next section, you will learn about the kinds of support victims need to recover from bullying.

Healing Victims

The most important—and, at times, the most difficult—part of helping victims heal is ending the bullying behavior that is causing them trauma. This may involve taking disciplinary action against the bully, conducting peer mediation or restorative justice circles (see chapter 2), removing abusive content from online forums, or, in extreme cases, filing court orders. Throughout, victims should feel safe and should be sheltered from potential reprisals from bullies angry about being held accountable for their actions. To learn more about the components of effective systems for reporting and responding to bullying, see chapter 10.

Once the bullying stops, victims must cope with the aftermath of the violence. They may require help overcoming anxiety and depression, integrating themselves into social groups, recovering ground academically, or regaining self-esteem. Mental health professionals such as therapists, psychologists, psychiatrists, and social workers can provide guidance and support in these cases.

Most school counselors are trained to deal with these issues. Unfortunately, some schools may not have a counseling staff. Other schools may have counselors, but they may not have the time or resources to provide individual students with sustained attention. Consequently, teens may have to seek services outside of their schools. Ideally, providers should be low cost or free, since some teens lack health insurance or want to approach counselors without the knowledge of parents or guardians. It can be helpful if providers come from the same background as the students, particularly in communities where teens may be hesitant to get help because they think it makes them weird or weak. In reality, mental illness affects more teens than many of us know, and seeking help is a sign of strength and willingness to heal and change, rather than a sign of weakness. A therapist who is familiar with the teen's background can help address this feeling and other issues in a culturally relevant manner.

Another way to help victims heal is to give them strategies to avoid being targeted in the future. For example, it can be helpful for them to learn to stand up for themselves, perhaps by role-playing what they will do the next time someone tries to bully them. Or, they may learn to value aspects of themselves that make them unique, but also make them more vulnerable to bullying, such as a disability, their sexual orientation, their gender identity, or their income level. Or, they may combat social isolation by building community through getting involved in extracurricular activities, building stronger connections with family members, or going out of their way to introduce themselves to someone new.

Sometimes teen victims need to change, not to please a bully, but to lead happier and healthier lives. For example, some victims may need practice controlling emotions such as anger or frustration. Others need to recover from feelings of vulnerability, insecurity, or shame. Many teens who experience trauma and violence deal with their emotions through doing something creative. They may enjoy painting or sketching, writing poems or stories, dancing or playing music, or acting in plays or comedy sketches. Creative activities are helpful not only because they give us outlets to express our feelings, but also because they help us feel talented and special. As artists, we can reveal parts of ourselves that make us proud, a process that is essential for healing. Nida Ruzzaq is an example of a teen who enjoys writing poetry. Her poem, "I Been Treated So Wrong" on page 48, portrays the progress a young person makes from insecurity to pride.

One of the most important things to remember is something discussed earlier: no teen is simply a victim. All teens have multiple identities and experiences. With the right support and care, no teen has to define him- or herself as a bullying victim for his or her entire life.

I Been Treated So Wrong

This poem by teen Nida Ruzzaq describes the journey of a teen who was a victim of bullying. The subject of the poem gained confidence and was able to stop her self-destructive behavior. This is a creative interpretation of what it feels like to recover from the depression and trauma of bullying.

I Been Treated So Wrong

The scars will stop the bullies,
The scars will stop my parents.
The scars will start letting me see my true beauty.
The scars are the ones who don't call me names
The scars are the ones who don't beat me up.
from their words
I am thinking, they are right
I am a failure,
I am a loser,
I am useless,
I am an ugly girl . . .
aren't I?

I've been treated so wrong,
as if I am becoming untouchable.

The blades and scars will never cry for me
The scars will ruin my skin
The tears will make me weaker
The pain will get stronger
The blood will always be coming out of this ugly body.
I am a slow dying flower
but . . .

inside I am a true beauty to me

I am a wild flower,

found in the most unlikely places

I am a true winner . . .

aren't I?

Start by making a change

Start by putting the blade down.

Start by loving yourself.

Start by loving others before . . .

someone cuts in the wrong place

and with their blood they write,

Am I Better For You Now WORLD?

. . . start by putting the blade down.

Healing victims and preventing bullying is not an individual responsibility. Rather, it is a collective responsibility. In the next section, you will learn about ways to build welcoming and tolerant communities that accept differences and reject bullying.

Creating Safer Schools

Being bullied can make victims feel helpless and alone. This can be particularly damaging for teens who do not have a strong sense of belonging at their schools or in their communities. Sometimes victims feel isolated because they have few friends. Other times they feel excluded because of their identities. Teens with physical disabilities, for example, may not be able to participate in academic or athletic activities with the rest of their class. Teens who identify as LGBTQ may not be interested in discussing romance with their peers who are interested in the opposite sex. Teens who have less money may not be able to participate in social events that require spending cash that they do not have. These differences not only make them more vulnerable to bullying, they also lead to social isolation.

Schools can combat social isolation by teaching teens that differences make people unique and interesting, not uncool or worthy of bullying. Teachers, students, and administrators can work together to give students who would ordinarily be bullying victims opportunities to interact with peers in a positive way. For example, rather than simply celebrating sports, schools might hold plays and talent shows where students who are not athletically inclined can show off their strengths. Having activities like these in schools can help teens discover talents that make them proud of themselves and allow them to define themselves in new ways.

Another way that schools can help integrate victims of bullying is to introduce clubs where teens can meet others who either have an identity in common with them or consider themselves allies, something you will read more about in the next chapter. Gay-Straight Alliances (sometimes called GSAs), for instance, are places where LGBTQ students can safely meet both LGBTQ and straight peers who are publicly supportive of queer issues. Another example might be a Students on Financial Aid club at a college campus, where young people who struggle to pay tuition can both exchange information and provide emotional support in the face of classism.

One of the reasons that teens are bullied is that their peers make assumptions about them without taking the time to get to know who they are and what makes them special. Some teens may feel trapped by cliques and may feel scared to venture out of the boundaries of their group of friends to meet new people. Or, they may avoid new students because they believe that doing the opposite will put them at risk for victimization. Situations like these can make it scary for teens to do something as simple as make a new friend.

An organization called Teaching Tolerance started an annual event to address these barriers and encourage teens to meet new people: Mix It Up at Lunch Day.[40] Every year on October 29, schools ask teens to simply have lunch with someone they have never spoken to before.[41] Schools do a variety of activities throughout the day, week, or year to help students implement inclusive practices like welcoming newcomers, finding commonalities with peers who may appear to be different, and practicing empathy.[42] Many teens say they enjoy Mix It Up at Lunch Day because they have a structured opportunity to make new friends. This helps them avoid some of the issues they would face if they approached a new person alone, such as overcoming timidity, worrying about what others will think, and feeling vulnerable to rejection. To find out how to bring Mix It Up to your school, check out www.tolerance.org.

Focusing on inclusion for a day, a week, or even a month is not enough to change a school environment. To build a truly inclusive space, adults and students in the building must set examples for each other. Adults must respect students and other adults. Students must question whether the criteria they use to judge others are based in reality or what they have been taught is cool. Adults and students alike must practice empathy by respecting the perspectives, feelings, and experiences of others.

Being an Ally

In this section, we have learned about what teens can do to help each other both cope with bullying and prevent it from happening. In the next section, you will learn about what you can do if you are not a victim or a bully, but a third party in a bullying incident: a witness. As you will see, being a bystander can be a powerful position for someone who wants to create change.

Notes

1. Danah Boyd and Alice Marwick, "Bullying as True Drama," *New York Times*, September 23, 2011, A35.
2. Shannon Maughan, "A Call to Action: Bullying and Books," *Publishers Weekly*, October 22, 2012, 22.
3. Maughan, "A Call to Action," 22.
4. Dan Olweus, *Bullying at School* (Oxford, UK: Blackwell Publishing, 1993), 32.
5. Olweus, *Bullying at School*, 32.
6. Olweus, *Bullying at School*, 32.
7. Olweus, *Bullying at School*, 44.
8. Olweus, *Bullying at School*, 44.
9. Emily A. Greytak, Joseph G. Kosciw, and Elizabeth M. Diaz, *Harsh Realities: The Experience of Transgender Youth in Our Nation's Schools* (Washington, DC: Gay, Lesbian, Straight Education Network, 2007), 14.
10. Greytak, Kosciw, and Diaz, *Harsh Realities*, 14.
11. Jessie Klein, *The Bully Society: School Shootings and the Crisis of Bullying in America's Schools* (New York: New York University Press, 2011), 83.
12. Greytak et al., *Harsh Realities*, 12.
13. "*Two Spirits*: About the Film," Independent Lens, PBS, 2013, http://www.pbs.org/independentlens/two-spirits/film.html (accessed April 12, 2013).
14. Klein, *The Bully Society*, 20.
15. Anahad O'Connor, "Autistic Pupils Face Far More Bullying," *New York Times*, September 4, 2012, D7.
16. O'Connor, "Autistic Pupils Face Far More Bullying," D7.
17. O'Connor, "Autistic Pupils Face Far More Bullying," D7.
18. O'Connor, "Autistic Pupils Face Far More Bullying," D7.
19. Break the Cycle, *2010 State Law Report Cards: A National Survey on Teen Dating Violence Laws* (Los Angeles: Break the Cycle, 2010), 4.
20. David A. Wolfe and Christine Wekerle, "Dating Violence Prevention with At-Risk Youth: A Controlled Outcome Evaluation," *Journal of Consulting and Clinical Psychology* 71, no. 2 (2003): 280.

21. DoSomething.org, *The Bully Report: Trends in Bullying Pulled from Student Facebook Interactions*, 2012, http://files.dosomething.org/files/campaigns/bullyreport/bully_report.pdf (accessed January 19, 2013), 7.

22. U.S. Department of Health and Human Services, "Effects of Bullying," Stopbullying.gov, 2013, http://www.stopbullying.gov/at-risk/effects/index.html#bullied (accessed April 13, 2013).

23. Danielle Jansen, René Veenstra, Johan Ormel, Frank C. Verhulst, and Sijmen A. Reijneveld, "Early Risk Factors for Being a Bully, Victim, or Bully/Victim in Late Elementary and Early Secondary Education: The Longitudinal TRAILS Study," *BMC Public Health* 11, no. 440 (2011): 2.

24. U.S. Department of Health and Human Services, "Effects of Bullying."

25. William E. Copeland, Dieter Wolke, Adrian Angold, E. Jane Costello, "Adult Psychiatric Outcomes of Bullying and Being Bullied by Peers in Childhood and Adolescence," *JAMA Psychiatry* 70, no. 4 (April 2013): 419–426. doi:10.1001/jamapsychiatry.2013.504.

26. U.S. Department of Health and Human Services, "Effects of Bullying."

27. Maughan, "A Call to Action," 22.

28. Dewey Cornell, Anne Gregory, Francis Huang, and Xitao Fan, "Perceived Prevalence of Teasing and Bullying Predicts High School Dropout Rates," *Journal of Education Psychology* 105, no. 1 (February 2013): 138–149. doi: 10.1037/a0030416.

29. Copeland et al., "Adult Psychiatric Outcomes of Bullying," 423.

30. John Cloud, "Bullied to Death?" *Time*, October 18, 2010, 60–63.

31. Copeland et al., "Adult Psychiatric Outcomes of Bullying," 423.

32. Faye Mishna, Mona Khoury-Kassabri, Tahany Gadalla, and Joanne Daciuk. "Risk Factors for Involvement in Cyber Bullying: Victims, Bullies and Bully-Victims," *Children and Youth Services Review* 43, no. 1 (January 2012): 64.

33. Mishna et al., "Risk Factors," 64.

34. Mishna et al., "Risk Factors," 64.

35. Mishna et al., "Risk Factors," 67.

36. Catherine Hill and Holly Kearl, *Crossing the Line: Sexual Harassment at School* (Washington, DC: American Association of University Women, 2011), 3.

37. Hill and Kearl, *Crossing the Line*, 3.

38. Hill and Kearl, *Crossing the Line*, 15.

39. Hill and Kearl, *Crossing the Line*, 15.

40. Teaching Tolerance, "What Is Mix It Up at Lunch Day?" Teaching Tolerance: A Project of the Southern Poverty Law Center, 2013, http://www.tolerance.org/mix-it-up/what-is-mix (accessed May 25, 2013).

41. Teaching Tolerance, "What Is Mix It Up at Lunch Day?"

42. Teaching Tolerance, "Mix It Up Activities (Grades 9 to 12)," Teaching Tolerance: A Project of the Southern Poverty Law Center, 2013, http://www.tolerance.org/mix-it-activities-grades-9-12 (accessed May 25, 2013).

a. Adam Kreitzman has given Rowman & Littlefield permission to publish his story in his own words.

b. Emery Cowan, "A Boy Remembered: Transgender Teen's Death 10 Years Ago Remains a Motivation for Education about Gender Diversity," *Durango Herald*, June 11, 2011, http://durangoherald.com/article/20110612/NEWS01/706129875/ (accessed April 12, 2013).

c. Cowan, "A Boy Remembered."

d. Two Spirits, "About," Twospirits.org, 2013, http://twospirits.org/about-the-film-2/ (accessed April 14, 2013).

e. Two Spirits, "About."

f. Cowan, "A Boy Remembered."

g. Cowan, "A Boy Remembered."

h. Two Spirits, "About."

i. Janine Rayford with Sydney Berger, "A Bullying Victim Bravely Speaks Out," *People*, July 9, 2012, 88.

j. Rayford with Berger, "A Bullying Victim Bravely Speaks Out," 88.

k. Rayford with Berger, "A Bullying Victim Bravely Speaks Out," 88.

l. Rayford with Berger, "A Bullying Victim Bravely Speaks Out," 88.

WITNESSES

Almost every American teen has watched someone else being bullied. Approximately eight in ten teens witness bullying at least once a week, and a quarter of teens witness it every day.[1] Nine out of ten teens have seen bullying occur online.[2] Teens become witnesses or bystanders when they see a bullying incident take place that they have not instigated. Witnesses can stop bullying or can encourage it to continue. Based on sheer numbers, giving bystanders the tools they need to defend victims could be one of the most powerful ways to end the cycle of violence. Yet, standing up to bullies can be risky and frightening. Plus, experts still do not have a full understanding of the psychological effects of witnessing bullying. In general, bystanders tend to be overlooked by teens and adults alike.

In this section, you will learn about different types of bystanders and what is known about the psychological effects of being a witness. You will also read about why witnesses may choose not to act on behalf of victims, and how to intervene in a bullying situation if it does not put you at personal risk. As you will find, if you have the courage to intervene in a bullying incident without being harmed, you have the power to positively impact the lives of both the bully and the victim.

Effects of Being a Witness

Even though witnessing bullying is a common experience among teens today, we know little about its psychological impact. A recent study suggests that witnesses are at risk for abusing alcohol or drugs, and feeling unusual levels of anxiety, depression, or paranoia.[3] They may have difficulty forming trusting relationships, and they may experience elevated heart rates, particularly during time periods when bullying commonly occurs, such as during lunch.[4]

For young people who currently are or have been bullying victims, the psychological effects of being a bystander can be more severe. For these teens, witnessing bullying may trigger memories of their own experiences as victims.[5] This in turn reminds them of the anxiety, depression, and other negative emotions they had when they were being bullied.

Regardless of past experiences, witnessing bullying can lead to feelings of helplessness and powerlessness.[6] Teens who see bullying occur and do not intervene or report what they have seen may feel that they should have done more.[7] They may be pressured into participating in bullying even if they do not want to, which also makes them feel guilty.[8]

A bystander's decision to support the victim, the bully, or neither can ruin relationships, end friendships, and leave lasting trauma. The role is painful and

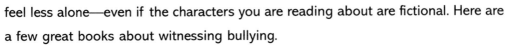

Witnessing Bullying: Read All about It!

Sometimes reading about the experiences of others can help you find ways to cope and to feel less alone—even if the characters you are reading about are fictional. Here are a few great books about witnessing bullying.

Bystander, by James Preller (2009, Feiwel and Friends, 240 pages). Eric, who is new in town, befriends popular and attractive classmate Griffin. Slowly, Eric starts to realize that Griffin is a bully. Eric watches from the outside at first, not joining in the bullying but not stopping it either. Then the tables turn, and Eric is Griffin's next victim.

The Hate List, by Jennifer Brown (2010, Little, Brown and Company, 432 pages). Valerie is devastated when her boyfriend, Nick, opens fire in school, killing several students and injuring many others, including Valerie. When she returns to school in the fall, her classmates are convinced that she was partially responsible, even though she was not. Worst of all, despite what he did, she still loves and misses Nick, who killed himself after the incident. This book is the story of how she and her community heal from this loss.

Orchards, by Holly Thompson (2011, Ember, 336 pages). Kana Goldberg is half Jewish, half Japanese American. After her friend commits suicide, Kana decides to go to Japan to stay with her family and work in the orchards. During the summer, she thinks about the role she and her clique played in allowing the bullying that led to her friend's suicide to continue. Eventually, she takes a courageous step to make things right. The story is told in the form of a poem.

complicated, which perhaps is why it is attractive to authors looking for nuanced plots and complex characters. There are a growing number of fiction books that are told from the viewpoint of witnesses. These stories explore what it's like to watch a friend become a bully, find yourself implicated in serious bullying incidents, and go from being a bystander to a victim. Try out some of the titles in Witnessing Bullying: Read All about It! on page 56.

Types of Witnesses

Witnesses can be classified according to the level of involvement they have in a bullying incident. Depending on their role, witnesses can be essential in stopping bullying. Unfortunately, they can also be instrumental in allowing the bullying to continue.

The first type of witness is called an *assistant*.[9] An assistant supports teen bullying without taking the lead role. Usually the assistant does not start the bullying, nor does he or she do the majority of the physical or verbal harassment. Instead, the assistant may encourage the perpetrator to continue the negative behavior or may contribute a few comments to verbal harassment. Assistants may justify their behavior by rationalizing that they did not instigate the behavior and that they are part of a group of people engaging in bullying and therefore do not bear complete responsibility.[10] By supporting the violence, though, assistants reinforce that bullying is socially acceptable and, in fact, can lead to popularity.

Bystanders could also be *reinforcers*, or individuals who do not participate in physical or verbal abuse but react to it positively by laughing, moving to get a better view of the incident, or otherwise showing that they are enjoying what is happening.[11] After the incident is over, they may tell others about what happened or laugh at the victim behind his or her back. Unlike assistants, reinforcers are not directly involved in bullying. However, like assistants, they send the message that bullying is fun and exciting. Having an audience makes some bullies feel powerful and popular, even though the way they behave should be considered socially unacceptable. Furthermore, by rallying positive responses to violence, reinforcers exacerbate victims' feelings of isolation and helplessness.

Witnesses can also be classified as *outsiders* who see the incident but do not react.[12] Many outsiders actively remove themselves from the situation, going so far as to pretend that they are not seeing what is happening. Outsiders may choose not to intervene because they feel powerless, unsure, or afraid that the bully will turn on them as well. While outsiders do not make the violence worse, they also do not make it better.

Finally, witnesses who stand up for the individual being victimized and actively try to stop the bullying are classified as *defenders*.[13] During the incident, they

Witnesses may choose to act as outsiders who do not influence the situation positively or negatively.

may intervene by defending the victim or attempting to stop the bully. After the incident is over, they may publicly take the side of the victim by helping him or her cope with the trauma. Sometimes defenders risk being bullied for their stance or being physically assaulted if there is a fight going on. Alternatively, they could be powerful and popular students who decide to use their social power to stand up for others. Either way, the defender can play an important role by helping others see bullying as something damaging rather than cool.

A recent study shows that 76 percent of teens say that "the best thing others can do to stop bullying is to intervene."[14] In fact, when a young person intervenes in a bullying incident, the odds of a physical fight occurring go down about 10 percent.[15] Considering how many teens witness bullying, it is likely that almost every bullying incident has at least one bystander who could try to stop it. Yet, about half of teens say that when bullying occurs, others rarely or never intervene.[16] If witnesses actually have the power to stop violence, then why do so few try to intervene? In the next section, you will learn about the reasons why bystanders stay out of bullying incidents, even if they want to help.

Why Witnesses Do Not Speak Up

When teen Alice Wong was in eighth grade, she was part of a group of girls who used to bully others. While Wong never directly participated, she never stopped her friends. She remembers, "I often thought about what would happen if I told them how I felt when they were mean, but I was afraid to because I didn't want to lose their friendship. I was used to them and thought it would be too difficult to get to know a new group of people. I was also afraid that if I spoke up, they'd all turn on me as well."[17]

Wong is not alone in her fears. Bullies are often popular members of the school community who choose to use their power violently. Students who are friends with bullies may also be a part of this popular group. Standing up to bullying could cause them to lose their social status. This can feel like a lot to give up, particularly if it involves long-term friendships. Another reason that teens hesitate to intervene in bullying is that they run the risk of becoming victims. In addition to social exclusion, teens who stand up to bullies may face verbal taunts, online harassment, or rampant rumors. In some cases, witnesses who stand up to bullies are dragged into physical fights, which could lead to suspension, expulsion, or criminal charges.

Some defenders avoid this possibility by reporting incidents to trusted adults. Unfortunately, many do not choose this route because they believe that adults cannot help.[18] Furthermore, they may be labeled a "rat" or a "snitch" for bringing adults into the situation and may be victimized themselves. Many students decide that reporting is not worth the risk, especially considering that there is no guarantee that telling an adult will actually stop the violent behavior. For more about the complex issue of reporting and responding, see chapter 10.

Being a witness is even more complicated in online violence, known as cyberbullying. Cyberbullying can be anonymous, so sometimes students do not know who is bullying them. Furthermore, it is rarely confined to one or more discrete incidents that last for a certain amount of time. Instead, it takes the form of a web page or photo or e-mail or text that remains alive for days, weeks, or months, giving other students the opportunity to escalate the violence by spreading the message further or contributing harmful and damaging comments. It is hard to know how to stop cyberbullying from continuing once it has begun. After all, a bystander cannot be present every time someone reads the offending material to defend the friend who is being victimized. Also, a witness cannot delete the information from every single device, particularly if it is an e-mail or text message.

A common reason witnesses do not intervene is because they do not know what to say or do in the moment. When bullying is happening, everyone involved experiences strong emotions that could impair judgment or slow down response time. However, defenders do not always intervene immediately. Some are supportive friends to victims, consoling them and helping them cope after the incident. Some confront the bully after the incident occurs, when being alone makes it easier to talk honestly. In the next section, you will learn a variety of techniques for being a defender.

Being a Defender

Teens sometimes think that the only way that they can help victims is by standing up to bullies while they are targeting others. This can be frightening and risky, and, most importantly, it is not the only option. If you know the student acting like a bully personally, you may want to intervene when you have time to talk alone. If you are not comfortable speaking to the bully, there are many other ways that you can show the victim your support. In this section, you will learn numerous ways to be a defender. You will also meet some teens who provide examples of what being a great defender can look like.

Support the Person Being Bullied

Teens who are bullied may feel alone, desperate, and helpless. This is why one of the common reactions to bullying is skipping school or avoiding social contact. One way to be a defender is to let the victim of bullying know that you care and that he or she can depend on you. This could mean calling or texting the person, inviting him or her to social events, visiting him or her at home, or sitting with him or her at lunch. It could also mean refusing to participate in conversations about the bullying or disputing rumors when you hear them. In the case of cyberbullying, it could mean choosing not to forward an e-mail or text or picture, or to refrain from commenting on a page. It may not be enough to stop the bullying, but it could help the teen who is being bullied have the strength to maintain friendships and relationships with others that will help him or her avoid sinking into anxiety or depression.

When teen Destiny Smith's friend Jessica was cyberbullied, Smith did not know who was responsible for creating the page that targeted her friend and several other female students. However, she still found a way to be a defender. Read more about Smith's story, as told in *YCteen*, on page 61.

Report the Bullying to an Adult

Some teens think that letting an adult know about a bullying incident is dishonorable because it betrays their classmates' privacy. Others fear that the bully will

Destiny Smith's Story of Being a Defender

When teen Destiny Smith found out about a Facebook page someone at her school had created to bully other students about their sexuality, the last person she expected to see on it was her friend "Jessica" (name has been made up). The page called Jessica, among other things, a "whore" and someone "who had abortions for fun."[a] Smith was horrified and called Jessica immediately. Jessica was distraught. Although Smith advised Jessica to move past it, she realized how seriously her friend was hurting.

Jessica began to avoid her friends at school, and started wearing clothing that hid her body and face. Smith remembers, "I asked Jessica why she was staying away from us. She said she felt nasty. Everywhere she went, she felt like everybody was talking about her or looking at her funny. At first I thought that maybe she was exaggerating, but then I walked her to her class. Sure enough, it seemed like everywhere I turned, somebody was looking at Jessica, whispering or shaking their head."[b] Eventually, Jessica stopped coming to school.

When Smith visited Jessica at home, she found out that Jessica had been sexually abused and that being cyberbullied about her sexual activity made traumatic memories resurface. Smith convinced her to come back to school despite the obstacles she was facing. On Jessica's first day back, Smith knew that she had to be there for her friend. She says, "I approached her with a smile to let her know that she was not going to endure the bashing by herself. For the next couple of days I walked her to all her classes and sat with her at lunch to get her back into the habit of being a productive student."[c]

Jessica is back at school, and although she is much less trusting and open than she used to be, she is surviving. Smith was able to be a supportive witness for Jessica without confronting the bully. In her role as a defender, Smith made a huge difference in Jessica's life.

find out and target them next. Still others think that reporting will not result in any action. Yet, adults in your school, campus, and community can sometimes be the most effective people to address bullying because they can help you with the individual incident as well as find ways to prevent bullying from occurring in the future.

When you are reporting an incident, you should speak to an adult you trust, even if that person is a neighbor or relative who may not work at your school or campus. If you have any evidence of the bullying, you should bring it, particularly if the incident is something that happened online or over your cell phone. If you think you may have trouble discussing what happened, try writing down everything you remember and giving it to the adult. Explain that it is hard for you to talk about, and that you were more comfortable putting it down on paper. Let the adult know if you have concerns about being a target. You may wish to remain anonymous, which is a decision that any adult should respect. You may also want to let the adult know you need him or her to look out for you and try to be around if the bully you are reporting is present. Finally, you may want to ask him or her for suggestions as to how to remain safe after you have made the report.

If your school does not have a mechanism for making anonymous reports—such as an e-mail address or a toll-free number—you should consider talking to faculty and administrators about starting a confidential system. If students are able to report bullying anonymously, they may be more likely to do so. Or, at the very least, those who choose to report bullying can feel safer about their decisions.

In the case of cyberbullying, you may have other options as well, such as calling service providers and asking them to remove inappropriate content, especially on platforms such as Facebook and Twitter. You may also be able to call your cell phone company and ask them for help blocking messages from certain callers. See page 63 for some resources you can turn to if you witness cyberbullying.

Talk to the Bully in Private

Sometimes it is better to talk to someone who is acting like a bully after an incident has occurred, rather than in the moment. This could make you feel calmer and safer, since you can take time to think about what you want to say. It may also be better for the bully, who may feel more comfortable being him- or herself when there is no audience to impress or reputation to maintain.

When you speak to an individual who is acting like a bully, it can be helpful to separate him or her from his or her action.[19] Start by saying something that you admire and respect about the person to show that you have his or her best interest in mind.[20] You might say something like, "One of the reasons that I like being friends with you is that you really care about me," or "I will always remember that time you stuck up for me in third grade," or "You mean a lot to me, and so does our friendship." Then try and ask questions that are not accusatory, but instead focus on his or her side of the story. Rather than asking "why"—many bullies cannot actually answer this question—ask "what" and "how" questions.[21]

Witnessing Cyberbullying

If you witness cyberbullying, you may be able to directly contact service providers who can help you remove the abusive content. Here are some websites and organizations you can call for advice.

Twitter: Reporting Abusive Behavior
https://support.twitter.com/forms/abusiveuser

YouTube.com: Content Reporting and Removals
http://support.google.com/youtube/bin/answer.py?hl=en&answer=178909

Facebook: How to Report a Violation
http://www.facebook.com/help/263149623790594/

Commonsense Media (a nonprofit that can help you with all cyberbullying complaints)
http://www.commonsensemedia.org/

You might also want to contact teachers, counselors, or administrators in your school or on campus who can put you in touch with local resources for combating cyberbullying.

For example, you could ask, "What were you doing earlier today when you were with Miguel?" Or "How did you feel when you were in the hallway today with Fatima?" Then ask your friend to reflect on how this made others feel. For example, "How do you think Ana felt when you said that?" This is also a good time to remind your friend about his or her good qualities. For example, you might say, "You are always so considerate of my feelings. That's why I was surprised about the way you acted. How do you think Casey feels right now?"

Throughout the conversation, try to be supportive of the bully. You may find out that he or she has something going on at home and needs help. You may find

Sometimes you can be a supportive witness by speaking to your friend alone after the incident has occurred.

out that something upsetting happened earlier that made him or her lash out in anger, fear, or frustration. You may find that he or she has started a pattern of bullying that he or she wants to break. In all these cases, you can work with your peer to address the problem and to repair the damage done to the victim.[22] Remember that bullies often act the way they do because of an underlying problem. Having a friend like you who is willing to confront the behavior and work through it with them can make all the difference in bullies' lives.

Before you speak to the bully, you may want to practice role-playing the conversation with a trusted adult or friend. Together, try anticipating some possible directions that the discussion may take, and brainstorm ways that you could react. Try using the Freeze Frame! exercise on page 65 to prepare yourself—and have some fun in the process.

Freeze Frame!

When you watch someone become a bully, it can be difficult to know how to tell that person that you do not approve of the behavior, particularly if he or she is your friend. You may feel scared and alone, or you may wish you had someone else there to support you. One way to avoid this feeling is to work with friends to anticipate reactions and prepare responses beforehand. This way you know what you are comfortable saying and doing, and you know you have a strong network to rely on when you intervene.

Here's a game you and your friends can play to help you problem-solve together. It's called Freeze Frame!

Directions:
1. Think of a time when you witnessed bullying and you wanted to intervene.
2. Ask a group of friends who know the two involved parties to get together. Pick a friend to play the role of the bully, and then pick a friend to play the role of the victim.
3. Describe the scene you witnessed and then ask your friends to act it out.
4. When you get to the part where you wish you had done something differently, say "Freeze!"
5. Discuss with your friends how you were feeling and why you didn't intervene. Brainstorm possible responses. As you are brainstorming, try and predict how the bully or the victim will act. What are some possible negative consequences? How could they be avoided?
6. Ask the friends to do the scene again. Then, allow other friends (including yourself) to yell "Freeze!" when you get an idea.
7. The actors should freeze. Walk over to the victim or witness and tap him or her on the shoulder.
8. Then try out the responses you have brainstormed. Make sure that the other friends act out a possible worst case scenario that could happen with this response, and try to deal with it. See if you change the situation.
9. When you're done, discuss which strategy you liked best. What will you use next time? What did you learn from this?

This activity was adapted from a game created by Augusto Boal, a Brazilian actor and activist who started a genre of theater called Theater of the Oppressed. If you liked this, check out Boal's book *Games for Actors and Nonactors* (1992). It's full of theater games you can use to come up with your own strategies for promoting nonviolence.

Stop the Show

One of the reasons that teens act like bullies is because they get positive reinforcement for their negative behavior. If they think that bullying makes them more popular or powerful, they will continue to do it. If they feel that they are not getting any benefit or, worse, are becoming less popular, they are more likely to stop. Consequently, sometimes the best thing you can do as a defender is to stop the bully from getting positive attention for his or her destructive behavior.

The simplest way to do this is to help the victim of bullying find an excuse to get away from the situation.[23] You might say something like, "Come on, we'll be late for practice," or "Hurry up, Ms. Jones is asking for you," or "You're going to make me late again, let's go!" Remember that sometimes bullies act out because they do not know where to channel their anger or other negative emotions. If you can get a friend away from the bully, it may diffuse the situation, giving the bully time to think rationally about his or her behavior and to find another way to cope with whatever he or she is feeling.

Another way to stop the show is to refuse to give the bully an audience. You could simply walk away from public bullying incidents, taking as many friends as you can with you. If you feel comfortable, you could also say something like, "I don't think that's cool," or "It's not funny," or "This isn't something I want to watch." This will help others around you realize that they do not need to be a part of the scene unfolding, or it may give them the courage to express their disapproval as well. Ideally, this could make the prospect of intimidating the victim less appealing since there is no audience to impress.

In both of these cases, you should consider the risk to yourself. If you feel that speaking out publicly could expose you to emotional or physical harm, it is perfectly acceptable not to act in the moment. As you've learned in this chapter, there are many ways to be a defender without putting yourself directly in harm's way.

Be an Ally

As you've read in previous chapters, bullying is all about power. Bullies act the way they do to become more powerful. Victims are often individuals who have less power in the social hierarchy. Witnesses are afraid to intervene because they feel powerless, or because getting involved threatens the power that they have.

One way to be a defender is to stand with those who may have less power in our society. An individual who chooses to use his or her privilege to try to make the world a safer, more just place is called an *ally*. Being an ally means more than just standing up for victims when bullying occurs. It means understanding and recognizing how and why we treat certain people differently than others. It also means using this understanding to try to change these unfair patterns of behavior.

Being an ally means actively learning about people who are not like you. At times, it can be uncomfortable. It may mean building relationships with individuals you would never normally talk to, or confronting the fact that you have certain advantages that your friends do not have that have contributed to your success. But it can also be a lot of fun. For example, it may mean attending events like fund-raisers, protests, marches, or cultural events where you might make new friends, develop new skills, and learn more about yourself. To find out more about what it's like to be an ally, check out Kristy Plaza's story below.

Being an Ally: Kristy Plaza's Story

Kristy Plaza is straight, but her friend "Tom" (name has been changed) is gay. Starting in middle school, Plaza watched Tom face homophobia in their Los Angeles area community, even though their high school was reputed to be accepting. "At my school same-sex couples are welcome to every school dance. The administration is trying to create an open-minded environment, but the reality is that not all students at my school are tolerant,"[d] Plaza says.

Although her friend said that he would no longer let hateful acts and comments hurt him, Plaza felt that he should not have to face hatred because of his sexual orientation. She was frustrated and wanted to create change, so she decided to join the school's Gay-Straight Alliance (GSA), a club for lesbian, gay, bisexual, and queer (LGBTQ) students and their straight allies. Plaza says, "I eventually realized that if I didn't stand up for gay rights, then I'd be just as bad as those who make fun of people who are gay."[e] As a straight person, Plaza realized that she had the power to convince other straight people to stop using violence to address something they do not understand.

At the first meeting, Plaza listened to gay and lesbian students talk about their experiences coming out to their families. Later, she learned more about the obstacles faced by both LGBTQ teens and adults: at one meeting, a member's father talked about how he had to quit his job because of speculation about his sexuality. Plaza began to understand not just what homophobia looks like, but also where it unfolds. This understanding helped her recognize how and when she could take action as a straight ally.

Plaza is a senior now, but feels that during her three years in the GSA, she has learned many ways to be a defender. To begin with, Plaza recruited other students to join the club, both LGBTQ and straight. She frequently talks to her peers about the importance of gay rights issues such as marriage equality. She also confronts students who use homophobic slurs in everyday conversation. She says, "When one guy says to another that he looks good, he feels like he has to immediately say, 'No homo.' When I hear someone say that, I tell them, 'Please don't say that. It's offensive and I'd appreciate it if you didn't say things like that. Thanks.'"[f]

Plaza sees that there are risks to her actions. For example, she thinks many people at her school believe that she is a lesbian, which could open her up to the same teasing her LGBTQ friends face. However, Plaza knows that there is nothing negative about being a lesbian and is not bothered by the speculation. She says, "I don't care because I think it's important for people to stand up for what they believe in, regardless of what anyone else might think."[g] Furthermore, Plaza recognizes that as someone straight, she has power and privilege in her school. She can use that power and privilege to change the way people think.

Plaza says, "Gay or straight, everyone can be hurt by words and we all deserve kindness and respect."[h] This is why she believes that playing the role of an ally is so important.

If you're interested in starting a GSA at your school, check out Gay-Straight Alliance Network at www.gsanetwork.org.

Being an ally is not always easy. You may face bullying, intimidation, or harassment because you choose to side with a group that is considered unpopular, uncool, weird, or different. But by being an ally, you will set an inspirational example. Furthermore, it may help others appreciate who you are and where you come from: while some of your identities may give you privilege, others may not. For example, you may be straight, but you may also be a woman, or a person of color, or working class, exposing you to sexism, racism, or classism. Who knows—perhaps one day, a male LGBTQ student you defended may stand up for your gender, or a White woman that you defended may stop her friend from being racist. The friends you make as an ally may have the opportunity to be *your* ally as well, giving you an opportunity to work together to fight bullying based on multiple identities.

Different Types of Bullying

If you have read this far in this book, you have learned a lot about bullying. You've learned who the key players are in a bullying situation, and what challenges teens face in incidents involving harassment and intimidation. Perhaps most importantly, you've learned about the power you have to address bullying, no matter who you are or what your role may be.

In the next section, you will learn how to recognize and combat multiple types of bullying, ranging from bias-based harassment to cyberbullying to sexual harassment. Understanding how and why bullying takes place will help you confront violence in your own life and the lives of others. Read on to find out more about the types of bullying you and your friends may face.

Notes

1. DoSomething.org, *The Bully Report: Trends in Bullying Pulled from Student Facebook Interactions*, 2012, http://files.dosomething.org/files/campaigns/bullyreport/bully_report.pdf (accessed January 7, 2013), 3.
2. Cecilia Kang, "Nine of 10 Teenagers Have Witnessed Bullying on Social Networks, Study Finds," *Washington Post*, November 9, 2011, http://articles.washingtonpost.com/2011-11-09/business/35282386_1_social-networks-social-media-amanda-lenhart (accessed January 7, 2013).
3. Ian Rivers, V. Paul Poteat, Nathalie Noret, and Nigel Ashurst, "Observing Bullying at School: The Mental Health Implications of Witness Status," *School Psychology Quarterly* 24, no. 4 (2009): 211–223, 220.
4. "Study Shows Bullying Affects Both Bystanders and Targets," *Penn State Live: The University's Official News Source*, October 11, 2011, http://live.psu.edu/story/55627 (accessed January 8, 2012).
5. Rivers et al., "Observing Bullying at School," 220.
6. National Youth Violence Prevention Resource Center, *Facts for Teens: Bullying*, accessed at Unified Solutions, http://www.unified-solutions.org/Pubs/what_is_bullying.pdf (January 8, 2013), 2.
7. National Youth Violence Prevention Resource Center, *Facts for Teens*, 2.
8. National Youth Violence Prevention Resource Center, *Facts for Teens*, 2.
9. Rivers et al., "Observing Bullying at School," 212.
10. Dan Olweus, *Bullying at School* (Oxford, UK: Blackwell Publishing, 1993), 44.

11. Rivers et al., "Observing Bullying at School," 212.
12. Rivers et al., "Observing Bullying at School," 212.
13. Rivers et al., "Observing Bullying at School," 212.
14. DoSomething.org, *The Bully Report*, 9.
15. DoSomething.org, *The Bully Report*, 9.
16. DoSomething.org, *The Bully Report*, 7.
17. Alice Wong, "Nasty Girls," *YCteen*, 2002, http://www.ycteenmag.org/topics/bullying/Nasty_ Girls.html?story_id=NYC-2002-11-05 (accessed October 21, 2012).
18. DoSomething.org, "11 Facts about Bullying," DoSomething.org, 2012, http://www.do something.org/tipsandtools/11-facts-about-school-bullying (January 19, 2013).
19. Bob Costello, Joshua Wachtel, and Ted Wachtel, *The Restorative Practices Handbook for Teachers, Disciplinarians, and Administrators* (Bethlehem, PA: International Institute for Restorative Practices, 2009), E-book.
20. Costello, Wachtel, and Wachtel, *The Restorative Practices Handbook*.
21. Costello, Wachtel, and Wachtel, *The Restorative Practices Handbook*.
22. Costello, Wachtel, and Wachtel, *The Restorative Practices Handbook*.
23. U.S. Department of Health and Human Services, "Be More Than a Bystander," Stopbullying.gov, 2013, http://www.stopbullying.gov/respond/be-more-than-a-bystander/index.html (accessed February 21, 2013).

a. Destiny Smith, "Smut Page Survivor," *YCteen*, 2011, http://www.youthcomm.org/topics/ bullying/Smut_Page_Survivor.html?story_id=NYC-2011-11-06 (accessed January 9, 2013).
b. Smith, "Smut Page Survivor."
c. Smith, "Smut Page Survivor."
d. Kristy Plaza, "Standing Up for Gay Rights," *LA Youth*, October 2011, http://www.layouth .com/standing-up-for-gay-rights/ (accessed July 21, 2013).
e. Plaza, "Standing Up for Gay Rights."
f. Plaza, "Standing Up for Gay Rights."
g. Plaza, "Standing Up for Gay Rights."
h. Plaza, "Standing Up for Gay Rights."

BIAS-BASED HARASSMENT

If you have been bullied, you have probably experienced some combination of verbal, physical, and emotional teasing. It probably happened on the way to school, in your front yard, in the hallway when no one was looking, maybe even on your Facebook page. You probably felt that the individual bullying you had power over you. You may have had this feeling because the bully was stronger or more popular, or because of your identity. These patterns are common to many types of violence, not just bullying.

Bullying differs from other forms of abuse because it happens repeatedly. Sometimes it is predictable, occurring always on the bus or in the locker room. Other times it is unexpected, occurring when the bully runs into you in the hallway or suddenly begins posting messages online. But the key is that it happens more than once over an extended period of time. This is why bullying is so painful: the victim does not know how to make it stop.

Although all bullying follows certain patterns, it is not all the same. In this section, you will learn about how specific types of bullying can be identified, addressed, and, ultimately, prevented. Since there are many different types of bullying, you may have to take different approaches depending on the type of violence you face.

In this particular chapter, you will learn about bias-based harassment, or bullying that targets individuals because of their identities. You will learn what bias-based harassment looks like and how teens have worked together with policy makers to draw attention to how their identities affect their chances of being bullied. You will also explore your own multiple identities, including those that give you power and privilege, and those that expose you to oppression. Perhaps most importantly, you will learn how you can use your power to help stop bias-based harassment from occurring.

Bias-Based Harassment

As you learned in chapter 1, identities are personal characteristics about ourselves that affect how much power we have in society. Examples of identities are race, ethnicity, faith, gender, class, and sexual orientation. All of us have multiple identities, and, as we discussed in chapter 1, some of our identities grant us power while others expose us to oppression. All of our identities contribute to our experiences and make us unique individuals; in an ideal world, our identities would make us proud rather than fearful or insecure.

Bullies who engage in bias-based harassment target people because of their identities, whether or not those identities are visible and powerful in mainstream society. Even if you have an identity that gives you privilege, if you experience bullying because of any of your identities (such as your race, disability status, or religion) then you are experiencing bias-based harassment. So, for example, if you are being bullied because you are male, it does not matter that your gender gives you power. It is still bias-based harassment because you are being bullied over a characteristic that you cannot control.

Bias-based harassment occurs when bullies target us because of our identities.

Bias-based harassment is common, and it is harmful. A recent national study of thousands of teens showed that about one-third of bullying incidents could be classified as bias-based harassment.[1] The same study indicated that teens who suffered from bias-based harassment had worse health outcomes than teens who experienced bullying for other reasons. Compared to their peers who had suffered other types of violence, victims of bias-based harassment were more likely to have used alcohol or drugs, to get lower grades, to have experienced depression, and to engage in unhealthy behavior like drunk driving and skipping school. They also ran the risk of becoming victims of relationship violence, another form of bullying we'll discuss later in this volume.[2] Currently, we do not have enough research on bias-based harassment to fully understand why these negative trends occur. We do know, though, that bias-based harassment makes victims feel insecure about fundamental aspects of themselves that they cannot—and that they should not—change. This leads to feelings of deep fear, loneliness, and insecurity that probably contribute to psychological and physical issues.

No one should suffer from violence because of their identities. Not only does this bias-based harassment harm individuals, it also harms communities: places where differences are punished instead of celebrated and are less diverse, less vibrant, and less peaceful. Fighting bias-based harassment benefits us all by making our worlds more welcoming and interesting places.

Common Types of Bias-Based Harassment

In this section, you will learn about types of bias-based harassment. The examples here are not exhaustive, but they are some of the more common cases you will likely see in your schools and communities.

Ethnicity and Race-Based Harassment

Ethnicity and race are closely related, but they are not the same. Ethnicity describes a person's heritage. For example, I identify ethnically as Indian even though I was born in the United States. This is because my parents are from India, and this heritage is an important part of who I am. Some teens may have more than one ethnicity because their parents come from two different countries, or because they were born in a different country than their family. Others may identify with the same ethnicity as their home country alone.

Race, on the other hand, has to do with a person's physical characteristics. Race is not biological: if you compared a Black person and a White person's DNA, they would have so many genes in common that it would be almost impossible to tell their races. Instead, race is determined by how others perceive us and how we perceive ourselves. This is why we sometimes say that race is a *social construct*. Take President Barack Obama, America's first Black president. President Obama's mother was White and his father was Black. President Obama identifies as biracial, but American society defines him as Black because of his physical characteristics, such as his skin color and his hair. (In other societies, he may be considered White for these same reasons.) Although President Obama can choose his racial identity, he cannot choose how society sees him. His race has nothing to do with his genes, but instead is about the way he looks.

Because our society perceives some races and ethnicities in certain ways, the way you look can affect your ability to succeed. For example, some people think that the media criticizes President Obama more harshly than other presidents because he is Black, and that in 2008 and 2012 Americans voted against him because they preferred to support a White candidate, not because of his policies, skills, or other characteristics.[3] Race affects more than just presidents: in schools, Black and Latino teens are sometimes assigned to easier classes because teachers and administrators make false judgments about their abilities based on their race and ethnicity,[4] while Asian American students may not receive tutoring or other help they need because they are perceived to be overachievers simply because of the way they look.[5]

Since the teen years are a time for figuring out who you are, many teens—especially teens of color—spend a lot of time thinking about how they identify racially and ethnically and about how others identify them. Teens who become comfortable with their identities often do better in school, have stronger relationships, and are less likely to experiment with drugs later or join gangs.[6] They are also more likely to recognize and understand racism because they know that their race or ethnicity makes them unique and different, rather than less capable, intelligent, or attractive, no matter what society says.[7] When teens are bullied because of their race or ethnicity, it makes it harder to feel comfortable with these identities, and to have a strong sense of self essential to success and happiness as an adult.

In the United States, teens who ethnically identify as something other than American are considered oppressed, as are teens who identify as non-White—often called "people of color." A recent study shows that Asian American teens suffer more bullying than any other racial or ethnic group. More than half (54 percent) of Asian Americans in a recent study said that they have been bullied, as compared to about one-third (30 percent) of the general population.[8] Some people think this is because Asian Americans are stereotyped as quiet and submissive, so bullies see them as easy targets who will not fight back.[9] Others attribute it to the fact that some Asian Americans are recent immigrants who speak English with an accent, or because they are often profiled as Muslim and therefore become victims of Islamophobia.[10] Still others cite the myth that Asian Americans are "model minorities" who are smarter, wealthier, and better behaved than other minorities, a false idea that may make non-Asian teens of color resentful and likely to bully Asian peers out of humiliation, anger, or fear. This was the case in one high school in Philadelphia, where fellow students of color attacked Asian American students repeatedly, making them fear for their safety. Instead of allowing the bullying to continue, the students banded together to stop the violence. Read about how these teen advocates stood up to bullying below.

Asian American Teens Stand Up to Bullying

In December of 2009, Asian American students at South Philadelphia High School lived through a nightmare. Starting at 9 a.m., groups of Asian American students were attacked: one had a table thrown on top of him, and another was dragged down the stairs by her hair. The problems continued at lunch, when a group of African American students attacked a group of Asian American students standing in line in the cafeteria. Asian American teen Duong Nghe Ly remembers that as the violence was happening, "a group of about 40 students cheered."[a]

Later that afternoon, another group of Asian American students was attacked walking home from school. Vietnamese American teen Trang Dang was hit in the face in the attack, and her glasses were smashed. She also suffered severe mental trauma. She remembers, "After I got hit, then my mind just went blank. I was crying. It wasn't that painful, I think, but I don't really remember. I think because I've tried to forget about that day."[b]

After the incidents, an investigation showed that the violence started because of an untrue rumor that a group of Asian American students had bullied a wheelchair-bound Black student. More disturbing to the victims, though, was the lack of response from adults in the school, some of whom ignored the violence or expressed their unwillingness to help. Instead of continuing to live in fear, the Asian American students decided they had had enough. About eighty students boycotted school for eight days, returning only when the school agreed to take action. They also worked with the Asian American Legal Defense and Education Fund (AALDEF) to file a case against the school.

Since the incident, a new principal has made serious changes, taking steps to integrate the Asian Americans into the school community, posting signs in multiple languages explaining how to get help if you feel your safety is being threatened, installing security cameras, and establishing an adult point person as a resource for all bullying incidents. The school district also created an anti-bullying policy for the school and began to report incidents of bullying publicly.

Ly says that now the school is "truly a safe space to come and learn."[c] As a result of the changes he created, Ly won the Princeton Prize in Race Relations in 2011. He and his peers, now in college, tour schools talking to teens about bias-based harassment. Teens such as Ly show the power young people have to end violence.

Just because Asian Americans experience the most bias-based harassment does not mean that they are the only racial or ethnic group to face this abuse. Unfortunately, there is little research on bullying due to race and ethnicity, so these rates are hard to come by. However, there are resources available for learning more about race- and ethnicity-based harassment. Groups such as Teaching Tolerance (www.tolerance.org), the School of Unity and Liberation (www.schoolofunity-andliberation.org), the Chicago Freedom School (www.chicagofreedomschool.org), and the People's Institute for Survival and Beyond (www.pisab.org) offer resources and training for young people who want to learn more about recognizing and combating racism and ethnic discrimination. All of these organizations welcome teens of color and teens who identify as White. In fact, White students who understand and fight racism can be important allies to teens of color at their schools and in their communities by educating themselves and their peers about race, ethnicity, and respecting others.

Religion and Faith-Based Discrimination

About 80 percent of Americans identify as Christians. Although Christians are the majority, the United States is religiously diverse: about three million Americans identify as Jewish, about a half a million identify as Muslim, and more than six hundred thousand follow Eastern religions such as Buddhism, Sikhism, or Hinduism.[11] Compared to Christians, though, these groups are small.

Throughout history, American teens and families have experienced bias-based harassment as a result of their religion, or for being atheists who do not believe in God or any religion. Lately, though, the religious groups that have experienced the most prevalent and visible bias-based harassment are Muslims and Sikhs. This is often because their peers associate these teens with the attacks on September 11, when fundamentalist Muslims flew planes into the World Trade Center in New York City, destroying two iconic buildings and killing thousands—including many Muslims and Sikhs. Muslim teens say that their peers verbally harass them by calling them names like "terrorist" and saying "your family blows things up."[12] Others have suffered from physical violence at the hands of bullies who target them because of their faith.[13]

It is hard to tell how much bias-based harassment happens to Muslim teens since Islamophobia tends to be underreported. A group called Muslim Mothers conducted a survey of fifty-seven Muslim teens in their areas and found that every single one of these teens had been harassed because of their religion, which may indicate that the problem is very widespread.[14]

Bullying because of Islamophobia is not limited to Muslims. This is one reason why Asian Americans are currently the most bullied racial group: many people think that South Asians *look* Muslim, even though Muslims can be Black or White, and come from almost every continent and country.[15] One group of teens that has been especially targeted is Sikhs, who practice a religion that requires them to grow beards and wear turbans. About 75 percent of Sikh male teens said that they experience bias-based harassment as a result of their choice to wear a turban and to grow a beard.[16] Like Muslim teens, they are often called names like "terrorist."

When it comes to bullying, attention is often focused on Sikh boys, who wear turbans. However, Sikh girls are also targets of violence. One Sikh young woman, named Balpreet Kaur, was publicly cyberbullied because of her religiously motivated choices not to remove her facial hair and to wear a turban (which traditionally only Sikh boys do). Kaur spoke out about the strength she finds from her faith and was shocked by the positive response. For more about Kaur's story, see below.

Balpreet Kaur's Story

Balpreet Kaur, who is Sikh, was used to attention: she wears a turban, something that is usually worn by the men who practice her religion, and she has visible facial hair. She says, "They didn't know me, and they probably haven't seen another Sikh. And of course, they've probably never seen a Sikh woman who doesn't remove any of her body hair, including her facial hair."[d] The combination of Kaur's gender and religion made her stand out among her peers.

Stares were one thing, but bullying was another. Last year, someone anonymously posted a photograph of Balpreet Kaur in the "funny" section of the social media site Reddit.com with the caption, "I am not sure what to conclude from this."[e] The post was soon followed by negative comments harassing Kaur for the way she looked. The bias-based harassment attacked both her faith and her choice to be gender nonconforming by wearing a turban.

Instead of allowing both layers of violence to hurt her, Kaur decided to speak up. She wrote a response, saying, "I'm not embarrassed or even humiliated by the attention [negative and positive] that this picture is getting because, it's who I am. Yes, I'm a baptized Sikh woman with facial hair. Yes, I realize that my gender is often confused and I look different than most women. However, baptized Sikhs believe in the sacredness of this body . . . by not focusing on the physical beauty, I have time to cultivate those inner virtues and hopefully, focus my life on creating change and progress for this world in any way I can."[f]

Kaur wrote to her bullies—who she did not know—because she saw it as an opportunity "to educate, to enrich, and to elevate."[g] To her surprise, she received an outpouring of support from strangers who respected her choice to stand up to bias-based harassment and to be proud of who she is. Her response drew thousands of positive comments, and articles about her appeared on popular Internet news sites.

Kaur is a trained interfaith leader who works with the Chicago-based organization Interfaith Youth Core (www.ifyc.org). She says that her interfaith training helped her find the words for her message. She also says that the experience of standing up to her bullies has inspired her to speak up about her faith and her personal choices. She says, "I started wearing my heart on my sleeve and seeing every stare as a chance for dialogue and friendship. I began to firmly believe in the power of the spoken and written word. I finally began to realize that I had to take charge of my own narrative; if I didn't, then that ignorance I saw in people's eyes would never change into knowledge."[h]

Kaur's example shows the power we all have to combat bias-based harassment through the simple acts of telling our own stories, and believing in ourselves.

Sikh and Muslim teens are not the only young people who face bias-based harassment because of their faith. Teens from all religions, including Judaism, Christianity, Hinduism, Buddhism, and others, are at risk. Young people like Kaur believe that the best way to fight faith-based bullying is to educate others about various religions. One way to do this is through participating in interfaith organizations, or groups with teens from multiple faiths who come together to build understanding between each other and the outside world. To learn more about interfaith organizing, check out the Interfaith Youth Council at www.ifyc.org.

Gender-Based Discrimination

To understand gender-based discrimination, we must first understand the difference between *sex* and *gender*. *Sex* refers to biological characteristics that are unique to males and females. These include having a high bone density (unique to males), the ability to bear children (unique to females), and parts of our bodies that are unique to each sex.[17] *Gender* refers to our society's ideas of what it means to be male or female.[18] For example, many people believe that boys should not wear dresses and play with dolls, and girls should not shave their heads or get into fistfights. These expectations have nothing to with biology, but instead are related to our perceptions.

Sex and gender do not always have to be the same. For example, some teens may be biologically female but identify as male. Other teens may be ambiguously sexed at birth. Teens in all of these categories will sometimes choose to identify as transgender.[19] But teens who identify with the same sex that they are born, sometimes called cisgender or same gendered, might still challenge ideas of what it means to be male and female. These teens sometimes identify as gender nonconforming. Balpreet Kaur, who you read about on page 77, is a Sikh woman who wears a turban even though turbans are usually worn by men. Kaur's decision to wear a turban is an example of behavior considered gender nonconforming.

In fact, many of us may practice gender nonconforming behaviors at some points in our life—it's not often that we want to do what society expects of us all the time, especially when those expectations can make us feel stifled or uncomfortable. Until recently, psychologists used to diagnose children who defied gender expectations as abnormal.[20] Now, though, a growing number of people recognize that our ideas about masculinity and femininity are arbitrary, and that experimenting with gender is a healthy part of growing up.

Unfortunately, despite the changing world, children who do not follow gender rules are still bullied: according to the National Women's Law Center, one-third of elementary school students say that they have heard girls being bullied for not "acting like girls"; 38 percent of these same students have heard boys being bullied for not "acting like boys."[21] As children get older, it gets worse: about 64 percent of teens report that they have been bullied because of their gender expression.[22]

Title IX is a federal law that protects teens who are bullied because of their gender identity or expression. Congress originally passed Title IX in response to another common form of bias-based harassment: discrimination against women and girls. In the United States, women have faced a history of discrimination and consequently have less access to power than men. This is clear if you look at our president, our government, our most successful business people, and the heads of many organizations: the vast majority of these individuals are men, not women. Girls and women who are excluded from activities because of their gender—who are told that they are not as capable as their male peers or that their responses or emotions are a result of being a woman—all experience bias-based harassment.

Title IX was intended to ensure that girls and boys got equal access to education.[23] It applies to schools across the country and includes provisions that cover issues ranging from school sports to career and technical education to pregnant and parenting teens to sexual harassment.[24] It also protects teens from bullying that occurs because of circumstances directly related to their sex. For example, teen girls may experience bias-based harassment because they are pregnant. Although a teen boy may be an expectant father, his peers cannot tell this by looking at him. Title IX protects pregnant teens from discrimination and harassment, which is a protection relevant only to teens whose sex is female.

Title IX also provides some protections against specific types of homophobia, or bias-based harassment related to students' sexual orientation. We will discuss this type of bias-based harassment in the next section.

Homophobia

The term *LGBTQ* is used to refer to individuals who identify as lesbian, gay, bisexual, transgender, or queer. These individuals may prefer to date individuals of the same sex. For example, they may be women who are attracted to women, or men who are attracted to men. Others may be born as male or female, but identify as the opposite gender, as we discussed in the previous section. Still others may be attracted to both women and men.

LGBTQ teens are often the target of *homophobia*, a term used to describe negative, hurtful, and abusive attitudes, behaviors, and feelings toward individuals who identify as LGBTQ. Bias-based harassment related to sexual orientation is driven by homophobia. Unfortunately, homophobic bias-based harassment is widespread and severe. A survey conducted in 2009 of over seven thousand LGBTQ youth showed that the majority of teens who do not identify themselves as heterosexual have been verbally or physically assaulted as a result of their sexual orientation; for transgender teens, these trends become more severe.[25] This makes LGBTQ youth vulnerable to mental, physical, and emotional harm, and has elevated suicide rates in the LGBTQ community.

Perhaps because they experience it so frequently and so severely, LGBTQ teens have been national leaders in the struggle against bullying, lobbying for policy changes at the school, district, city, state, and national levels. These teens work by themselves or with allies who do not identify as LGBTQ, but also believe that bias-based harassment is wrong. Blake Danford is an LGBTQ teen leader who worked with allies at his school to challenge homophobic violence. Read about Danford's leadership below.

Youth Empowered to Act: Blake Danford's Story

Openly gay teen Blake Danford writes, "I was aware of my sexuality from a very young age, and, for many years, grew up thinking the whole world hated me. Homophobia was a constant presence in my life, whether it was from my family or the world around me."[i] At his high school, Danford said that "students would always make snide remarks at me in the halls. Having words like 'f*ggot' and 'queer' thrown my direction became an almost daily occurrence for me, and I was sick of it."[j]

Some LGBTQ teens choose to hide their sexual orientation to avoid violence. At first, this was Danford's strategy. He remembers, "When I finally got to high school, I was very afraid. I was only out to a few people and generally shied away from anything that would put me in the spotlight. I dressed plainly, walked quietly, and did what I could to avoid calling attention to myself."[k] However, despite his attempts to hide his sexuality, the bias-based harassment continued.

During his junior year at Fullerton High School, Danford grew increasingly frustrated. For one thing, the principal and assistant principal were unsupportive of the Gay-Straight Alliance, which was not allowed to participate in events like the National Day of Silence designed to raise awareness about LGBTQ youth. Then, in the spring semester, an openly gay student named Kyle Giertz entered the "Mr. Fullerton" fund-raiser. This annual event is a beauty pageant where the contestants are asked to answer questions, including where they see themselves in ten years. Giertz answered that he hoped gay marriage would become legal so that he could be married to a man he loved. The school disqualified him from the competition.[i]

This discrimination was an example of structural violence, and it was the final straw for Danford and his friend Katelyn Hall, who identifies as straight. Hall comes from a conservative Christian family. She is close to both Danford and Giertz, and said she wanted to do something because, "I was outraged. I felt that it displayed blatant disregard for my friend's rights and was completely uncalled for. . . . I knew something had to be done to combat what was essentially an act of bullying."[m]

Hall's family felt that supporting LGBTQ youth like Danford was a violation of Christianity. Hall disagreed. She wrote,

> After a heated debate with my grandmother, I opened my Bible in tears, trying to find solace in what I had relied on so long for peace. The page fell open to something I had highlighted long ago, Matthew 12:31: "Love your neighbor as yourself." I realized that it said neither "love your straight neighbors" nor "love your white neighbors" nor even "love your Christian neighbors." It said to love your neighbors. And that means all of them. I think that is something that so many Christian people, and people in general, forget. We should show everyone love, and that includes treating them equally.[n]

Together, Danford and Hall started a letter-writing campaign with the theme, "Where do you see yourself in ten years?" The campaign became an opportunity for teens to envision a world free of bullying. Hall and Danford then started a youth blog, ran a Know Your Rights project informing teens about the laws in California that they can use to combat bullying, and created resources for ending bias-based harassment of LGBTQ youth. The site has been so successful that they were asked to present at the 2012 GLAAD media awards in Los Angeles. You can check it out at http://yetaoc.moonfruit.com/#

Danford says that he spoke up about his sexual orientation because, "I wanted no one to have to go through what I went through,"[o] a decision that has made him a role model. With the help of teens like Danford and Hall, perhaps this vision can become a reality.

Some teens may choose to hide their sexuality to avoid bullying. However, sometimes bullies target individuals they perceive to be LGBTQ even if they are not open about their sexuality or if they are heterosexual but are gender nonconforming, as discussed in the last section. If a bully targets a student because of his or her perceived gender or sexual orientation, it is still considered bias-based harassment, even if the victim is not openly gay.

Currently, no federal laws protect teens from bias-based harassment related to sexual orientation.[26] Title IX, discussed in the previous section, provides protections for certain types of homophobic bias-based harassment, such as calling a student "gay" or worse because of gender nonconforming behavior.[27] Some states and school districts also have laws that protect LGBTQ teens from bias-based harassment.[28]

In response to this lack of legal protection, members of Congress introduced the Student Non-Discrimination Act (SNDA) in the summer of 2013.[29] Modeled after Title IX, the SNDA prohibits schools and individuals from discriminating against teens based on their sexual orientation or their perceived sexual orientation.[30] If SNDA had been in effect, Danford's principal would not have been allowed to use structural violence to exclude Giertz from a school-based activity because he was openly gay. As of October 2013, the law has not passed. If it does pass, it will be one of the first legal protections for students who identify as LGBTQ and an essential tool in the fight against bias-based harassment.

Disability-Based Discrimination

Teens with special needs are some of the most frequent targets of bias-based harassment. They are about two to three times more likely to be bullied or harassed because of their disabilities, and they are also more likely to experience physical and verbal harassment on a long-term basis than their able-bodied peers.[31]

Disabilities can be visible, like being in a wheelchair, or invisible, like having a learning disorder like dyslexia. Students who have disabilities sometimes stand out from their able-bodied peers because they have trouble doing things like reading, following a conversation, or responding to jokes. Other times, these teens have an obvious impairment that keeps them from doing things like taking the stairs, participating in gym class, giving a speech without stammering, or speaking without sign language.

Teens who have developmental issues that affect their ability to socialize or interact with others are some of the most common victims of bias-based harassment. Bullies may target these teens because they get frustrated easily or do not understand when others are exploiting or manipulating them. About 65 percent of parents of students with Asperger's say that their child has been bullied in the last year, and about 40 percent of these students are bullied consistently for a year or longer.[32] Bias-based harassment of emotionally delayed young people is particularly harmful because it can prevent them from overcoming their disabilities: being bullied makes it more difficult to trust others and learn how to function socially, two key elements of overcoming emotional delays.[33]

Teens with physical disabilities may be directly targeted because they are unable to fight back against physical threats. Teen Kevin Kaneta, who has a condition called cerebral palsy, says that he thinks "[t]hey go after me because they see me as a vulnerable target."[34] Bullies forced Kaneta to eat dog food and tied his shirt around his face and took pictures that they posted on Facebook. Kaneta's condition makes it impossible for him to avoid his tormentors.

Besides being targets of direct physical and verbal violence, teens with physical disabilities may suffer from social isolation because they are unable to fully participate in activities where young people make friends and form strong emotional bonds. Sometimes they are unable to participate in athletic activities because they are wheelchair bound, lack stamina, or are fragile. Other times they may not be able to attend events or take classes because places like schools lack facilities such as wheelchair ramps, sign language interpreters, or properly fitted restrooms. In these cases, institutions act like bullies, not individuals: this is a form of structural violence.

Title II of the Americans with Disabilities Act (ADA) of 1990 provides protections to teens with disabilities. The ADA protects people with disabilities from discrimination, including bias-based harassment.[35] It also says that public institutions such as schools need to provide services to people with disabilities that allow them to participate as equally as possible.[36] This is further explained in the Individuals with Disabilities Education Act (IDEA), which outlines the services and procedures schools need to implement to serve students with special needs.[37] This network of laws came about as the result of years of activism from individuals with disabilities and their families, who demanded protections under the law.

Teens with special needs certainly face challenges. However, they also have numerous strengths and talents, and many are more than able to stand up for themselves. Teens such as Kaneta and television star Lauren Potter have worked hard to raise awareness about bullying because of disability status. For more on what you can do to stand in support of teens with disabilities, read about Lauren Potter on page 85.

Class-Based Harassment

After the recession of 2008, more and more teens and their families are struggling economically. Census data from 2010 shows that about one in five children under

Lauren Potter: *Glee* Star and Activist

Lauren Potter is one of the stars of the popular television show *Glee*. She also has Down syndrome, an inherited condition that affects her both physically and mentally. Although she is now one of the most famous actresses in the country, she experienced bias-based harassment as a teen. Potter and her mother, Sheryl Young, have partnered with an organization called Ability Path (www.abilitypath .org) to start a campaign called Disable Bullying to raise awareness about bias-based harassment of students with special needs.

Potter says that her example shows that no matter who you are, if you believe in yourself, you can achieve your dreams. She says the emotional pain bullies cause may make special needs teens doubt themselves and their abilities, which is why it is all of our responsibilities to stop bias-based harassment when we see it. Young fully supports Potter, helping her write about the issue to raise awareness of it. Potter and Young recently wrote, "We have seen the power behind what happens when individuals, schools and communities band together. It's time to take back our neighborhoods and put bullies on alert that all eyes are on them and any act of violence or manipulation will result in severe consequences. This may seem strong but we cannot stand around waiting for the next student to be hospitalized or worse, die."[p]

Potter and her mother are looking for visible supporters of their mission, and have created a video on YouTube inviting testimony from people who believe in their cause. If you would like to post a video on YouTube showing your support for Potter, check out abilitypath.org.

the age of eighteen lives in poverty, which is the highest rate the country has seen in thirty years.[38] This means for more and more teens, it is harder for their families to make ends meet, and there is less money to spend on things like clothes, music, or going out with friends, all things that make teens fit in.

We use the terms *class* or *socioeconomic status* to describe how wealthy or poor we are. All over the world, teens from lower socioeconomic statuses tend to be bullied more often than their wealthier peers.[39] Other than this, however, little is known about bias-based harassment related to class. This may be because teens who experience bullying due to their income levels may be harassed not for being poor, but because of decisions they make or the way they look as a result of poverty. For example, teens from families who are suffering economically may not have stable housing or a steady income, which means that they may not be able to do basic activities like take daily showers or buy new shoes or afford to go on school trips. Other students may harass these teens for being different, but they may not make the connection that it is because the teens are poor.

One group of teens who experience bias-based harassment and poverty are runaway and homeless youth. Many of these young people leave home because they are experiencing bias-based harassment or abuse because of their identities. For example, one in five runaway teens identify as LGBTQ; about one-third of runaway youth were thrown out of their homes because of their sexual orientation.[40] While there is not much research on whether these low-income teens are bullied for being homeless, we know that many of them actually became impoverished because they were forced to leave families due to bias-based harassment.

Even if they do not live in extreme poverty, teens who are not wealthy may be bullied because they are unable to afford what it takes to be popular. For example, they may not have the money to attend social events, such as dances or concerts, with their peers, or they may not have the money to purchase items that give them status in school, such as the right shoes or clothes.[41] Alice, a teen who used to be part of a group of girls who bullied others, remembers, "One day, I was wearing a Tommy Hilfiger shirt and she [the bully] came over to check the label. 'Is that real?' she said in a very obnoxious and loud tone as she peered and tugged on the back of my shirt. Everyone just stared. My cheeks turned red from embarrassment."[42] Asking if the shirt was really from the designer was a way for the bully to question whether Alice could actually afford a Tommy Hilfiger shirt, and was therefore based on Alice's class status.

Intersectionality

As you read this chapter, you may recognize yourself in multiple places. Maybe you are a teen woman of color, or a student with a disability who identifies as LGBTQ, or a Muslim from a working-class family. In other words, you have multiple oppressed identities that intersect and influence your experiences of bias-based harassment.

Sometimes having more than one identity means that you experience different kinds of bias-based harassment in different situations. Take, for example, Loan Tran, who is sixteen years old and identifies as Asian American and gay. In middle school, she experienced bias-based harassment because of her race and ethnicity. She remembers, "In middle school, I got teased for having an immigrant identity. People would call me names like 'rice picker' or 'fresh off the boat.'" When she got to high school, she was a victim of homophobia. She says, "Other Asian Americans have said to me [about my sexuality], 'Is that something that the Asian culture really wants to support?' I find that it's really interesting that they would use one aspect of me to bully the other aspect of me."[43] Tran was disappointed that her friends and family, who commiserated with her about one form of bias-based harassment (related to race), were so ready to engage in another form of bias-based harassment despite their past experiences.

Tran always felt that the harassment she faced was connected to both her race and her sexual orientation. She said, "I feel like the bullying I have faced has my ethnicity always intertwined with my LGBT identity."[44] What Tran experiences is called *intersectionality*, or the combination of two or more identities. In Tran's case, intersectionality means that she has trouble fitting into her community because part of her identity does not fit with their view of normal. It also exposes her to bullying for multiple reasons.

Other teens may experience bias-based harassment that is specific to one combination of their identities. For example, nineteen-year-old Sonia[45] says she experienced bias-based harassment because of the intersection of her gender and her faith. Sonia is a Muslim American woman, and she says that when she was in high school, "my principal . . . didn't really care about me and my sister going to college because she automatically assumed that our father wasn't going to let us go to college." Although in reality, Sonia's father supported her dreams, Sonia's counselor did not believe her and refused to give her the recommendation letter she needed to apply to a competitive private college. "I was like well just let me apply. And then she said this to me and I was so upset she said, 'It's not like your father's gonna let you go,'" Sonia remembers. She says that her principal had this attitude because she thought that all Muslim teen girls were married young and were not allowed to go to college away from home. If Sonia had been another religion or a boy, her principal would not have treated her this way.

All of us have multiple identities. Some of us have multiple identities that make us prone to bias-based harassment, while some of us have multiple identities that give us privilege and power. We should all be allowed to embrace all parts of ourselves and to live without fear of who we are. Any bullying that threatens our ability to embrace one or more aspects of our identities is considered bias-based harassment.

Responding to Bias-Based Harassment

Bias-based harassment has a hugely negative impact on the lives of young people, leading to lower grades, higher rates of absenteeism, and a greater likelihood of depression and even suicide.[46] Bias-based harassment also negatively affects communities because it makes unique individuals feel unsafe expressing their identities, thereby creating a world that is less diverse and less rich. Across the country, teens are standing up to bias-based harassment in multiple ways. Two key avenues for change are through passing laws and policies and through education.

In this chapter, we've discussed numerous laws and policies that protect teens from bias-based harassment. These include Title IX, the ADA, and the IDEA. There are also laws at the state and local level that provide protections against bias-based harassment: there are far too many to discuss here. You can combat bias-based harassment by educating yourself about these laws and learning how to use them to stop bullying at the individual and the school level. Another option is to work with groups that are trying to get stronger laws passed at all levels of government. Sometimes that means campaigning for existing laws that have not yet been passed, like the SNDA, discussed earlier. Sometimes that means working together to draft new laws, something you'll learn about in chapters 10 and 11 of this volume.

Another effective way to combat bias-based harassment is to educate communities about building cultures of tolerance. In chapter 1, you learned about

Groups That Combat Bias-Based Harassment in Schools

If you are interested in combating bias-based harassment at your school, or if you are experiencing bias-based harassment and do not know who to turn to, these organizations can help.

Ability Path
www.abilitypath.org
(650) 259-8500

American Civil Liberties Union
www.aclu.org
125 Broad Street, 18th Floor
New York, NY 10004
(212) 549-2500

Human Rights Campaign
www.hrc.org
1640 Rhode Island Avenue NW
Washington, DC 20036-3278
HRC Front Desk: (202) 628-4160
TTY: (202) 216-1572
Toll-Free: (800) 777-4723

Anti-Defamation League
http://www.adl.org/
(Search online for the location nearest you.)

Asian American Legal Defense and Education Fund
www.aaldef.org
99 Hudson Street, 12th Floor
New York, NY 10013
(212) 966-5932
info@aaldef.org

COLAGE: People with a Lesbian, Gay, Bisexual, Transgender or Queer Parent
http://www.colage.org/
4509 Interlake Avenue N #180
Seattle, WA 98103
(855) 4-COLAGE
collage@colage.org

Gay, Lesbian and Straight Education Network (GLSEN)
http://www.glsen.org
90 Broad Street, 2nd Floor
New York, NY 10004
(212) 727-0135
glsen@glsen.org

Rainbow Rumpus Magazine

www.rainbowrumpus.org

PO Box 6881

Minneapolis, MN 55406

(612) 721-6442

Southern Poverty Law Center

http://www.splcenter.org/

400 Washington Avenue

Montgomery, AL 36104

(334) 956-8200

The Sikh Coalition

http://www.sikhcoalition.org/

50 Broad Street, Suite 1537

New York, NY 10004

(212) 655-3095

39055 Hastings Street, Suite 210

Fremont, CA 94538

(510) 659-0900

cultural violence, which is a sometimes invisible form of violence that demeans or disparages individuals for their traditions, identities, and choices. Education and training can help groups of people recognize the attitudes and behaviors that create cultural violence. It can also give these same people tools to combat cultural violence and promote acceptance. Education could be as formal as workshops with expert trainers or as informal as book clubs where friends and family read about and discuss issues related to oppression. You can also talk to others about why you support students who are the victims of bias-based harassment, even if you are not exposed to it yourself. While it may be difficult to stand up to bullies at the exact moment when they are being violent or abusive, you can help show your solidarity with other teens by joining or starting clubs like Gay-Straight Alliances, making YouTube videos or posters about respecting everyone, and expressing your opinions about bias-based harassment when you are simply having a conversation with a group of friends you trust. Not only will this make bullying less acceptable at your school, it will also help students who may feel unsafe to be more comfortable knowing that they can turn to someone like you. Plus, it will help your peers examine their own biases and learn about how to overcome them.

See page 88 for a list of organizations that work to combat bias-based harassment nationally. Visit their websites or call them to find out more about how you can make your school a community free of bias-based harassment, where every teen feels free to be him- or herself.

Notes

1. Stephen Russell, Katerina Sinclair, V. Paul Poteat, and Brian Koenig. "Adolescent Health and Harassment Based on Discriminatory Bias," *American Journal of Public Health* 102, no. 3 (2012): 493.
2. Russell et al., "Adolescent Health and Harassment," 494.
3. Ta-Nehisi Coates, "Fear of a Black President," *Atlantic Monthly*, August 22, 2012, http://www.theatlantic.com/magazine/archive/2012/09/fear-of-a-black-president/309064/ (accessed August 6, 2013).
4. Tara Yosso, *Critical Race Counterstories along the Chicana/Chicano Educational Pipeline* (New York: Routledge, 2006), 9.
5. Robert Teranishi, "Asian Pacific Americans and Critical Race Theory: An Examination of School Racial Climate," *Equity and Excellence in Education* 35, no. 2 (2002): 146.
6. W. Wakefield and C. Hudley, "Ethnic and Racial Identity and Adolescent Well-Being," *Theory into Practice* 46, no. 2 (2007): 150.
7. Teranishi, "Asian Pacific Americans," 145–146.
8. Monisha Bajaj, Ameena Ghaffar-Kucher, and Karishma Desai, *In the Face of Xenophobia: Lessons to Address the Bullying of South Asian Youth* (Washington, DC: South-Asian Americans Leading Together, 2013), 2.
9. Helen I. Hwang, "In the Face of Bullying: Asian American Teens Bear the Brunt of Bullies, but a Group of Philadelphia Teens Show It Can Be Stopped," *Hyphen* 24 (Winter 2011). http://www.hyphenmagazine.com/magazine/issue-24-survival/face-bullying (accessed December 4, 2013).
10. Hwang, "In the Face of Bullying."
11. Barry Kosmin and Ariela Keysar, *American Religious Identification Survey (ARIS 2008): Summary Report* (Hartford, CT: Trinity College, 2009). http://commons.trincoll.edu/aris/files/2011/08/ARIS_Report_2008.pdf (accessed August 8, 2013), 3.
12. Omar Sacirbey, "9/11 Bullying: Muslim Teens Push Back," *Huffington Post*, September 8, 2011, http://www.huffingtonpost.com/2011/09/07/bullying-muslim-teens-push-back_n_952947.html (accessed August 8, 2013).
13. Sacirbey, "9/11 Bullying."
14. Sacirbey, "9/11 Bullying."
15. Hwang, "In the Face of Bullying."
16. Breakthrough, "Mansimran: How a Teen Deals with Bullying," Breakthrough.tv, http://breakthrough.tv/video/mansimran/ (accessed August 3, 2012).

17. World Health Organization, "What Do We Mean by 'Sex' and 'Gender'?" World Health Organization: Gender, Women, and Health, 2013, http://www.who.int/gender/whatisgender/en/ (accessed August 9, 2013).
18. World Health Organization, "What Do We Mean by 'Sex' and 'Gender'?"
19. Sylvia Rivera Law Project, *Fact Sheet: Transgender and Nonconforming Youth at Schools*, 2012, http://srlp.org/wp-content/uploads/2012/08/youth-rights-bw.pdf (accessed August 9, 2013).
20. Ruth Padawer, "Boygirl," *New York Times Sunday Magazine*, MM18, August 12, 2012.
21. National Women's Law Center, *It's Your Education: How Title IX Protections Can Help You*, June 2010, http://www.nwlc.org/sites/default/files/pdfs/NWLCItsYourEducation2010.pdf (accessed August 9, 2013).
22. National Women's Law Center, *It's Your Education*.
23. Joanne N. Smith, Mandy Van Deven, and Meghan Huppuch, *Hey, Shorty! A Guide to Combating Sexual Harassment and Violence in Public Schools and on the Streets* (New York: Feminist Press at the City University of New York, 2011).
24. National Women's Law Center, *It's Your Education*.
25. Emily A. Greytak, Joseph G. Kosciw, and Elizabeth M. Diaz, *Harsh Realities: The Experience of Transgender Youth in Our Nation's Schools* (Washington, DC: Gay, Lesbian, Straight Education Network, 2007), 14.
26. Human Rights Campaign, "Issue: Coming Out," Human Rights Campaign, June 4, 2013, http://www.hrc.org/laws-and-legislation/federal-legislation/student-non-discrimination-act (accessed August 10, 2013).
27. National Women's Law Center, *Fact Sheet: Title IX Protections from Bullying and Harassment in Schools: FAQs for LGBT or Gender Nonconforming Students and Their Families*, October 2012, http://www.nwlc.org/sites/default/files/pdfs/lgbt_bullying_title_ix_fact_sheet.pdf (accessed August 10, 2013), 1.
28. National Women's Law Center, *Fact Sheet: Title IX*, 2.
29. Human Rights Campaign, "Issue: Coming Out."
30. Human Rights Campaign, "Issue: Coming Out."
31. AbilityPath.org, *Walk a Mile in Their Shoes: Bullying and the Child with Special Needs*, 2012, http://www.abilitypath.org/areas-of-development/learning--schools/bullying/articles/walk-a-mile-in-their-shoes.pdf (accessed August 9, 2013), 9.
32. AbilityPath.org, *Walk a Mile in Their Shoes*, 11.
33. Nirvi Shah, "Children with Autism More Likely to Be Bullied," *Education Week Blog: On Special Education*, March 27, 2012, http://blogs.edweek.org/edweek/speced/2012/03/children_with_autism_more_like.html (accessed September 2, 2012).
34. AbilityPath.org, *Walk a Mile in Their Shoes*.
35. U.S. Department of Justice, Civil Rights Division, "Title II Highlights," ADA.gov, August 29, 2002, http://www.ada.gov/t2hlt95.htm (accessed August 10, 2013).
36. U.S. Department of Justice, "Title II Highlights."
37. American Psychological Association, "Individuals with Disabilities Education Act (IDEA)," American Psychological Association, 2013, http://www.apa.org/about/gr/issues/disability/idea.aspx (accessed August 10, 2013).
38. Sabrina Tavernise, "Soaring Poverty Casts Spotlight on 'Lost Decade,'" *New York Times*, September 13, 2011, http://www.nytimes.com/2011/09/14/us/14census.html?pagewanted=all (accessed September 3, 2012).
39. Pernille Due, Juan Merlo, Yossi Harel-Fisch, Morgens Trab Damsgaard, B. Holstein, J. Hetland, C. Currie, S. Grabhainn, G. Gaspar de Matos, and John Lynch, "Socioeconomic

Inequality in Exposure to Bullying during Adolescence: A Comparative, Cross-Sectional, Multilevel Study in 35 Countries," *American Journal of Public Health*, 99 (2009): 907.

40. National Runaway Switchboard, *Why They Run: An In-Depth Look at America's Runaway Youth* (Chicago: National Runaway Switchboard, 2010), 8.
41. Jessie Klein, *The Bully Society: School Shootings and the Crisis of Bullying in America's Schools* (New York: New York University Press, 2011), 20.
42. Alice Wong, "Nasty Girls," *YCteen* 2002, http://www.ycteenmag.org/topics/bullying/Nasty_Girls.html?story_id=NYC-2002-11-05 (accessed October 21, 2012).
43. Helen I. Hwang, "Voices of Bullying Victims," *Hyphen Blog*, 2011, http://www.hyphen magazine.com/magazine/issue-24-survival/voices-bullying-victims (accessed August 3, 2012).
44. Hwang, "Voices of Bullying Victims."
45. Not her real name. (She asked to have her name protected so she could not be identified.)
46. Greytak, Kosciw, and Diaz, *Harsh Realities*, 25.

a. Helen I. Hwang, "In the Face of Bullying: Asian American Teens Bear the Brunt of Bullies, but a Group of Philadelphia Teens Show It Can Be Stopped," *Hyphen* 24 (Winter 2011). http://www.hyphenmagazine.com/magazine/issue-24-survival/face-bullying (accessed December 4, 2013).
b. Hwang, "In the Face of Bullying."
c. Hwang, "In the Face of Bullying."
d. Balpreet Kaur, "Turning Ugliness into Beauty through Interfaith Leadership," *Huffington Post*, October 5, 2012, http://www.huffingtonpost.com/balpreet-kaur/turning-ugliness-into-beauty-through-interfaith-leadership_b_1943244.html (accessed August 8, 2013).
e. Kaur, "Turning Ugliness into Beauty."
f. Kaur, "Turning Ugliness into Beauty."
g. Kaur, "Turning Ugliness into Beauty."
h. Kaur, "Turning Ugliness into Beauty."
i. Blake Danford, "From Bullied Gay Teen to Anti-Bullying Activist: Why I Decided to Make a Difference," *Huffington Post*, July 10, 2012, http://www.huffingtonpost.com/blake-danford/from-bullied-gay-teen-to-anti-bullying-activist_b_1662490.html (accessed August 31, 2012).
j. Danford, "From Bullied Gay Teen to Anti-Bullying Activist."
k. Danford, "From Bullied Gay Teen to Anti-Bullying Activist."
l. Katelyn Hall, "How This Straight, Christian Girl from a Conservative Family Found Herself Fighting for LGBT Youth," *Huffington Post*, July 9, 2012, http://www.huffingtonpost.com/katelyn-hall/lgbt-youth-bullying_b_1660026.html (accessed August 8, 2013).
m. Hall, "How This Straight, Christian Girl."
n. Hall, "How This Straight, Christian Girl."
o. Danford, "From Bullied Gay Teen to Anti-Bullying Activist."
p. Sheryl Young and Lauren Potter, "Doing Nothing Is Not an Option," *Huffington Post: Impact*, February 15, 2011, http://www.huffingtonpost.com/sheryl-young/doing-nothing-is-not-an-o_b_823505.html (accessed August 9, 2013).

6

CYBERBULLYING

···

One of the major changes bullying has undergone in the past decade is that now, it does not just occur in person; it also occurs online. Bullies harass victims through text messages, Facebook, Twitter, e-mails, instant messages, and other forms of social media. Some bullies even create web pages dedicated to harassing victims. Bullying that occurs in the virtual world is called "cyberbullying." In a recent study, about 16 percent of American teens reported they had been cyberbullied in the past year.[1] One in five teen girls say they were cyberbullied in 2011,[2] and 62 percent of transgender youth said they had been harassed online.[3]

In this chapter, you will learn more about what cyberbullying looks like and who it affects. You will also learn how cyberbullying is different than in-person bullying, how to prevent and respond to cyberbullying, and how teens, educators, and policy makers are working together to eliminate it. You may notice that this chapter is full of questions and debates. Since it is a relatively new form of bullying—so new that most adults did not experience it during their teenage years—we are still learning about what cyberbullying looks like, how it affects teens, and how best to respond to it.

The fact that cyberbullying does not occur in physical space raises questions about what institutions are responsible for responding to it. For example, if a teen posts a rumor about a classmate on Facebook after school hours and off school grounds, does the school have the authority to address it? Should Facebook have the authority to take bullying content off of personal web pages? Should cyberbullying lead to consequences like prison? These are all questions that educators, teens, and lawmakers grapple with daily, and that you will grapple with in this chapter.

Types of Cyberbullying

Cyberbullying, also called *electronic bullying* or *online cruelty*, is any form of bullying, intimidation, or harassment that occurs in virtual or electronic spaces.[4] Examples of cyberbullying include sending threatening text messages, starting a rumor online, creating a web page dedicated to insulting the victim, or forwarding a compromising photograph through e-mail. In all of these cases, huge numbers of people can participate in the abuse through posting comments and forwarding messages for days or even weeks at a time, making this form of bullying particularly severe and hurtful.

Another form of cyberbullying takes advantage of the fact that online, we can conceal our identities. Some cyberbullies impersonate victims, sending embarrassing e-mails in their name or posting humiliating status messages from their Facebook accounts. Other times, cyberbullies impersonate someone else, such as a victim's romantic interest, and communicate with the victim using this false identity. They may use this identity to find out compromising information about the victim, which they then reveal publicly.

In fact, the most common form of cyberbullying is disseminating private photos, instant messages, e-mails, or other communications.[5] Cyberbullies may forward e-mails to a group of people without the sender's permission, or post the contents of a chat conversation on a public page such as Facebook, or distribute photos taken on cell phones that are supposed to remain private. This is why teens that are active on social media are more likely to be victims of cyberbullying than those who have a less visible online presence.[6] Some teens put themselves at particular risk by oversharing, or publicly revealing information about themselves that should be kept private. Examples of oversharing include everything from posting contact details such as addresses and phone numbers to expressing opinions about an incident witnessed at school to talking openly about personal or health problems. Read more about oversharing—and how to avoid it—below.

Oversharing

When you are playing on a computer or cell phone by yourself, it can be difficult to remember that even though you are alone, your online actions are public, and that everything that you put on the Internet is part of a permanent record. In some ways, this is exciting: it means that you have an outlet to express your views and creativity to a wide audience. In some ways, though, it is dangerous, particularly if you share information that you later realize could be hurtful to your friends, family, or yourself. One of the best ways to protect yourself from cyberbullying is to limit what you share online or on mobile devices.

Here are a few guidelines to help you think about what you are sharing and to avoid oversharing. Can you think of any others?

1. Do not share personal information about where you live or how to contact you. You may think that your friends are the only ones who can see this information, but when you put it on the Internet, it becomes available to everyone—including people who may not have your best interests at heart.
2. Do not share your passwords with others. No matter how much you trust your friends, do not give them access to your accounts.
3. Do not allow others to take compromising pictures of you, no matter how much you trust them. If someone is pressuring you to do something that you find uncomfortable, that person is not someone you can trust.
4. Do not reveal private information about yourself or your family in online spaces. Instead, try writing it down or talking about it with someone you trust.
5. Avoid expressing yourself publicly in the heat of the moment. Instead, write your thoughts in a private place, like a journal, or have a conversation with a friend. That way, if you change your mind once you calm down, you will not have to face the consequences of a public statement made because of anger, sadness, or frustration.
6. Remember that these rules do not just apply to platforms such as Facebook—they also apply to e-mail, photos, or anything else that can be easily forwarded.

As a general rule, when you are online, think about what would happen if someone you care about saw what you are writing or producing. How would it hurt them? How would it hurt you? How would you feel if it remained online permanently, which is a possibility? Thinking this way can help protect you and the people you love.

Other forms of cyberbullying mirror bullying that happens in the real world. Cyberbullies might send insults over text messages, for example. Or they may deliberately exclude individuals from electronic groups or pages to make them feel ostracized.

As cyberbullying evolves, so does the vocabulary we have to talk about it. The Internet community has coined a number of terms to describe specific types of cyberbullying. For example, *flaming* is having an online fight that includes an exchange of insults and, at times, inappropriate language. *Trolling* is starting a fight between two people online, a behavior that can lead to flaming. *Cyberstalking* is persistently sending intimidating or harassing messages through online platforms. It is also sometimes used to describe adults that are cyberbullying minors. *Sexting* is sending a sexual text message that might include an inappropriate photo or comment, and can be considered a form of sexual harassment. As technology develops and new forms of cyberbullying emerge, this list of terms is sure to expand.

Differences between Cyberbullying and In-Person Bullying

There are several differences between cyberbullying and off-line bullying. Face-to-face bullying requires the bully to be physically present. This means that victims can get relief by removing themselves from the situation. Cyberbullying, on the other hand, does not require the bully's physical presence: it can occur twenty-four hours a day, seven days a week, no matter where the bully or the victim is located. There is no way to escape. Furthermore, in face-to-face bullying, the bully immediately sees the victim's response, which helps them understand the negative effects of their behavior. As they see the consequences of their actions, bullies may realize they have gone too far, or they may feel empathetic and stop. In contrast, in cyberbullying, bullies do not see the victim's body language, making it difficult for them to comprehend the impact of their actions and giving them less incentive to stop.[7]

Unlike face-to-face bullying, cyberbullying can be anonymous. E-mails can be forwarded, text messages can be sent, and websites can be created without a bully ever revealing his or her identity. Websites like Formspring.me allow users to ask questions and receive anonymous feedback.[8] While these electronic forums were originally intended to be survey tools, teens have used them to invite people they know to anonymously comment on their personalities, friendships, and character traits. Unfortunately, some teens use this as an opportunity to post insulting comments about their peers without revealing their identities, a behavior that can devastate victims: although teens may not know who specifically posted the cruel words, they know that the bullies are members of their community and, quite possibly, peers who they considered friends. One of the most famous cases of cyberbullying on Formspring.me was the tragic suicide of Alexis Pilkington, who killed herself because of the abusive comments she received on both Formspring .me and Facebook—comments that continued even after she had taken her own life.[9]

Cyberbullying is also different for witnesses. First of all, depending on the form it takes, cyberbullying can be visible to many more people than in-person bullying. While a few dozen students may witness bullying that happens in a locker room or a cafeteria, a Facebook message or text message can reach hundreds of people instantly, including adults and family members. Cyberbullying is therefore much more public than face-to-face bullying and can be far more humiliating.

Although some witnesses may be present when the cyberbully is producing abusive content, many are present only after the message has been sent, the picture posted, or the website created. This means that witnesses cannot stand up to the bully in real time to prevent the act from occurring. However, they can still support victims behind the scenes, just as in face-to-face bullying. Since cyberbullying is fairly new, not much research has been done on the role of witnesses. As the issue is better understood, witnesses may find creative ways to protect their friends and peers from bullies online.

Cyberbullying and Gender

Young people who identify as male are much less likely to be cyberbullied than their peers who identify as female or transgender. Seventy percent of girls say that they are bullied online, compared to only 59 percent of boys.[10] Furthermore, only 26 percent of boys say they are bullied through their cell phones, whereas about 40 percent of girls say that they are routinely bullied through texting.[11] About 56 percent of girls say that they experience sexual harassment both online and in person, and they are 12 percent more likely to experience online sexual harassment compared to boys.[12] Sixty-two percent of transgender teens report that they have been cyberbullied in the past, and studies show that they are more likely to be electronically harassed than gender conforming male or female teens.[13] While little research exists as to who is harassing transgender teens, the fact is that they are the most common victims of cyberbullying.

Some experts believe that straight, cisgender boys are more likely to be responsible for cyberbullying than their peers, although research remains inconclusive. This may be because negative behavior such as posting compromising pictures of female intimate partners or teasing individuals who are gender nonconforming are seen as evidence of masculinity, and therefore make boys more popular and powerful.[14] In other words, our society may be sending male teens the message that cyberbullying actually makes them cooler.

In 2013, a teen Radio Rookies reporter at WNYC in New York City, Temitayo Fagbenle, produced a piece about cyberbullying in schools. After extensive research, she concluded that there is a double standard when it comes to cyberbullying: while girls lose social status when they are cyberbullied (and, in particular, when the cyberbullying involves sexual harassment), boys gain social status. Read more about Fagbenle's expert opinion below.

Temitayo Fagbenle's Story

Temitayo Fagbenle was a reporter for Radio Rookies in New York City from 2012 to 2013. She produced a piece about cyberbullying that aired in 2013. Fagbenle said that she chose to focus on cyberbullying because, "as a teenage girl, I see bullying every day. The only difference now is that the medium is through Facebook, a tool that connects millions of people around the world and makes the overall bullying effect, in my opinion, much more damaging. This was something that I've seen happen to girls countless times on Facebook and I wanted to report on it."

One of the focuses of Fagbenle's piece is the difference between how cyberbullying affects girls and boys. She said that double standards are not limited to bullying and that she has experienced them her whole life. She said, "Whether it was being told of my 'physical inabilities' as a girl vs. boys, or being told I couldn't do something BECAUSE I was a girl, the double standard is an apparent aspect of our society. And the sexual stigma against women has been in place for millennia."

Fagbenle had a lot to say about how bullying and popularity are closely intertwined. She said, "Teenage girls (and boys) are always in competition with each other. Bullying is just another means to crawl up to the top of the social ladder. . . . Facebook has a new thing where you can get subscribers and [consequently, now] people really want to get 'Facebook Famous' so they use these kinds of pictures and videos to get there."

For boys, the connection between cyberbullying and popularity was especially clear, Fagbenle says. She explained, "When these boys post these photos and videos, they do it because it raises their status and because most of the time they aren't reported." She also believes that some teens are so focused on gaining popularity that they lack empathy. She said, "Most of the time the audience these pictures reach are immature and unaware (or just uncaring) of the emotional damage this can cause the victim of this act."

Fagbenle talked about the key role that witnesses can play in reporting cyberbullying—that is, if the companies who receive the reports are responsive. She said,

> Oftentimes teens who comment on these pictures by trying to call out the boys for their wrongdoing are targeted as well. I think the best approach to avoid this is to report it. While I was reporting the story I tried to report a half-naked picture of a 16-year-old girl three times to Facebook but it still stayed up, I don't understand why. The boy who put up the photo I reported, and boys who tend to put up these kinds of photos, post a lot of this material so I'm sure a lot of people report them. I think the institutions, like Facebook, that are used as the medium for cyberbullying need to step up and fully accept their role in modern day bullying and strive to help end it.

What else could help end bullying? Fagbenle says, "The possibility of jail time."

To hear Fagbenle's story, and the stories of other Radio Rookies, check out radiorookies.org.[a]

The Effects of Cyberbullying

In many ways, the effects of cyberbullying are similar to the effects of off-line bullying. Just like the victims of face-to-face bullying, the victims of cyberbullying suffer physically and psychologically. Cyberbullying victims report that they feel unsafe, have frequent headaches and nausea, and have trouble sleeping.[15] They are more likely to skip or drop out of school, get poor grades, take alcohol and drugs, and have low self-esteem.[16]

In other ways, cyberbullying can be more severe than in-person bullying. For example, one study found that young people who are cyberbullied are twice as likely to consider suicide as teens who are bullied off-line.[17] Another researcher speculated that cyberbullying victims feel traumatized because they are at the mercy of cyberbullies at any time or any location, provided the victim has cell phone or Internet connectivity.[18]

Since cyberbullying is a relatively new phenomenon, we still do not have much information about how it affects young people. We do know that cyberbullying is a form of violence and, therefore, is unacceptable. Unfortunately, eliminating and preventing cyberbullying remains challenging.

Cyberbullying Laws and Policies

As of this writing, only sixteen states have anti-bullying laws that include the term *cyberbullying*.[19] While most school officials and lawmakers agree on the need to address cyberbullying, many are unsure how to do so.

Although cyberbullying may happen outside the classroom, being cyberbullied can affect a teen's physical and emotional safety at school. Given this reality, should a school be responsible for addressing cyberbullying, even if it does not happen on school grounds?[20] Some policies (such as those in the state of Massachusetts and in New York City public schools) state that schools must address cyberbullying if it directly affects a student's ability to learn, even if the harassment does not occur at the school itself or during school hours.[21] Other policies do not clarify this issue, and teens who are cyberbullied by peers outside of school may not know who to turn to or where to go, even if the bullying affects their educational experience.

The Tyler Clementi Case

In 2010, Tyler Clementi was a freshman at Rutgers who identified as LGBTQ (lesbian, gay, bisexual, transgender, or queer). He was just starting the process of coming out to friends and family, and was finally ready to start dating. One night, Clementi invited a man to his dorm room. At the time, he did not know that his roommate, teen Dharun Ravi, was filming him with this new romantic interest. In fact, Ravi twice filmed Clementi on his web cam and used Twitter, among other platforms, to publicize the videos. Clementi found out, and soon after, he committed suicide. In 2012, Clementi's family took the case to court, and, one month after the case began, Ravi was found guilty. The court was then charged with sentencing Ravi, which led to a series of legal questions regarding Ravi's actions in particular and cyberbullying in general.

Since this was one of the first cases of cyberbullying to be tried publicly, and certainly one of the most famous, lawmakers, advocates, teens, and parents knew that the decision would be used as an example for all future incidents. It also meant that there was no prior case that could serve as an example for a sentence.

Some argued that Ravi should be charged with murder because Clementi died as a result of his cruelty. Others thought that Ravi did not intend to cause Clementi's death and that he should be imprisoned for a lesser crime. Still others believed that Ravi needed counseling rather than a prison sentence. Since Ravi is not an American citizen, any criminal charge he incurred would make him eligible for deportation, a consequence that some people felt was too severe, and others felt was appropriate.[b]

In the end, the judge sentenced Ravi to thirty days in prison, three hundred hours of community service, and eleven thousand dollars in fines.[c] Ravi was also required to attend counseling related to the cyberbullying.[d] Some thought this was an appropriate sentence because it not only publicly showed that cyberbullying is a serious crime, it also gave Ravi the chance to redeem himself.[e] Others felt that the sentence was too lenient given that he was found guilty of multiple offenses, including invasion of privacy.[f]

Although many debate whether the sentence was fair, one thing became very clear as a result of this tragedy: cyberbullying is a serious offense that needs legal attention and dedicated prevention efforts.

Another question is whether cyberbullying should be considered a criminal offense. Some argue that jailing cyberbullies illustrates that cyberbullying is a serious offense, a message that is particularly important given how many teens believe that it is humorous rather than harmful. Supporters say that knowing the possibility of incarceration exists will stop teens from engaging in this negative behavior. Critics of criminalization say that cyberbullying is symptomatic of deeper biases such as racism, sexism, and homophobia. Sending young people to jail for cyberbullying could ruin their future, but it will not solve the problem, nor will it address the underlying causes of bullying. Some also argue that cyberbullies have deeper psychological problems that need to be addressed, such as anger management issues or a lack of social skills. Prison does not address these problems, they say, and therefore is not an effective solution.

The debate about the role of the criminal justice system in cyberbullying became especially heated after the case of Tyler Clementi, an eighteen-year-old freshman at Rutgers University, who committed suicide after his roommate, Dharun Ravi, used social media to broadcast Clementi's romantic encounter with another man. Read more about Tyler Clementi on page 102.

Another question is what should be done once cyberbullying is reported. Should the authorities be allowed to search students' e-mails and text messages? Or are these invasions of privacy and violations of our right to free speech? In fact, one of the biggest challenges addressing lawmakers is how to balance protecting teens' right to privacy and their right to safety from harassment.[22] Additionally, questions remain about how much responsibility companies that create social media platforms should take for preventing or reacting to cyberbullying. Social networking platforms such as Facebook (http://www.facebook.com/help), Twitter (https://support.twitter.com/articles/15794-abusive-behavior), YouTube (http://support.google.com/youtube/bin/request.py?contact_type=abuse), and Formspring.me all have pages that explain what electronic abuse looks like and how to report it. Some of these platforms are responsive, taking down content immediately after it is flagged. Others are not responsive at all.

Some corporations have taken an active role in preventing cyberbullying. One of these is MTV, which created the "A Thin Line" campaign to raise awareness about the effects of cyberbullying and digital dating violence, and to help teens protect themselves and their privacy. The site also has opportunities for teens to post the actions they have taken to prevent cyberbullying, and hosts contests for teen-produced content designed to raise awareness about this important issue. To find out more, check out www.athinline.org.

What to Do If You Are Cyberbullied

In some ways, reacting to cyberbullying is similar to reacting to any kind of bullying. Just as in face-to-face bullying, your first step should be to talk to a trusted adult who can help you make the harassment stop and navigate the aftereffects. However, cyberbullying also requires specific actions that are different than those utilized in other kinds of bullying.

If you are being cyberbullied, do not respond.[23] This is for your own protection: you are in a much better position when you report the harassment if you have not acted abusively or tried to engage the bully in conversation. Plus, the more you respond, the more attention the bully gets, and the more interested witnesses become, a cycle that just perpetuates the bullying and makes it worse.

Do not forward any evidence of the cyberbullying to anyone.[24] If you are upset and need to talk, tell your friends verbally or show them the evidence on your device. Remember that the fewer people who have the content, the easier it is to stop it from spreading.

If possible, block the person who is bullying you so that he or she can no longer access your Facebook page, Twitter account, cell phone, or other electronic devices.[25] If the content is on a site such as Facebook, contact the company to see if they will take it down.[26] Most electronic platforms and phone companies have web pages that give clear instructions about how to block unwanted contacts and remove damaging content. You can ask an adult or a friend to help you find the information, or call the company's helpline.

Keep a record of everything that happened.[27] Since it is easy to delete electronic content, make sure you have hard copies of it that you can show when you are explaining what happened, just in case the bully or the corporation or anyone else decides to erase it. Print out any images or texts or e-mails, save your text messages, and keep a written record of what occurred when. If the bullying makes you feel afraid for your safety, talk to an adult about whether it would be appropriate to speak to a law enforcement official.[28] If you are worried about the bully finding out that you reported his or her actions, make this clear. The officials can advise you about how to protect yourself. You should also inform officials at your school or campus about the cyberbullying so that the adults in the building are aware of your situation and can help you.[29]

Cyberbullying can feel more overwhelming than in-person bullying because it is impossible to avoid: no matter where you are, as long as you are carrying an electronic device, the bully can reach you. While it is often recommended that victims of bullying talk to a counselor or a therapist, this is especially important when it comes to cyberbullying. Discussing what you are going through with a professional can help you work through insecurity and anxiety that naturally accompanies this type of intensive bullying, and can help you move on with your life. Also talk to people you love and trust and let them know how they can support you. You can talk to a professional for ideas about what to ask from friends and family.

Responding to cyberbullying is yet another area that requires more research. As the phenomenon spreads, more and more adults in your life will become familiar with it and will be able to help you. However, like all types of bullying, it is not enough for communities to know how to respond to cyberbullying. They must also push for prevention. In the next section, you will learn about digital citizenship and how it is becoming an essential element of the fight against cyberbullying.

Digital Citizenship

One of the best ways to prevent cyberbullying is to train teens and adults about what it looks like, how it is harmful, and how it can be prevented. A concept called *digital citizenship*, developed by Common Sense Media, describes a new approach to promoting positive and responsible online behavior.

Just like we learn how to be responsible members of our community, state, and country, we must all learn how to be responsible members of online spaces. In the real world, there are some behaviors that we do not practice because they harm individuals, which in turn makes all of us feel unsafe. These behaviors include stealing, lying, vandalizing property, or physically assaulting others. Similarly, in online spaces, we can choose whether we want our behavior to support and welcome others or to make them feel unsafe. Cyberbullying is an example of a behavior that makes a community unsafe. Digital citizenship describes positive behaviors that make online spaces more welcoming and secure for all of us, regardless of our identities.

An increasing number of resources describe responsible online behavior. Since the electronic world is constantly changing—as are electronic devices—our ideas of what counts as acceptable participation in virtual worlds also changes. However, there are a few guidelines that will likely remain constant as the online world develops, evolves, and grows.

If You Wouldn't Do It in Person, You Shouldn't Do It Online

Sometimes it can be scary to say or do something to someone standing in front of us. Being online can give us the courage to do things that we would not normally do. This is why cyberbullying is tempting: because we do not see the emotional impact we are having on the victim, nor do we fear for our safety; we only feel the power we have to act without facing the consequences of our behavior. Furthermore, abusing others online may help us gain attention from others, even if we are anonymous. For someone who may not be used to popularity or attention, this can be addictive, even if it causes others pain.

Just because others may be commenting on your Facebook post or congratulating you on something you forwarded does not mean that the person you are affecting feels the same way. Before you act in the digital world, think about whether you would do the same thing in person. For example, would you pass a humiliating picture of your significant other around your social studies class? Would you complain about your best friend to his or her face, or just in a Facebook status? Are you writing an abusive text message because you are too afraid to say what you mean in person? Remember, just because some behavior feels acceptable online does not mean that it would be acceptable in person.

Electronic Messages Do Not Just Disappear

When you send a text message, tweet an opinion, send a chat, write a blog post, or post on Facebook, it may feel like what you have created is temporary because it is not on paper. However, the truth is that electronic information is saved and archived. Whether or not you save the information, others can find it through searches, or they may save it themselves if you sent it to them.

The mark you leave in cyberspace is sometimes called a *digital footprint*. Your digital footprint is detailed, widely available, and permanent. Take a moment to think: in ten years, will you will be proud of your words and actions, or will you regret them? What if a potential employer saw what you had written? Or a close friend or significant other? Before you put something into cyberspace, think about the people you could possibly hurt—including yourself.

Nothing Is as Private as It Seems

When you send someone a text message or post a status, a handful of people may respond to you. However, keep in mind that many more people will have viewed your content. All of these individuals are capable of forwarding electronic information to people you may never have imagined. Even your most trusted friend may innocently share something you created in confidence, making your private information instantly public.

It is important to keep this in mind when you share information electronically. Do not just think about who the content is going to, but also who it *could* go to. Think also about whether you could just as easily share with someone verbally or in person. Keeping your thoughts and images out of the virtual world may not make you "Facebook Famous," as Fagbenle said on page 100. However, it may preserve your reputation, an important relationship, or your future success, all of which could prove to be more important than fleeting popularity.

The Internet Is More Than Facebook and Twitter

When you are thinking about your safety and privacy, remember that your electronic interactions include searches, shopping, and other personal tasks. Before you enter data such as a credit card number or social security number or contact

Remember that anything sent using a cell phone can be easily forwarded to others. Limit your texting and protect your privacy.

details, Google search anything related to a private issue, or look up information such as your bank balance or your grades, make sure that you carefully consider the security of the website you are using. Think about who is maintaining the site—is it a renowned expert or a famous company? Or is it something you've never heard of before? If something goes wrong, who can you talk to about it? If you have any doubts about the site, avoid it. Also think about the device you are using. Is it a shared computer that anyone can log onto? Is it a cell phone that your friends sometimes use to make calls? If so, think twice before entering personal information.

In addition to these guidelines to digital citizenship, which are recommended by adult experts, you may want to think about what you want your digital world to look like. What rights should you have when you go online? What protections do you think you and your friends need? To think about what your digital world might look like and what rights you want in that world, try the following exercise.

Although this chapter has focused on the potentially negative effects of electronic communications, there is one more tenant of digital citizenship that is important to remember: the online world is a powerful place for creating change. Teens have used the Internet to bully each other, but they have also used it to improve the off-line world, advocating for teen-friendly policies, raising money for good causes,

Digital Rights

Throughout history, nations or groups of nations have created documents outlining the rights of their citizens. Rights are what we are entitled to regardless of our race, class, gender, sexual orientation, immigration status, or any other identity. These rights become the basis of how we treat others, how others treat us, and how our institutions grant us protection. Individuals are encouraged or penalized depending on whether or not their behaviors limit the ability of others to enjoy their rights.

Some of these documents, like the Bill of Rights in the United States Constitution or the Magna Carta in England, are hundreds of years old. Others, like the Universal Declaration of Human Rights, are much newer. Still, the authors of these documents probably could not imagine that the world would go from being a purely physical place to having a virtual space as well.

Here is a list of some of the most important declarations of rights in history. Try reading through a few and ask yourself the questions that follow:

Famous Statements of Rights:

- The Magna Carta (created in England in 1215): http://www.constitution.org/eng/magnacar.htm
- The Declaration of the Rights of Man (the foundation of the French Revolution published in 1789): http://avalon.law.yale.edu/18th_century/rightsof.asp
- The U.S. Bill of Rights (the ten amendments to the Constitution that went into effect in 1791): http://www.archives.gov/exhibits/charters/bill_of_rights_transcript.html

- The Universal Declaration of Human Rights (created by the United Nations General Assembly in 1948): http://www.un.org/en/documents/udhr/index.shtml
- The Declaration of the Rights of the Child (created by the United Nations in 1959): http://www.un.org/cyberschoolbus/humanrights/resources/child.asp
- The South African Bill of Rights (published in South Africa in 1996 as part of the post-apartheid government): http://www.info.gov.za/documents/constitution/1996/96cons2.htm

1. What do you think the societies that produced these documents valued? How can you tell?
2. What are the best parts of these documents? What could be improved?
3. Who did the authors of these documents have in mind when they wrote them? Who was included? Who was left out? (For example, the U.S. Bill of Rights was written by White, landholding men. Do you think that they considered women, people of color, those who identify as LGBTQ, or low income communities when they were writing it? Why or why not?)

Now think of your digital community. Who is part of it? What problems do they face? What rights should they have? What can you do to make your community a safer place where your rights are protected?

Try writing your own Statement of Digital Rights. Ask your friends to do so as well. Compare and contrast what you've written. If possible, share with administrators or faculty on your school or campus. Your work could be a great start to a conversation about making your digital community safer for all of its citizens.

and educating themselves about one another's differences. Think about how many anti-bullying campaigns you have read about in this book that began as videos on YouTube or as blog posts by a few concerned young men and women.

Being a good digital citizen does not have to be limited to making sure that you do not harm others. It can also include creating positive change. When you are online, you are powerful. The question is whether you choose to use your power to intimidate and exclude others, or to make them feel comfortable, warm, and safe. The choice is yours.

Notes

1. U.S. Department of Health and Human Services, Centers for Disease Control and Prevention, "Youth Risk Behavior Surveillance—United States, 2011," *Morbidity and Mortality Weekly: Surveillance Summaries* 61, no. 4 (accessed June 8, 2012): 9.
2. U.S. Department of Health and Human Services, "Youth Risk Behavior Surveillance," 9.
3. Emily A. Greytak, Joseph G. Kosciw, and Elizabeth M. Diaz, *Harsh Realities: The Experience of Transgender Youth in Our Nation's Schools* (Washington, DC: Gay, Lesbian, Straight Education Network, 2007), 21.
4. Robin M. Kowalski, Susan P. Limber, and Patricia W. Agatson, *Cyberbullying: Bullying in the Digital Age*, 2nd ed. (Malden, MA: Blackwell Publishing, 2012), 1.
5. Amanda Lenhart, *Pew Internet & American Life Project: Data Memo*, June 27, 2007, http://www.pewinternet.org/~/media//Files/Reports/2007/PIP%20Cyberbullying%20Memo.pdf .pdf (accessed January 10, 2013), 1.
6. Lenhart, *Pew Internet & American Life Project*, 2.
7. Lenhart, *Pew Internet & American Life Project*, 3.
8. Tamara Lewin, "Teenage Insults, Scrawled on Web, Not on Wall," *New York Times*, May 5, 2010, http://www.nytimes.com/2010/05/06/us/06formspring.html?src=me&ref=homepage&_r=0 (accessed January 1, 2013).
9. Edeico Martinez, "Alexis Pilkington Brutally Cyberbullied, Even after Her Suicide," *CBS News*, March 26, 2010, http://www.cbsnews.com/8301-504083_162-20001181-504083.html (1 January 2013).
10. DoSomething.org, *The Bully Report: Trends in Bullying Pulled from Student Facebook Interactions*, 2012, http://files.dosomething.org/files/campaigns/bullyreport/bully_report.pdf (accessed January 19, 2013), 6.
11. DoSomething.org, *The Bully Report*, 6.
12. Catherine Hill and Holly Kearl, *Crossing the Line: Sexual Harassment at School* (Washington, DC: American Association of University Women, 2011), 11.
13. Greytak, Kosciw, and Diaz, *Harsh Realities*, 21.
14. Jessie Klein, *The Bully Society: School Shootings and the Crisis of Bullying in America's Schools* (New York: New York University Press, 2011), 26.
15. Andre Sourander, Anat Brunstein Klomek, Maria Ikonen, et al., "Psychosocial Risk Factors Associated with Cyberbullying among Adolescents: A Population-Based Study," *Archives of General Psychiatry* 67, no. 7 (2010): 722.
16. U.S. Department of Health and Human Services, "What Is Cyberbullying?" Stopbullying .gov, 2013, http://www.stopbullying.gov/cyberbullying/what-is-it/index.html (accessed January 10, 2013).
17. Sameer Hinduja and Justin W. Patchin, *Cyberbullying Research Summary: Cyberbullying and Suicide*, 2010, http://www.cyberbullying.us/cyberbullying_and_suicide_research_fact_sheet .pdf (accessed December 2, 2012).
18. Sourander et al., "Psychosocial Risk Factors," 725.
19. Hinduja and Patchin, "State Cyberbullying Laws: A Brief Review of State Cyberbullying Laws and Policies," 2010, http://www.cyberbullying.us/Bullying_and_Cyberbullying_Laws .pdf (accessed January 10, 2013).
20. Marlene Sandstrom, "More Insidious Harassment," *New York Times*, September 30, 2010, http://www.nytimes.com/roomfordebate/2010/09/30/cyberbullying-and-a-students-suicide/ more-insidious-harassment (accessed January 10, 2013).

21. Sandstrom, "More Insidious Harassment."

22. Laurie L. Levinson, "What Isn't Known about Suicides," *New York Times*, September 30, 2010, http://www.nytimes.com/roomfordebate/2010/09/30/cyberbullying-and-a-students -suicide/what-isnt-known-about-suicides (accessed January 10, 2013).

23. U.S. Department of Health and Human Services, "Report Cyberbullying," Stopbullying .gov, 2012, http://www.stopbullying.gov/cyberbullying/how-to-report/index.html (accessed February 9, 2013).

24. U.S. Department of Health and Human Services, "Report Cyberbullying."

25. U.S. Department of Health and Human Services, "Report Cyberbullying."

26. U.S. Department of Health and Human Services, "Report Cyberbullying."

27. U.S. Department of Health and Human Services, "Report Cyberbullying."

28. U.S. Department of Health and Human Services, "Report Cyberbullying."

29. U.S. Department of Health and Human Services, "Report Cyberbullying."

a. Temitayo Fagbenle has given Rowman & Littlefield permission to publish her story in her own words.

b. Kate Zernike, "Rutgers Webcam-Spying Defendant Is Sentenced to 30-Day Jail Term," *New York Times*, May 21, 2012, http://www.nytimes.com/2012/05/22/nyregion/rutgers-spying -defendant-sentenced-to-30-days-in-jail.html?pagewanted=all (accessed January 10, 2013).

c. Zernike, "Rutgers Webcam-Spying Defendant."

d. Zernike, "Rutgers Webcam-Spying Defendant."

e. Zernike, "Rutgers Webcam-Spying Defendant."

f. Zernike, "Rutgers Webcam-Spying Defendant."

SEXUAL HARASSMENT

Sexual harassment is bullying related to gender and sexuality, which includes one's perceived or actual sexual orientation or sexual preferences. It includes any unwanted romantic advances. If someone you have a crush on gives you welcome attention, it is not considered abusive. If you are not interested in the attention, then the behavior could be classified as a form of bullying. Sexual harassment also encompasses some types of homophobic bias-based harassment. For example, calling someone a homophobic epithet is an example of sexual harassment whether or not the person identifies as LGBTQ.

Sexual harassment is one of the most common types of bullying. The American Association of University Women (AAUW) found that during the 2010–2011 school year, almost half of teens had been victims of sexual harassment, and one-third of girls and one-fourth of boys had witnessed it.[1] Yet, only about half of students who experienced it said that they did anything to respond to it, and less than 10 percent reported it to an adult at their school.[2] Yet, 87 percent of students said that the abuse negatively affected them.[3] These statistics indicate that sexual harassment is a widespread problem that goes unnoticed and unaddressed.

In this chapter, you will learn how to identify, respond to, and prevent sexual harassment. You will learn about laws and policies that protect you and your peers from discrimination based on your gender identity or sexual orientation. You will learn about why sexual harassment has been acceptable in our society for so long and what you and your peers can do to change this. Finally, you will learn about teens who have joined together to end sexual harassment in their schools, streets, and communities.

What Sexual Harassment Looks Like

One of the reasons why sexual harassment is so commonly experienced but so rarely reported is that many teens and adults do not recognize it when it occurs. Unfortunately, in our society, many disrespectful behaviors are considered harmless or acceptable. In fact, some types of sexual harassment are even encouraged.

Is This Sexual Harassment?

Sexual harassment is often ignored because we excuse this unacceptable behavior as normal. Take this quiz and see whether you can tell what is considered sexual harassment and what is not.

1. Someone touches you in a sexual way without your permission.
2. You are walking down the street and a stranger yells out that you are beautiful.
3. Your friend asks if you want to see a sexual picture on her phone. You say no, but she shows you anyway.
4. Your friend calls you "gay" for doing something socially unpopular.
5. The person who you have had a crush on asks you on a date, and you say yes.
6. You are fooling around in the locker room, and a friend pulls your gym shorts down.
7. A female friend of yours wears an extremely short skirt to school, and boys begin to comment on how attractive her legs look.
8. You flirt with a friend who you are interested in and who is interested in you.
9. Someone in your class tells a sexual joke.
10. Someone starts a rumor on Facebook that one of your friends had sex with several other students in your school.

Answers:

1. Yes. Any touching without your permission is considered sexual harassment.
2. Yes. Even if the stranger claims he or she is giving you a compliment, he or she is targeting you without your consent.
3. Yes, especially if it makes you feel uncomfortable. You should not have to look at anything of a sexual nature against your will.
4. Yes. This is an example of homophobia.

5. No. If you are interested in this person romantically, and you feel comfortable, then it is simply going on a date.
6. Yes. Taking off someone else's clothes without his or her consent is considered sexual harassment.
7. Yes. It does not matter how someone dresses, it does not give others the right to make comments about how he or she looks.
8. No. If you are both comfortable, then it is not considered sexual harassment.
9. Yes. A sexual joke could make someone feel uncomfortable.
10. Yes. Starting a rumor about someone else's sexual conduct is considered harassment.

Try the quiz on page 114 to see if you can recognize sexual harassment when you see it—you may be surprised.

Sexual harassment is more than just touching. In fact, most sexual harassment is verbal or written, rather than physical.[4] Plus, increasingly, sexual harassment occurs in cyberspace. For example, showing someone a sexual picture that he or she does not want to see, starting a sexual rumor about someone, or sending someone a provocative text message are all examples of sexual harassment. In fact, sexual jokes, gestures, and comments are the most commonly experienced forms of sexual harassment.[5] Anything sexual in nature that makes you uncomfortable is considered sexual harassment. If, on the other hand, someone you are interested in is flirting with you and you enjoy it, then this is not considered sexual harassment. The key is how it makes you feel.

Researchers estimate that as many as 80 percent of teens experience some form of sexual harassment while they are in high school.[6] Girls are more likely than boys to experience most forms of sexual harassment, including being shown sexual pictures they do not want to see, being physically intimidated or touched in a sexual way, and being harassed online.[7] Girls who reach puberty earlier than their classmates are more likely to be sexually harassed than their peers.[8] Both girls and boys who do not conform to gender stereotypes have a higher risk of being sexually harassed than their peers.[9] For example, girls who have short hair and like to wear masculine clothing or boys who have long hair or participate in feminine activities may be targeted because of these choices and behaviors.

The highest rates of sexual harassment are not among cisgender boys or girls, but are recorded among transgender youth. A study from 2007 indicates that

Sexual harassment disproportionately affects women and girls.

around 90 percent of transgender teens experience routine verbal sexual harassment, over half experience physical violence, and three-fourths experience sexual harassment because of their gender identity or sexual orientation.[10] While this group of teens is often overlooked, clearly more needs to be done to protect them from this type of bullying.

No More Excuses for Sexual Harassment

Most teens who sexually harass their peers are male. In the AAUW study, two-thirds of students said that their harassers were either individual boys or a group of boys, whereas less than 20 percent of students said their harassers were individual girls or groups of girls (transgender statistics were not reported).[11] About 45 percent of students who admitted to sexually harassing others thought that what they were doing was "no big deal," and 39 percent said that they were just being funny, indicating that many do not realize how damaging and inappropriate their behavior can be.[12] Similarly, some people believe that practices such as aggressive flirting, telling dirty jokes, or engaging in unwanted advances are signs of masculinity, rather than bullying. For example, teen women from the New York City–based group Girls for Gender Equity (GGE) say that adults in their schools excused aggressive behavior from male students by saying that they were "just acting like boys."[13] Some researchers take this rationale a step further, arguing that teen boys feel social pressure to engage in sexual harassment to prove their masculinity and heterosexuality, particularly through visibly and actively pursuing girls.[14] By this logic, sexual harassment almost seems like a rite of passage. In reality, expectations about masculinity are unfair to all teens regardless of their gender or sexuality, since they encourage disrespectful behavior and force young men to act in ways that are uncomfortable or wrong.

Just as boys feel pressure to be masculine and girls feel pressure to be feminine, most students feel pressure to be straight. Because of this, teens may use words like *gay* or *lesbian* as insults, even though in reality they describe an individual's sexual orientation and, therefore, are not negative terms.[15] About one in five teens say that they were sexually harassed by being called gay or lesbian; about the same percentage of teens say they had used the terms to insult their peers either online or in person.[16] Students may feel that if they insult others in this way, they are proving to the world that they are straight.[17] In reality, they are communicating that they believe being LGBTQ is a bad thing and being straight is a good thing. This is damaging to students and adults who may not be straight and is a serious form of bullying.

Another reason why adults and students ignore sexual harassment is because they believe that the victims deserve to be harassed because of their behavior. Teens from GGE say that when they reported sexual harassment at their schools, the adults who received the reports said that the victims invited sexual harassment because they dressed or acted provocatively.[18] The teens said that the harassment was not addressed, and the bullies continued their unacceptable behavior.

No one deserves to be sexually harassed. Ever. In this case, both the young women and their harassers made choices. The young women chose to wear clothing that may have been tight or revealing, or to become consensually involved with their peers romantically or sexually. These decisions did not harm others. On the other hand, their harassers made the choice to engage in bullying behavior that directly and intentionally hurt others. It is not fair to blame the young women who did nothing to harm anyone else, rather than to hold bullies accountable for their actions. In fact, most teens agree with this assessment: about 91 percent of teens say that sexual harassment victims "don't bring sexual harassment on themselves."[19] Teens recognize that their choices are their own, and that nobody deserves to be hurt for being themselves.

Yet another reason that sexual harassment is accepted is because it is mistaken for flirting or an innocent way to pursue someone romantically. Unfortunately, this is rarely true. Only about 3 percent of teens who admit to sexually harassing others did so because they were interested in dating the victim, and only 6 percent of teens thought their target enjoyed being harassed.[20] Most sexual harassment has nothing to do with romance, and most teens who engage in sexual harassment know that the individuals they are targeting are not open to their advances.

One final reason why sexual harassment continues is because both victims and their confidantes feel uncomfortable discussing and addressing it. Young women from GGE said that when they reported sexual harassment to teachers they trusted, the adults felt the issue was too sensitive or felt helpless to respond and so did nothing.[21] Additionally, some schools do not want to educate their staff about sexual harassment because they fear that teachers and students will report incidents and that they will consequently be labeled "the sexual harassment school."[22] This logic is bad for both teens and adults: until we can openly talk about sexual harassment, it will be impossible to eliminate it. Some educators and policy makers actually see an increase in reporting as a positive sign that individuals in the building feel comfortable talking about bullying problems, which is the first step in developing effective prevention methods. Reporting desensitizes the issue, which in turn makes adults comfortable talking to students or getting help from their colleagues in stopping the behavior.

Excusing harassment as being funny or masculine, blaming the victim, feeling helpless, and attempting to cover up the problem all illustrate the need to educate both students and adults about what sexual harassment is, how to respond to it, and how to prevent it. All over the country, teens are working together to raise awareness about sexual harassment. The young women of GGE, for example, conducted research, developed an educational campaign, fought for legislative change, made a film about their work, and even contributed to a book. Read more about their work on page 119.

The Negative Consequences of Sexual Harassment

Victims of sexual harassment suffer long-term effects on their mental and physical health. Transgender students who are sexually harassed are more likely to be absent, have lower grades than their peers, and show less interest in education because they feel unsafe coming to school.[23] Regardless of their gender identity, students who are sexually harassed tend to experience physical problems such as insomnia, an inability to concentrate, and a feeling of being sick to their stomach.[24] These problems are exacerbated when the harassment occurs online: almost half of students who experience sexual harassment both online and in person do not want to come to school or consider transferring to escape their harasser.[25] The effects also differ by race: Latina and Black teens are more likely than their White peers to ask for a transfer from their schools because of sexual harassment, change their route to school to avoid harassers, and to drop out of activities to avoid the bullying.[26] Similarly, teens from low-income communities are more likely than

Girls for Gender Equity:
Participatory Action Research

In 2001, Joanne T. Smith, the daughter of Haitian immigrants and an avid basketball player, founded Girls for Gender Equity (GGE). The purpose of the organization was to empower teen girls through sports and leadership development, all with the ultimate goal of preparing them to fight for gender equity. As the organization grew, the teen participants took a leadership role in shaping the group's focus.

One of the key issues they wanted to address was sexual harassment. They began by trying to work with the New York City public school system to enforce Title IX, the law that outlines the steps schools need to take to prevent and respond to sexual harassment. After a series of disappointing conversations in which school system personnel either ignored them or told them that nothing could be done, the teens felt that the administration did not see ending sexual harassment as a priority because they did not realize the extent and the severity of the problem. They felt they needed to prove how widespread sexual harassment is and how much it negatively affects the daily lives of women and girls. It seemed as though no one had collected the information that policy makers and officials would find compelling enough to take action.

The girls decided to take matters into their own hands. With the help of trained researchers from the City University of New York, they designed a study that would answer the question, "What is the impact of sexual harassment in New York City schools?"[a] They came up with a research design that included a survey and focus groups, as well as less traditional methods such as passing around slam books, or notebooks where their peers could make anonymous comments.

Although their initial goal was to survey 600 middle school and high school students, they ended up reaching 1,189! They also conducted three focus groups and collected data from their slam books and blogs. The girls found some important results: 67 percent of students did not think sexual harassment was a problem in their schools.[b] Yet, about a quarter of students said they were harassed daily, and another 14 percent said they were harassed weekly.[c] Almost three-quarters of students said that they had witnessed verbal sexual harassment, and almost two-thirds had witnessed physical sexual harassment.[d] These results clearly demonstrated that sexual harassment was a real problem in New York City schools.

The young women used what they learned to organize a coalition of groups dedicated to fighting sexual harassment. They presented their results at a conference they organized to bring the coalition together, and used what they had learned to testify at a hearing held by the city council. They also produced a film about street harassment, a specific type of sexual harassment that occurs in neighborhoods and on the street. Their work has shifted the power dynamic in their conversations: instead of being the objects of research, they are the researchers. They hold the power of information that they have collected themselves, and, when it comes to sexual harassment in schools, they are the experts.

To find out more about GGE, check out their book *Hey, Shorty! A Guide to Combating Sexual Harassment and Violence in Public Schools and on the Streets*, which describes in detail how the teens conducted the study. As you read, think about what kinds of issues are important to you and how collecting your own data could help you fight for what you believe in.

their wealthier peers to stay home from school in reaction to harassment.[27] Although it is not clear why these differences exist, it is important to remember that all of us have unique experiences because of our multiple identities, and, as a result, we each face different kinds of trauma, and we each cope with violence in different ways.

Sexual harassment impacts more than just the victims. Studies show that whether or not they are victims, teens who attend schools where severe sexual harassment takes place experience negative psychological effects because they realize that they are in an institution where harassment is tolerated and permitted, a fact that makes them feel fundamentally unsafe.[28]

One of the most disturbing consequences of sexual harassment is that it creates bullies: about 92 percent of girls and 80 percent of boys who are sexually harassed become harassers.[29] About a quarter of these teens report that they become bullies specifically because they want revenge.[30] The damaging logic of blaming the victim and excusing the bully is a one of the reasons why this happens: by sending the message that victims are to blame and bullies are not, we communicate that bullying is acceptable and grant bullies power. Instead, we should focus on making teens who engage in sexual harassment stop their harmful behavior.

In fact, by law, both school officials and young people are supposed to learn about sexual harassment every year. The law that mandates this is called Title IX.

Title IX

Title IX, which was briefly discussed in chapter 5, is a law designed to address gender equity issues in schools. It is probably most famous for mandating that girls and boys should have equal access to sports. However, it addresses other issues as well, including career education, technology access, and sexual harassment. It is a federal law, which means that it affects every school in the United States, and it was signed into law by the president.

Title IX passed in 1972. Although it may seem surprising that a law that simply requires schools to treat boys and girls fairly would be contentious, it has been the source of controversy ever since it was enacted. Read more about the history of Title IX, and why it was controversial, below.

Under Title IX, schools and universities are required to provide a number of services related to preventing sexual harassment.[31] First, every school district is supposed to have a Title IX coordinator. So is every university. This coordinator is an adult who is supposed to ensure that all sexual harassment or gender-based discrimination complaints are addressed appropriately and efficiently. Your school

A History of Title IX

In 1964, President Lyndon B. Johnson signed into law the historic Civil Rights Act, a piece of legislation that officially outlawed racism and segregation. It remains one of the most important laws in U.S. history, making it illegal to discriminate against anyone on the basis of race. Eight years later, President Richard Nixon signed Title IX, an amendment to the Civil Rights Act that addressed gender discrimination against young women, particularly in schools. An amendment is a piece of legislation that extends the existing law to cover more than its original form.

President Nixon assigned the Department of Health, Education and Welfare to create regulations that specified what schools and universities would have to do to comply with Title IX. When the law was posted for public comment, the Department received over ten thousand comments specifically on the issue of women's sports.[e] Other parts of the law were controversial as well: the *New York Times* editorial board called Title IX "educationally unsound" for establishing requirements for colleges to admit more women.[f] Clearly, many people had strong opinions about what Title IX should and should not do.

After the regulations were written, Title IX became famous for mandating that schools fund women's and men's sports equally. However, it also contains sections that promote girls' access to math, science, and technology; outlaw discrimination against pregnant teens; and mandate a process for schools to respond to sexual harassment.[g]

While the Nixon administration was supportive of the law, everything changed when President Ronald Reagan was elected in 1980. President Reagan chose not to enforce Title IX because he believed that giving money to women's sports would reduce funding for men's sports.[h] In fact, critics of Title IX have made the same argument as recently as the 2000s.[i] These issues have led to a series of Supreme Court cases focusing on enforcing the law.

Perhaps the most interesting thing about Title IX is that when it was written, its authors thought that it would soon be outdated. That's because at the time, Congress had just passed the Equal Rights Amendment (ERA), a constitutional amendment that made gender discrimination illegal.[j] Since it would change the U.S. Constitution, the ERA had to be approved by the states by 1982, ten years after it was drafted. Unfortunately, not enough states ratified it, and it never passed.[k] Had it become law, the ERA would have more than covered the regulations in Title IX. Plus, it would have superseded Title IX, meaning that in a court of law, it would have been a stronger way to argue and justify a case.

To this day, the U.S. Constitution does not guarantee equal treatment for women. Every few years members of Congress try to reintroduce the ERA, but it never passes. Luckily, Title IX provides some protections for women, even if the Constitution does not.

should inform you and the community who the Title IX coordinator is and how to contact him or her.

If you are sexually harassed, you have the option of reporting the incident to the Title IX coordinator or another adult you trust. If the adult you speak to is not the Title IX coordinator, you should let this adult know that he or she can contact the Title IX coordinator to find out the appropriate procedures. This is important since many adults do not know how to respond to sexual harassment and, therefore, may want help or get guidance from an expert. You can also make a report if you witness sexual harassment. In fact, according to Title IX, as long as it is clear that a student is being harassed, then any adult who notices the harassment must put an end to it.

Title IX guarantees you the right to get an education without being afraid of sexual harassment or gender discrimination. Once you have reported the incident, your school or university is required to investigate and respond to the harassment quickly and fairly. Officials must not only respond to this specific incident of sexual harassment; they must also take steps to prevent it from happening in the future. The National Women's Law Center says that some examples of actively addressing the problem could include separating you and the person who is bullying you and referring one or both of you to counseling.[32] Another action you might suggest is to do school- or university-wide training on sexual harassment to raise awareness and to send a message that it will not be tolerated.[33]

Sexual harassment is the bully's fault, not the victim's fault. Therefore, anyone who reports sexual harassment should not be punished or penalized. If you are a victim of sexual harassment at your school or university, you do not have to change your classes, where you live, or anything about your routine. The harasser is the one who must make the changes. Therefore, if a counselor or another school official asks you to alter something about your life to separate you and your harasser, consider whether you feel comfortable doing so. If you do not want to make a change, you do not have to: it is up to your harasser to alter his or her behavior, not you.[34]

Although Title IX is a federal law, many school districts and universities are not in compliance with all of its regulations. The girls of GGE, for example, found that when they called New York City public school teachers and administrators in a random phone survey, the majority of adults in school buildings could not identify their Title IX coordinator.[35] If this is the case in your district, you have several options. Your school or university may have an anti-bullying policy. While federal law requires compliance with Title IX regardless of other existing rules and regulations, you may be able to take advantage of the structures put in place through an anti-bullying policy—such as an adult anti-bullying coordinator or a counseling program—to deal with a sexual harassment situation. You can also file a complaint with the U.S. Department of Education's Office of Civil Rights

(OCR).[36] The complaint could be about your situation or about the fact that your school is not in compliance with Title IX. The OCR accepts complaints online at http://www2.ed.gov/about/offices/list/ocr/complaintintro.html.

You have a right to learn in a safe and secure environment. If you are being sexually harassed, talk to an adult you trust to make sure that the issue is addressed quickly and effectively. Federal law is on your side.

Sexual Harassment Outside of School

Schools are not the only places where teens experience sexual harassment. Some researchers estimate that 80 percent of young women experience street harassment, or sexually aggressive behavior from strangers, before the age of nineteen.[37] Street harassment ranges from inappropriate comments about your body to inappropriate touching. It can be difficult to address because it happens in so many locations and because it often involves strangers. Experts on street harassment say that if you feel safe, you should respond in the moment by firmly telling the harasser to stop.[38] Doing so can make the harasser break the pattern and can make you feel confident and in control, which in turn could reduce the trauma you feel afterward. If you do not feel safe, then you should not respond. If you do choose to respond, say something short and firm, such as, "Don't do that," or "Street harassment is not acceptable," then keep walking. If your harasser follows you or tries to talk to you, do not answer or engage him or her in conversation.[39] You might also choose to respond in this way when you see someone else being harassed, particularly if one of your friends is acting as the harasser. By pointing out that street harassment is unacceptable, you are helping to change the way our culture views this damaging behavior.

If you choose not to respond when the harassment happens, you have another option: you could tell your story on www.ihollaback.org. Read about Hollaback! on page 125.

Increasingly, students experience sexual harassment both in person and online.[40] About one in three girls and one in four boys have experienced sexual harassment through the Internet, receiving unwanted text messages, Facebook posts, and e-mails, or having their personal information revealed online, among other experiences.[41] Approximately one in five teens have received unwanted electronic messages of a sexual nature, while about 13 percent say rumors were started about them online.[42] Since online sexual harassment—a form of cyberbullying—is relatively new, schools may not know what their obligations are to address it. If cyberbullying is making you feel unsafe and unable to learn, you can ask your school community to help stop it. For more on cyberbullying, see chapter 6 of this volume.

Hollaback!

Hollaback! started in 2005 when a group of young people got into a discussion about street harassment. During the conversation, the women realized that sharing their experiences with others made them feel less alone. The men, on the other hand, were shocked—they had no idea that women and LGBTQ youth faced these issues every day. They wanted to do something, but what? Most street harassment comes from strangers. How do you send a message to people that you don't even know? Plus, it happens everywhere, from the United States to India to Nigeria to France. How do you start a worldwide movement?

Hollaback! decided that the first step was to create a community where victims of street harassment could share their stories and feel supported, so they started a blog called *Hollaback!* (www.ihollaback.com). Victims of street harassment were encouraged to upload photos of their harassers and to tell their stories. The photos publicly humiliated street harassers and sometimes even made them stop their behavior. The stories created a bond between victims and their supporters. The blog helped people realize that street harassers are not the majority and that there is a growing movement of concerned citizens committed to making streets safe for all genders. The blog became popular not just in the United States, but globally.

Now, Hollaback! is much more than just a blog. It's a nonprofit organization that provides trainings in addressing and preventing street harassment, facilitates public art projects, promotes safe streets, and conducts its own research. The stories that individuals tell about harassment remain one of the most powerful aspects of the organization. To find out more, and to find a chapter near you, check out www.ihollaback.org. Who knows, after exploring the blog, you may be inspired to tell your own story!

Responding to Sexual Harassment

Since sexual harassment involves sex and gender, two topics that many of us feel uncomfortable discussing, it can be difficult to know what to do when you experience or witness it. If you are sexually harassed or you witness sexual harassment, there are a few things you can do immediately. First, tell the harasser that his or her behavior is unacceptable and needs to stop immediately. Use words that focus on your feelings or the feelings of your peer who is being harassed. For example, you may say something like, "That makes me feel uncomfortable. Please stop."[43] Or you could say, "I know you think that is a joke, but I don't think it's funny. Please don't tell jokes like that anymore."[44] This may be difficult to do at first, but keep trying. Practice with your friends when the bully is not around. Or ask a friend to support you when you speak up. Remember that studies show that many teens who sexually harass others think that their behavior is not serious. Letting them know that what they are doing is wrong could change their perspective. Your words are powerful.

Whether or not you are comfortable confronting a bully when you witness sexual harassment, you should always report what you have seen to a trusted adult after it occurs. If you or someone you know is being harassed through e-mail or texts, do not respond. Instead, show the messages to an adult and ask for help. You may want to work with the adult to contact your Title IX coordinator to make sure that you know the procedures for responding to the incident. Make sure you also ask about the school's plans to prevent sexual harassment in the future. Remember that this is a requirement under federal law.

Just like teens, adults that you trust may not know what to do about sexual harassment. Education and training for everyone in your university, school, or community can help adults learn how to help you, not to mention raise awareness among students about what sexual harassment is and why it is wrong. You could work with friends and adults to find out about groups in your area that provide training. You could distribute books or pamphlets or make posters that educate others about sexual harassment. You could even become involved in a program yourself, becoming a researcher and a trainer like the girls in GGE. Note that training on sexual harassment should include information on cyberbullying and LGBTQ issues: these are areas that many teens and adults know little about, so including them in any training is key.[45]

One of the best ways to combat any kind of violence is to create spaces where teens feel comfortable talking and taking action. You could work with an adult in your school to start an after-school club dedicated to fighting for gender equity. You could also work with an existing club, such as a Gay-Straight Alliance, to discuss these issues. The club could be responsible for asking the school or university administration to take specific actions. For example, there are some places in schools where sexual harassment is more likely to occur than others. Often, places like hallways, locker rooms, cafeterias, school buses, and other areas without adult supervision are places where harassers feel confident they will not be stopped. One way to try to reduce the amount of sexual harassment in schools is to identify these places and make them safer. The activity below can help you think about ways to make your school a sexual-harassment-free zone.

Mapping Sexual Harassment and Bullying

This activity is adapted from the *Shifting Boundaries* curriculum developed by educators concerned about the rise in dating violence in middle schools.[1] For more information, check out the National Institute of Justice website at www .nij.gov.

One of the strategies schools use to combat bullying is to identify the places in the school building where it is likely to occur. Most bullying occurs outside of the classroom in hallways, locker rooms, school buses, or other spaces that are hard to monitor. Sometimes, just making sure that an adult is standing in a place where students don't feel safe is enough to deter bullies.

Try this activity to identify the places in your school where sexual harassment and bullying might happen:

1. Draw a map of your school. Include hallways, classrooms, restrooms, and outside areas where students may congregate.
2. Use green to color the areas where you feel safest.
3. Use yellow to color areas where you sometimes feel safe and sometimes do not.
4. Use red to color the areas where you feel unsafe.
5. Ask your friends to do the same activity and compare your maps.

When you look at your maps, discuss the following:

1. Look at the green spaces where you feel safe. What do they have in common? For example, is there always an adult there? Is it well lit? Is it open and does it have easy exits?

2. Look at the yellow and red spaces where you feel unsafe. What do they have in common? For example, are they often empty of students and adults? Are they dark or enclosed?

3. What are some differences between your map and your friends' maps? Why do you think these differences exist? Are they because of your gender, age, class, sexual orientation, or size? Are they because of who you trust in the building and who you know?

4. What can you do to make your building safer? What adults can you talk to about your maps? What can you as students do together?

5. Your map does not include online spaces such as text messages, Facebook, or Twitter. How could you add these to your map? How could you make them safer?

When sexual harassment occurs, remember that your personal choices can have a huge impact. Earlier in this chapter, we learned that victims of sexual harassment often become bullies themselves. Although it can be difficult, if you are sexually harassed, make a pledge that you will not become a bully. Instead, make a choice to make positive change, and to help bullies, witnesses, and victims work together to stop sexual harassment from happening again.

Notes

1. Catherine Hill and Holly Kearl, *Crossing the Line: Sexual Harassment at School* (Washington, DC: American Association of University Women, 2011), 2.
2. Hill and Kearl, *Crossing the Line*, 2.
3. Hill and Kearl, *Crossing the Line*, 2.
4. Hill and Kearl, *Crossing the Line*, 2.
5. Hill and Kearl, *Crossing the Line*, 11.
6. Debbie Chiodo, David A. Wolfe, Claire Crooks, Ray Hughes, and Peter Jaffe, "Impact of Sexual Harassment Victimization by Peers on Subsequent Adolescent Victimization and Adjustment: A Longitudinal Study," *Journal of Adolescent Health* 45 (2009): 250.
7. Hill and Kearl, *Crossing the Line*, 12.
8. Chiodo et al., "Impact of Sexual Harassment Victimization," 247.
9. Chiodo et al., "Impact of Sexual Harassment Victimization," 247.
10. Emily A. Greytak, Joseph G. Kosciw, and Elizabeth M. Diaz, *Harsh Realities: The Experience of Transgender Youth in Our Nation's Schools* (Washington, DC: Gay, Lesbian, Straight Education Network, 2007), 18.
11. Hill and Kearl, *Crossing the Line*, 13–14.

12. Hill and Kearl, *Crossing the Line*, 15.
13. Joanne N. Smith, Mandy Van Deven, and Meghan Huppuch, *Hey, Shorty! A Guide to Combating Sexual Harassment and Violence in Public Schools and on the Streets* (New York: Feminist Press at the City University of New York, 2011), 62.
14. Jessie Klein, *The Bully Society: School Shootings and the Crisis of Bullying in America's Schools* (New York: New York University Press, 2011), 76.
15. Klein, *The Bully Society*, 82.
16. Hill and Kearl, *Crossing the Line*, 13–14.
17. Klein, *The Bully Society*, 82.
18. Smith, Van Deven, and Huppuch, *Hey, Shorty!* 62.
19. Hill and Kearl, *Crossing the Line*, 16.
20. Hill and Kearl, *Crossing the Line*, 15.
21. Smith, Van Deven, and Huppuch, *Hey, Shorty!* 62.
22. Smith, Van Deven, and Huppuch, *Hey, Shorty!* 62.
23. Greytak, Kosciw, and Diaz, *Harsh Realities*, 25.
24. Hill and Kearl, *Crossing the Line*, 20–22.
25. Hill and Kearl, *Crossing the Line*, 22.
26. Hill and Kearl, *Crossing the Line*, 24–25.
27. Hill and Kearl, *Crossing the Line*, 24–25.
28. Alayne J. Ormerod, Linda L. Collingsworth, and Leigh Ann Perry, "Critical Climate: Relations among Sexual Harassment, Climate, and Outcomes for High School Girls and Boys," *Psychology of Women Quarterly* 32, no. 2 (2008): 123.
29. Hill and Kearl, *Crossing the Line*, 15.
30. Hill and Kearl, *Crossing the Line*, 15.
31. National Women's Law Center, "Title IX Protections from Bullying and Harassment in Schools: FAQs for Students," National Women's Law Center, 2012, http://www.nwlc.org/resource/title-ix-protections-bullying-harassment-school-faqs-students (accessed December 12, 2012).
32. National Women's Law Center, "Title IX Protections."
33. National Women's Law Center, "Title IX Protections."
34. National Women's Law Center, "Title IX Protections."
35. Smith, Van Deven, and Huppuch, *Hey, Shorty!* 121.
36. U.S. Department of Education, Office for Civil Rights, "Frequently Asked Questions about Sexual Harassment," Ed.gov, April 3, 2011, http://www2.ed.gov/about/offices/list/ocr/qa-sexharass.html (accessed December 3, 2012).
37. Holly Kearl, *Stop Street Harassment: Making Public Places Safe and Welcoming for Women.* (Santa Barbara, CA: Praeger Press), 3.
38. Hollaback! "What to Do If You Experience/Witness Harassment," Hollaback! You Have the Power to End Street Harassment, 2012, http://www.ihollaback.org/resources/responding-to-harassers/ (accessed December 3, 2012).
39. Hollaback! "What to Do If You Experience/Witness Harrassment."
40. Hill and Kearl, *Crossing the Line*, 13.
41. Hill and Kearl, *Crossing the Line*, 13.
42. Hill and Kearl, *Crossing the Line*, 13.
43. Hill and Kearl, *Crossing the Line*, 37.
44. Hill and Kearl, *Crossing the Line*, 37.
45. Hill and Kearl, *Crossing the Line*, 40.

a. Joanne N. Smith, Mandy Van Deven, and Meghan Huppuch, *Hey, Shorty! A Guide to Combating Sexual Harassment and Violence in Public Schools and on the Streets* (New York: The Feminist Press at the City University of New York, 2011), 77.

b. Smith, Van Deven, and Huppuch, *Hey, Shorty!* 77.

c. Smith, Van Deven, and Huppuch, *Hey, Shorty!* 77.

d. Smith, Van Deven, and Huppuch, *Hey, Shorty!* 77.

e. Tamar Wilder Carroll, "Assessing the History of Title IX: Review," *Thirdspace: A Journal of Feminist Theory and Culture* 9, no. 2 (2010), http://www.thirdspace.ca/journal/article/view Article/reviews_carroll/366 (accessed November 30, 2012).

f. Karen Blumenthal, "The Truth about Title IX," *Daily Beast*, June 22, 2012, http://www .thedailybeast.com/articles/2012/06/22/the-truth-about-title-ix.html (accessed December 3, 2012).

g. Caroll, "Assessing the History of Title IX."

h. Caroll, "Assessing the History of Title IX."

i. Caroll, "Assessing the History of Title IX."

j. Blumenthal, "The Truth about Title IX."

k. Blumenthal, "The Truth about Title IX."

l. Nan Stein, "Shifting Boundaries: Lessons on Relationships for Students in Middle School," National Institute of Justice, 2010, http://www.ncdsv.org/images/ShiftingBoundariesLessons RelationshipsStudentsInMiddleSchool_12-2010.pdf (accessed November 7, 2012), 18.

DATING VIOLENCE

. . . .

About 30 percent of teens are bullied by individuals that they ought to love and trust: their romantic partners.[1] This type of bullying is commonly referred to as dating violence, domestic violence, or intimate partner violence, and it affects teens of all gender identities and sexual orientations.[2]

It is one thing to be bullied by someone who is a peer, acquaintance, or friend. It is another thing entirely to be bullied by one of the most important people in your life. Everything from recognizing that bullying is happening to gathering the strength to confront the abuse to ending the relationship is emotionally charged. But being involved in dating violence at an early age puts you at risk of continuing these patterns throughout your adult life. Consequently, learning how to stop the cycle as a teen is essential for developing healthy relationships in the future.

In this chapter, you will learn what dating violence looks like, who it affects, and why it happens. You will also learn what you can do to stop it, whether you are a survivor of abuse, an abuser, or a bystander. As you will see, bullying in romantic relationships looks very different from bullying between acquaintances, but it is just as problematic.

Types of Dating Violence

The Center for Disease Control (CDC) in the United States has identified four distinct types of dating violence: emotional, physical, sexual, and stalking.[3]

An individual who constantly insults, degrades, or manipulates his or her intimate partner is using emotional violence.[4] It may begin as teasing or name calling, behavior that at first seems harmless or could be mistaken for flirting.[5] The problems start when these practices escalate into public humiliation, shaming, or other behavior deliberately designed to make an individual feel hurt or degraded.[6] Manipulation and extreme possessiveness are also examples of emotional violence. For example, some bullies prevent their partners from seeing friends and family, control their movements, and act excessively and irrationally jealous. Emotional violence can occur in person, online, or both. Since emotional violence does not necessarily involve direct physical contact, some teens do not recognize it at first.

Victims of dating violence must face the fact that they are being betrayed by the people they love.

However, emotional violence has serious consequences: not only is it damaging in and of itself, it can also be the first stage in a cycle of bullying that can lead to physical and sexual assault.

Examples of physical dating violence include hitting, kicking, pinching, shoving, biting, or other types of assault.[7] Just like emotional violence, physical violence can mask itself as harmless teasing or "horsing around." This is particularly true for teens who grow up watching parents or other loved ones using physical violence at home: although the behavior of the adults around you may make you believe that violence is an inevitable part of relationships, it does not have to be. In fact, love should never hurt. We will discuss this later in the chapter.

Sexual violence occurs when a bully forces a partner to engage in a sexual activity against his or her will.[8] Sexual violence is not limited to sexual intercourse. It also includes any physical intimacy that is unwanted, including touching and kissing. It can be difficult to talk to others about sexual violence, particularly if you are dating someone who you find physically attractive: you may feel that you have no right to complain because you genuinely want to be intimate with your partner—just not in the way he or she is asking you to be intimate. Similarly, you may not know how to communicate your boundaries to your partner for fear of ruining your relationship. In reality, someone who loves you should not force you to do anything that makes you uncomfortable. Likewise, true friends will not judge you for being attracted to your partner but wanting to slow things down. Anyone who does not understand this may not have your best interests at heart.

A final type of dating violence is stalking, which is when a romantic interest harasses you until you fear for your safety.[9] This type of violence is not limited to current or former partners, but can be perpetrated by anyone who has made it clear that he or she is attracted to you. Stalking can happen in person, online, or both. It is a serious offense that usually requires legal or police intervention. If you believe that someone is stalking you, you should speak to an adult immediately, even if the stalker is someone that you were intimate with in the past or that you are currently dating. No one has a right to make you feel unsafe, no matter how much they love you or how much you love them. This is another recurring theme in this chapter: someone who truly loves you will never want to hurt you.

Dating Violence in LGBTQ Communities

The rates of dating violence among same-sex couples are roughly the same as the rates of dating violence among heterosexual couples.[10] However, teens who identify as LGBTQ face special challenges when it comes to both recognizing intimate partner violence and addressing it.

Some teens may not be out to their parents, friends, and family about their sexuality. Reporting the violence would require them to reveal information about their identity that they are not yet comfortable sharing.[11] Unfortunately, some teens fear that coming out may lead to verbal or physical abuse from their loved ones. For these young people, reporting intimate partner violence will only incite violence from others that they care about, making the decision almost impossible.

Even if LGBTQ teens report the abuse, they may not be able to access services appropriate for same-sex couples.[12] Most existing anti-domestic violence resources are tailored for heterosexual couples and do not meet the needs of LGBTQ youth. For example, survivors may escape abusive partners by entering a shelter system that protects them from their abusers. Often, the shelters are same sex: most commonly, they admit only women, and their locations are kept secret from men. However, entering a single-sex shelter does not help a survivor whose partner is of the same sex and therefore can access the shelter.[13] This is an example of how the current system does not adequately consider the needs of same-sex couples in general and dating violence in particular.

Additionally, nonprofit staff, law enforcement officers, counselors, and others who are traditionally resources for teens in abusive relationships sometimes falsely believe that same-sex partner violence does not exist or is not as serious as heterosexual partner violence. For example, they may believe that same-sex couples share the same physical power and therefore individuals can defend themselves in abusive situations, or that same-sex relationships in general are unnatural or unhealthy and therefore undeserving of services.[14] Not only are these attitudes untrue, they are unfair. Abuse is abuse no matter who is involved, and no one deserves to be the victim of violence. Likewise, no one has the right to inflict violence on others. Perhaps most importantly, many of us learn the basics of romantic relationships when we are teens, and all of us need support to make healthy choices about relationships in the present as well as the future. Denying the existence of same-sex dating violence denies LGBTQ teens the chance to change their relationship patterns before they enter a cycle of violence that could continue into adulthood.

Yet another reason why it can be difficult to report same-sex intimate partner violence is that LGBTQ communities can be tight-knit, and partners may be friends with the same people.[15] Teens may be afraid to report or address the bullying because they feel that the community will not believe them, or that they will

Resources for LGBTQ Teens Experiencing Dating Violence

LGBTQ teens face unique choices when coping with intimate partner violence. The following organizations provide resources specifically tailored to ending abuse within same-sex couples.

The Antiviolence Project

This New York City–based organization provides counseling and support to LGBTQ individuals who experience abuse or trauma.

http://www.avp.org/

Twenty-four-hour hotline: 212-714-1141

Emerge

This group provides services for both survivors and bullies, and for same-sex and opposite-sex couples.

http://www.emergedv.com/

Phone number: 617-547-9879

The Gay Men's Domestic Violence Project

This organization provides resources to men who identify as gay and are the victims of relationship abuse.

http://gmdvp.org/

Twenty-four-hour hotline: 800-832-1901

The Network/La Red

This organization supports lesbians and transgender individuals who experience partner abuse. The services are in English and Spanish.

http://tnlr.org/

Twenty-four-hour hotline: 617-742-4911 (v), 617-227-4911 (tty)

Sojourner House

This organization addresses domestic violence issues for same-sex and different-sex couples.

http://www.sojournerri.org/

Twenty-four-hour hotline: 401-765-3232

lose important relationships that they will need to cope with the emotional fallout of ending the abuse.[16] They may also fear that they will never have another chance to date, or that they are somehow denying their status as LGBTQ.[17] In these cases, it is important for teens to feel that they have a solid support system of people who care about them and are willing to both support them and validate their identity when they are single.

There are a number of groups that now specialize in supporting individuals who experience same-sex intimate partner violence. See page 134 for a list of resources that may be useful to you if you or someone you know is a victim or an abuser in a same-sex relationship.

Effects of Dating Violence

Most of the research about dating violence has been focused on adults rather than teens, and on heterosexual relationships rather than same-sex partners.[18] Consequently, we are still learning about how intimate partner bullying affects young people. Despite the lack of research, it is clear that, like other types of bullying, dating violence has negative effects on both the bully and victim.

In the short term, teens who are bullied by their partners expose themselves to a higher risk of being injured, both physically and mentally.[19] Girls are at a greater risk of these injuries than boys, a pattern that holds true in both different-sex and same-sex partner violence.[20] Dating violence also causes emotional damage by making teens question their self-worth and feel anxious, inferior, or insecure. Teen Haley Robinson, for example, did not realize how much her partner's bullying affected her until she was able to leave the situation. For more on Robinson's story, see below.

Haley Robinson's Story

When teen Haley Robinson started dating Dylan [a pseudonym], everything was wonderful. Then, suddenly, his behavior changed. Robinson remembers, "I started receiving over 100 texts from him within an hour. At first, I thought Dylan was thinking of me, but it turned out he was really quizzing me on my whereabouts."[a] In addition to texting her and calling her constantly, Dylan followed her and exhibited violent, angry behavior when she spoke to other boys.

Robinson knew something was wrong and went to Dylan's house to discuss the possibility of going to counseling together. In response, he held her hostage for twelve hours. Despite his behavior, Robinson cared about Dylan and did not want to give up on the relationship. Consequently, she told him that she was willing to give him a chance if he was willing to change. Her offers were in vain. Robinson only escaped the abuse after she decided to transfer to a boarding school in Michigan, where she could start over and, at long last, live without fear.

The move helped Robinson realize how badly Dylan had made her feel about herself. She remembers, "Once I was removed from Dylan, I was able to realize just how much he had made me doubt myself. In Michigan I was surround by supportive friends and faculty who helped me see that I deserved better."[b] Furthermore, Robinson was able to see how damaging her relationship was. She says that after being in such a healthy environment, "At least I was able to see my relationship with Dylan for the threat it was."[c]

When Robinson returned from her new school to visit her family during spring break, Dylan physically threatened her. She decided to file a restraining order, which she was able to accomplish through the help of a supportive local police department and her loving family. She says that unfortunately, not all teens are able to stop the cycle as she did. She says, "Being a middle-class student in a good high school and having a supportive and involved father was not enough in my case. I needed the court and local law enforcement on my side as well."[d] Robinson believes that schools need to teach teens more about dating violence so they are aware of it and understand that it is a common problem. She says, "I know that if I had learned that I am not alone in this fight, I could have stood up to Dylan and ended the relationship. I don't want any teenager to go through what I did."[e]

In the long term, victims of dating violence are more likely to develop eating disorders, abuse alcohol and drugs, do poorly in school, and experience depression.[21] They are also at greater risk of considering suicide.[22] Perhaps more importantly, once a teen enters into a cycle of dating violence, it can be difficult to break that cycle later on: individuals who are in violent relationships as teens are more likely to be in violent relationships in college and as adults.[23] This is one of the reasons why it is essential for teens to get help with relationship abuse as early as possible.

Just like victims, bullies who enter into a cycle of abusing their partners run the risk of developing a pattern that they will carry into adulthood. Teens who bully their intimate partners are more likely than their peers to suffer from depression and to have problems with aggression.[24] Often, addressing these underlying issues helps the bully stop his or her destructive behavior. In the next sections, you will learn more about why individuals become bullies and how the cycle of violence can be broken.

Why Teens Experience Dating Violence

If you have a friend who has experienced dating violence or you have experienced it yourself, you may have wondered why it was so hard for the person being bullied to leave the relationship. Similarly, if you have a friend who bullied an intimate partner, you may wonder why he or she engaged in such abusive behavior with someone he or she loved. We do not know as much about teen dating violence as we do about adult dating violence, but there are a few theories as to why teens choose to bully their partners and why some teens might be more likely to become victims of dating violence than others.

Many young people have their first intimate relationships when they are teenagers. Although romantic relationships can be fun and rewarding, they also require

During the teenage years, we experience relationships for the first time. Sometimes it can be difficult to recognize dating violence because we do not know what is considered normal behavior in relationships.

maturity, sacrifice, and compromise. Teens develop these qualities through a variety of experiences, including relationships. As they are starting out, many teens model their relationships on the relationships they see around them. This is why teens who live with parents or guardians who are survivors or perpetrators of intimate partner violence are more likely to be victims of dating violence themselves as adolescents: based on what they see around them, these teens falsely believe that violence is a normal part of all relationships.[25] Likewise, teens who bully their partners are more likely than their peers to come from households where violence is used to solve problems and where parenting is inconsistent or overly harsh.[26]

Not all teens who come from homes where they see relationship violence automatically become victims or bullies. In fact, many of these teens have rewarding, healthy, and loving relationships with supportive partners.

Some people believe that our ideas about gender affect individuals' choices to bully their intimate partners. For example, studies suggest that boys engage in dating violence because they want a sense of control over their partner, regardless of whether that partner is male or female.[27] Furthermore, boys who were in violent relationships reportedly were more likely to say they felt powerless than their peers in healthy relationships.[28] This was true both of boys who were bullies and who were bullied. Some researchers argue that boys may feel social pressure to act masculine, which many mistakenly associate with violence and aggression; they say that this pressure makes some male teens feel that they have to bully their partners to prove their masculinity.[29] Not all experts agree. Some say that power imbalances are common among adults where one person in the relationship may earn more, be responsible for children, or be dependent on the other partner for basic needs; the same is not true with teens.[30] Furthermore, this research does not explain why some girls bully their partners as well.

The one thing we do know about dating violence is that it can happen to anyone. Being a survivor of dating violence when you are a teen does not make you weak. Additionally, being a bully does not mean that you cannot change. There are many ways to break the cycle and plenty of resources for support.

Family and Friends

In a recent study of Latino teens, participants said they were unlikely to speak to adults such as doctors, lawyers, teachers, school nurses, or others in their schools and communities about intimate partner violence.[31] There are several reasons for this. Some teens may not feel close to any adults outside of their family. Others may have negative experiences with institutions such as hospitals or police departments and may think that people who work in these places will exacerbate the problem rather than address it. Community-based programs designed to support couples experiencing dating violence routinely have low enrollments of teens, a fact that reflects teens' uncertainty in turning to people outside of their relatives and social circle about sensitive issues related to dating violence.[32]

Consequently, family and friends play a major role in teen dating violence issues—sometimes negative, sometimes positive. When asked who they are most likely to turn to if they experience dating violence, teens routinely name either friends or family members.[33] In the aforementioned study, boys reported that they were more likely to talk to family for fear of being laughed at by their friends, while other participants said they preferred to speak to friends because they expected parents to overreact.[34] In fact, there appears to be a big difference between how boys and girls react to realizing they are in a violent relationship: while girls are likely to seek out help, boys hesitate because they feel embarrassed, perhaps because they believe that being bullied makes them seem weak or less masculine.[35] Teen boys and girls alike specify that they prefer to speak to friends, siblings, or adults who are outside their communities or who they trust to keep their secrets. This is because they do not want rumors about their relationship to spread and because they worry that they may lose control of the situation if the information about their situation gets to the wrong people, and they may be forced to take legal action or counseling or other actions that they find uncomfortable or suspect will be ineffective.[36] Unfortunately, there is not yet enough research to determine whether these trends also hold true for transgender teens.

Family and friends tend to be the first to notice that something in a relationship has gone wrong. Researchers estimate that about half of all incidents of adolescent dating violence occur in front of others, most often friends or other teens in the same social circle.[37] While peers can be supportive, they can also be unresponsive. Sometimes teens choose not to intervene when they witness dating violence because they are friends with both partners and do not feel that they can take sides even though one partner's behavior may be unacceptable.[38] Others worry that the bully may begin victimizing them or that getting involved would be disrespectful of the couple's privacy.[39] It is also likely that many teens and adults do not know what to do when they witness domestic violence. They may not know what to say or how to help the victim protect him- or herself in case there is retribution for their intervention later. They may not know the appropriate time to call the authorities. As a result, they may decide that they would do less harm by simply keeping out of it.

In the worst case, peers become part of the problem. When bullies face the consequences of mistreating their partners, friends of the bully may blame the victim. They might tell the victim that he or she is overreacting or, in extreme cases, threaten the victim for his or her actions. This may be because peers do not understand the severity of the bullying, or they may not believe that their friend is capable of such violent behavior.

Sarah Van Zanten's Story

At first, teen Sarah Van Zanten's boyfriend was perfect: handsome, attentive, and kind. Soon, though, he became a bully, insulting her, monitoring her whereabouts, and physically abusing her. Although the violence got worse, the spontaneous romantic acts continued. For example, Van Zanten's boyfriend often delivered flowers to her. Van Zanten was confused and embarrassed. "I felt ashamed of sticking with him. . . . I think it has to do with being in one of the first relationships of your life. You don't really know where to draw the line," she said.[f]

Van Zanten's friends noticed she was spending less and less time with them, but did not know something was wrong. After a particularly violent incident at school, Van Zanten got her parents and a teacher involved. She broke up with her boyfriend but soon started seeing him again after he convinced her to forgive him.

The turning point for Van Zanten came at a party where her boyfriend was drunk. He became angry at her and kicked her in the stomach. She was unconscious for three hours, but none of the people at the party—many of whom knew her boyfriend—called an ambulance. Finally, Van Zanten woke up and called one of her friends, who came and picked her up. Her friend, teen Brian Knott, was a fellow crew team member. He remembers, "You could tell she had been crying. . . . I came and asked [her boyfriend] to leave; then I gave her a ride home."[g] Despite Knott's presence, Van Zanten's boyfriend tried to follow them home.

Van Zanten went to the police, and her school expelled her boyfriend. Although the decision was clearly in the interest of her safety, many of Van Zanten's peers criticized her and told her she was overreacting. Van Zanten's now ex-boyfriend was handsome and popular, and her peers did not believe that he could have been a batterer. Some of her ex-boyfriend's friends told Van Zanten that because of her actions, she and "her dog" were "in danger."[h] After this threat, Van Zanten also decided to leave the school.

Van Zanten's friend Knott was instrumental in helping her remove herself from a dangerous situation. However, her peers also blamed her for the abuse, even though the violence was not her fault. Van Zanten's story shows what research has proved over and over again: for teens who are bullies or survivors of bullying in intimate relationships, peers can make all the difference in either repairing the situation or making it worse.

Some of Sarah Van Zanten's peers were instrumental in helping her leave her abusive relationship. However, other peers ostracized her for finally taking action against her bullying partner. Read about Van Zanten's story on page 141.

Reacting to Dating Violence

Although it can be uncomfortable or scary to bring up an abusive relationship with a friend or to admit that you are a bully or a victim in a dating violence situation, it is also critical to making sure that you and the people you love stay healthy and happy. If you show courage now, you, your friends, and your current and future partners will all benefit from your actions.

In the Moment

If you witness dating abuse, it can be frightening to try to intervene. Remember that you should never do anything that makes you feel unsafe. However, you should also keep in mind that intervening does not have to involve yelling or assaulting someone or even breaking up a fight. Sometimes it can be as simple as changing the direction of the conversation, particularly if the situation is heating up but has not yet become physical. You could say something as simple as, "Why are you guys fighting? We're here to have fun." Or you could make an excuse to get one of your friends out of the situation, such as, "Sorry to interrupt, but we're late—the two of us should get going," or "I'm starving; why don't we grab something to eat?" You may then have the opportunity to get one of the two partners alone and to either calm down the bully or ask the victim what is going on.

Another strategy is to agree on a code word, gesture, or action that you can share with a trusted friend as a signal that you are afraid and need to diffuse the situation. If you are the victim or a witness, the code may indicate that you need an excuse to leave, or you need someone to call a trusted adult or sibling or friend who has the power to de-escalate the situation. If you are the abuser, you may feel as though your anger is getting out of control, and you are about to do something you regret. Having a code with a friend will help you protect your privacy and safety even when you panic.

If you are a victim or a witness, make sure you document abuse when you see it or right after it happens. Although it might be painful, try and remember the details. Where were you? What time was it? What day? What happened and in what order? Who else was there? If you are physically hurt, try to document your injuries through photographs. Again, it can be extremely emotional to do this, but it can be vital if you decide to take legal action or to report what is happening to a health or counseling professional. Try to have a friend you care about with you when you do this to help you cope emotionally.

Victims and Survivors

If you are in an abusive situation, the most important step is to end the bullying. More often than not, this means ending the relationship. While it may seem like an obvious solution, it is much more difficult than it appears. After all, you may have once been in love with someone who is now hurting you.

Remember that you do not have to go through a breakup alone. Ending an abusive relationship often requires support from a counselor, friend, or community-based organization. Do not be afraid to reach out to someone you trust to talk about your feelings. Do not be afraid to admit that you have an emotional attachment to your partner, even if your partner is a bully. A true friend and ally will help you cope with these emotions and do the right thing for you. Furthermore, if you truly love the person who is bullying you, it is important for you to acknowledge that this person also needs help. If one of you can be strong and admit that there is a problem, it makes it easier for the other person to do the same.

Unfortunately, simply breaking up with your partner does not necessarily guarantee that you, or your friend, are safe. Bullies frequently try to resist break-ups using emotional blackmail. They might also aggressively try to restart the relationship even if their partner has been firm about ending things. Therefore, it is important to create a plan for staying safe both while the abuse is occurring and after you or your friend have attempted to end it. Generally, this means developing strategies to avoid dangerous situations with the abuser and building a support system you can turn to before, during, and after you or someone you know experiences violence. Consider times and places where you feel unsafe, such as walking to school, staying home alone, or commuting to a job.[40] Think about ways to either avoid or escape these situations by making sure you have someone you trust with you at all times, and memorize or have handy a list of phone numbers of people who have agreed to come to you wherever you are in a time of crisis.[41] Also consider your digital life: block your partner from Facebook, e-mail, and your phone; if possible, change your usernames and passwords even if you do not think your partner knows them, and avoid computers your partner can access.[42] Finally, consider your emotional health. Consider who you can call and what types of activities you can do if you are feeling depressed or unsure of your decision.[43] Create a list of qualities that you like about yourself that you can refer to when you are feeling vulnerable, depressed, or inferior. Ideally, you should write your safety plan down and give copies to a friend or family member (but make sure that your partner does not have a copy). To go through this exercise, check out the template on http://www.loveisrespect.org/get-help/safety-planning.

Bullies

If you are abusing your romantic partner, the first step is to accept your responsibility for the situation, admit that you are engaging in negative behavior, and believe that you can change.[44] The second is to face the experiences you have had and the beliefs you hold that have caused you to act this way, and to understand what you need to break this pattern of violence.[45] While these steps may sound simple, they are often challenging, particularly because usually you will undertake this process while you are separated from someone who is important to you emotionally but is also the survivor of your abuse.[46] Consequently, it is important to build a support system of people who love you and truly believe that you can change, and for you to connect with mental health professionals who can guide you through the process of ending your violent behavior. With the right support and guidance, you can change.

Friends and Witnesses

If you are a friend of someone who is the victim of abuse, remember that even though it may be obvious to you that the relationship has to end immediately, your friend could take some time to realize this. If you see a violent pattern developing, tell your friend about your concerns.[47] Be there to listen, but do not pass judgment on your friend's decisions. Most importantly, do not pass judgment on your friend's partner. Instead, acknowledge your friend's feelings and focus on what he or she can do to be safe. Furthermore, let your friend know that healthy relationships do not involve abuse and that the bullying is not his or her fault.[48] Help your friend connect with people, organizations, and resources that can help, and, if possible, go with your friend to check out programs or counselors or social workers. By being there, you are sending a message that your friend is not alone and that he or she can survive (and, in fact, thrive) without the bully.

You can also play a critical role if your friend is a bully. Often bullies end up with no one to turn to, either because people are afraid of them or because people define them by their violent choices. With the right support, abusers can change. By supporting the bully, you may face anger from the victim or your friends who blame the bully for the hurt he or she has caused. Remember that standing by someone does not mean ignoring the violence or its consequences. It does mean recognizing that your friend is more than his or her worst mistakes and is therefore capable of successfully tackling difficult changes, such as breaking abusive patterns.

Do not be afraid to let your friend know that you are worried about him or her. Emphasize that you are concerned, and do not pass judgment. Just as you would with the survivor, acknowledge your friend's feelings and help him or her connect with the resources he or she needs to change.[49] However, do not allow your friend to blame the victim for the abuse. Try to help him or her focus on the hurt he or she is causing and see that violence is not an acceptable part of love, or life in general.[50] Most importantly, stand by your friend the same way you would stand by a victim. Remember that the bully has also lost a partner he or she loves. Being there through this period can make the difference between a bully changing his or her ways or persisting with damaging behavior in yet another relationship.

Another way that you can help friends who experience dating violence is to help them connect with legal resources to escape abuse. The next section discusses laws and policies developed to try to stop dating violence.

Dating Violence Laws and Policies

Several American laws protect victims of dating violence. Perhaps the most famous is the federal Violence against Women Act (VAWA), which Congress reauthorized in 2013. The original version of VAWA, passed in 1994, had two primary purposes. The first is to ensure that abusers can be held legally responsible for their actions, and the second is to provide grants for programs that could further criminal investigations, provide services to victims of abuse, and prevent domestic violence from occurring in the first place.[51]

The importance of the act is both practical and symbolic. The legislators who authored and updated VAWA felt that in the United States, violence against women is largely ignored or dismissed, which is why there were few resources dedicated to ending dating violence.[52] Now, the reauthorized VAWA includes provisions that protect individuals who identify as LGBTQ, has special provisions for young people, and has language that extends protections to Native Americans and to men who face domestic abuse.

For undocumented immigrants in particular, dating violence poses legal complications. Calling the police to get help could mean alerting the authorities to your status, which many fear could lead to deportation. But staying in an abusive relationship could expose you to physical and emotional harm. To address this, the federal government designed the U-Visa program, which gives survivors of substantial abuse temporary protection from deportation.[53] If you are a victim of a crime that puts you in danger, including domestic violence, incest, sexual assault, or rape, you can apply for a U-Visa that will grant you four years of legal status in the United States.[54] It also gives American law enforcement officials the chance to investigate those who have caused you harm and to protect you from further abuse.[55] To be eligible for a U-Visa, though, you must agree to cooperate with the police and prosecutor on the case investigating your abuser, a choice that can be difficult for those who face bullying at the hands of loved ones. Furthermore, you will need someone in your local law enforcement agency to certify you to receive the visa.[56] To investigate your options concerning U-Visas, speak to an immigration lawyer or visit the federal government's website on immigration policies at www.uscis.gov.

When it comes to actually getting protection, counseling, and other services, victims of dating abuse must appeal to state laws. Unfortunately, when lawmakers think about violence between partners, they do not always recognize the specific needs of teen victims. For example, although forty-five states and the District of Columbia explicitly allow minors to access protection orders, or legal documents that contain mandatory steps for keeping abusers away from their victims, only nine states and the District of Columbia legally allow young people to petition for a protection order from their abuser without the help of an adult.[57] Some teens do not have trustworthy adults in their lives who can help them, and thus may not have access to legal protection from their abuser. Additionally, only fifteen states allow for individuals to file protection orders against minors. This means that in most states, teens who are abused by fellow teens face obstacles in getting legal protections because their abusers are too young to be affected by protection orders.[58] Three states specify that protection orders only extend to opposite-sex couples, making it difficult for LGBTQ youth to take legal action.[59] Additionally, many states limit teens' ability to access services such as birth control and HIV/STI (human immunodeficiency virus/sexually transmitted infection) counseling that can be helpful in coping with the consequences of abuse.[60] And only about seven states require school districts to implement educational programs designed to prevent teen dating violence.[61] As these facts show, generally, local laws need to be strengthened to help teens cope with bullying at the hands of their romantic partners.

Preventing Dating Violence

Title III of VAWA outlines a series of grants for organizations to use to design prevention programs that specifically address issues like teen dating violence and campus violence.[62] The purpose of this section is to encourage schools and community-based groups to stop negative behaviors, attitudes, and practices that lead to abusive relationships. While knowing how to react to dating violence while it is happening to you or someone you love is vitally important, the long-term solution to ending intimate partner bullying is to help everyone recognize it, understand it, and stop it before it begins.

There are a wide variety of organizations and curricula designed to help teens recognize, address, and prevent dating violence. Available programs help participants understand their personal assumptions about romantic relationships, some of which may lead them to falsely believe that either being a victim or a bully is a normal part of being intimate. Teens who grow up in households where they or their family members are regularly mistreated often harbor unhealthy attitudes about relationships: they may be unable to recognize dating violence because they believe violence is a normal part of intimacy.[63]

Another key component of any prevention program is building communication skills. Teens need to learn how to communicate anger, frustration, and fear to their partners without causing them physical or emotional harm. This is a skill adults develop through romantic and platonic relationships, a skill that young people having their first romantic experiences have not had a chance to master. At times, teens' lack of experience can be a positive thing: teens are frequently more open to learning about relationships than adults because romance is a world that they are just beginning to explore. Furthermore, teens have not yet had enough romantic relationships to develop patterns of behavior, which makes it easier for them to grow and change.[64] For all of these reasons, experts, educators, and advocates believe that training and education starting as early as middle school are essential for helping teens make the right choices about the ways in which they treat their intimate partners and the behaviors they will tolerate in romantic relationships.

With or without education and training, issues like teen dating violence can be difficult to talk about. Often, it seems that there is never a good time to bring up a topic that is so sensitive, private, and serious. For taboo topics like dating violence, it can be helpful to set aside a time and a space to talk about the issue without singling out individuals or making people feel scared, embarrassed, or threatened. This is the idea behind Teen Dating Violence Awareness month, which started in February 2010. Schools and communities across the country recognize this month with special programming and activities designed to destigmatize the issue and to raise awareness about the resources available to teens experiencing abuse. The theme also attracts media attention, so it is a great time to hold press conferences, publish editorials, run trainings, and hold events to educate the public about what they can do to support teens who experience bullying from their intimate partner. To find out more about how you can get involved in Teen Dating Violence Awareness Month, check out http://www.teendvmonth.org/.

Dating Violence among Adults

Throughout this chapter, we have focused on teens bullying other teens. Unfortunately, dating violence is not just restricted to young people. Adults also bully each other, and their behavior can affect the young people who live with them and love them. In the next chapter, we will discuss adult bullies.

Notes

1. Jagdish Khubchandani, James Prince, Amy Thompson, Joseph A. Dake, Michael Wib-lishauser, and Susan K. Telljohann, "Adolescent Dating Violence: A National Assessment of School Counselors' Perceptions and Practices," *Pediatrics*, July 9, 2012, http://pediatrics.aap publications.org/content/early/2012/07/03/peds.2011-3130 (accessed January 10, 2013), 2.
2. Khubchandani et al., "Adolescent Dating Violence," 2.
3. Centers for Disease Control and Prevention, "Understanding Teen Dating Violence: Fact Sheet," 2012, http://www.cdc.gov/ViolencePrevention/pdf/TeenDatingViolence2012-a.pdf (accessed February 20, 2013).
4. Centers for Disease Control and Prevention, "Understanding Teen Dating Violence."
5. Centers for Disease Control and Prevention, "Understanding Teen Dating Violence."
6. Centers for Disease Control and Prevention, "Understanding Teen Dating Violence."
7. Centers for Disease Control and Prevention, "Understanding Teen Dating Violence."
8. Centers for Disease Control and Prevention, "Understanding Teen Dating Violence."
9. Centers for Disease Control and Prevention, "Understanding Teen Dating Violence."
10. Brown University, "Dating Violence in LGBTQ Communities," Brown University Health Education, 2013, http://brown.edu/Student_Services/Health_Services/Health_Education/sexual_assault_&_dating_violence/dating_violence_in_LGBTQ_communities.php (accessed March 14, 2013).
11. Brown University, "Dating Violence in LGBTQ Communities."
12. Brown University, "Dating Violence in LGBTQ Communities."
13. Brown University, "Dating Violence in LGBTQ Communities."
14. Brown University, "Dating Violence in LGBTQ Communities."
15. Brown University, "Dating Violence in LGBTQ Communities."
16. Brown University, "Dating Violence in LGBTQ Communities."
17. Brown University, "Dating Violence in LGBTQ Communities."
18. Khubchandani et al., "Adolescent Dating Violence," 2.
19. Beverly Weidmer Ocampo, Gene A. Shelley, and Lisa H. Jaycox, "Latino Teens Talk about Help Seeking and Help Giving in Relation to Dating Violence," *Violence Against Women* 13, no. 2 (February 2007): 173.
20. Khubchandani et al., "Adolescent Dating Violence," 2.
21. Centers for Disease Control and Prevention, "Understanding Teen Dating Violence."
22. Carl D. Maas, Charles B. Fleming, Todd I. Herrenkohl, and Richard F. Catalano, "Childhood Predictors of Teen Dating Violence," *Violence and Victimization* 25, no. 2 (2010): 132.
23. Centers for Disease Control and Prevention, "Understanding Teen Dating Violence."
24. Centers for Disease Control and Prevention, "Understanding Teen Dating Violence."
25. Maas et al., "Childhood Predictors of Teen Dating Violence," 132.
26. Centers for Disease Control and Prevention, "Understanding Teen Dating Violence."
27. Carrie Mulford and Peggy C. Giordano, "Teen Dating Violence: A Closer Look at Adolescent Romantic Relationships," *National Institute of Justice Journal*, no. 281 (October 2008), http://www.nij.gov/journals/261/teen-dating-violence.htm (accessed March 13, 2013).

28. Mulford and Giordano, "Teen Dating Violence."
29. Mulford and Giordano, "Teen Dating Violence."
30. Mulford and Giordano, "Teen Dating Violence."
31. Khubchandani et al., "Adolescent Dating Violence,"181.
32. Khubchandani et al., "Adolescent Dating Violence,"174.
33. Khubchandani et al., "Adolescent Dating Violence,"179.
34. Khubchandani et al., "Adolescent Dating Violence,"181.
35. Khubchandani et al., "Adolescent Dating Violence,"174.
36. Khubchandani et al., "Adolescent Dating Violence,"174.
37. Mulford and Giordano, "Teen Dating Violence."
38. Khubchandani et al., "Adolescent Dating Violence,"186.
39. Khubchandani et al., "Adolescent Dating Violence,"187.
40. Loveisrespect.org, "Safety Planning," Loveisrespect.org, 2013, http://www.loveisrespect.org/get-help/safety-planning (accessed March 29, 2013).
41. Loveisrespect.org, "Can I Stop Being Abusive?" Loveisrespect.org, 2013, http://www.loveisrespect.org/get-help/can-i-stop-being-abusive (accessed March 29, 2013).
42. Loveisrespect.org, "Can I Stop Being Abusive?"
43. Loveisrespect.org, "Can I Stop Being Abusive?"
44. Loveisrespect.org, "Can I Stop Being Abusive?"
45. Teen Dating Violence Awareness Month, "Research," Teen Dating Violence Awareness Month, 2013, http://www.teendvmonth.org/research (accessed March 29, 2013).
46. Teen Dating Violence Awareness Month, "Research."
47. Loveisrespect.org, "Help a Friend," Loveisrespect.org, 2013 http://www.loveisrespect.org/get-help/help-others/help-a-friend (accessed March 29, 2013).
48. Loveisrespect.org, "Help a Friend."
49. Loveisrespect.org, "Help a Friend."
50. Loveisrespect.org, "Help a Friend."
51. Lisa M. Seghetti and Jerome P. Bjelopera, *The Violence against Women Act: Overview, Legislation, and Federal Funding* (Washington, DC: Congressional Research Service, May 10, 2012), 3.
52. Seghetti and Bjelopera, *The Violence against Women Act*, 3.
53. U.S. Department of Homeland Security, "Questions & Answers: Victims of Criminal Activity, U Nonimmigrant Status," U.S. Citizenship and Immigration Services, November 22, 2010, http://www.uscis.gov/portal/site/uscis/menuitem.5af9bb95919f35e66f614176543f6d1a/?vgnextoid=1b15306f31534210VgnVCM100000082ca60aRCRD&vgnextchannel=ee1e3e4d77d73210VgnVCM100000082ca60aRCRD (accessed April 12, 2013).
54. U.S. Department of Homeland Security, "Questions & Answers."
55. U.S. Department of Homeland Security, "Questions & Answers."
56. Cristina Constantini, "The Problem with the 'Victim Visa,'" *ABC News/Univision*, January 31, 2013, http://abcnews.go.com/ABC_Univision/visas-problem-victim-visa/story?id=18357347#.UWfcSqL-Hzw (accessed April 12, 2013).
57. Break the Cycle, *2010 State Law Report Cards: A National Survey on Teen Dating Violence Laws* (Los Angeles: Break the Cycle, 2010), 7.
58. Break the Cycle, *2010 State Law Report Cards*, 7.
59. Break the Cycle, *2010 State Law Report Cards*, 7.
60. Break the Cycle, *2010 State Law Report Cards*, 4.
61. Break the Cycle, *2010 State Law Report Cards*, 8.

62. Cornell University, "42 USC Chapter 136, Subchapter III—Violence against Women," Legal Information Institute, 2013, http://www.law.cornell.edu/uscode/text/42/chapter-136/subchapter-III (accessed August 10, 2013).

63. David A. Wolfe and Christine Wekerle, "Dating Violence Prevention with At-Risk Youth: A Controlled Outcome Evaluation," *Journal of Consulting and Clinical Psychology* 71, no. 2 (2003): 280.

64. Wolfe and Wekerle, "Dating Violence Prevention with At-Risk Youth," 280.

a. Haley Robinson, "No One Will Love You More Than I Do," *Huffington Post*, February 6, 2013, http://www.huffingtonpost.com/haley-robinson/teen-dating-violence-awareness-month_b_2635623.html (accessed March 13, 2013).

b. Robinson, "No One Will Love You More Than I Do."

c. Robinson, "No One Will Love You More Than I Do."

d. Robinson, "No One Will Love You More Than I Do."

e. Robinson, "No One Will Love You More Than I Do."

f. Nina Burleigh, "A High School Student's Nightmare: Dating Violence," *People* 68, no. 11 (September 10, 2007): 99.

g. Burleigh, "A High School Student's Nightmare," 99.

h. Burleigh, "A High School Student's Nightmare," 99.

9

ADULT BULLIES

··

Unfortunately, not all adults actively oppose bullying. Some are unresponsive because they do not recognize it when it happens, or they do not know what to do when they see it. Worse, some adults bully teens. These adults do not just ignore the problem of bullying: they contribute to it.

Adults can be passive or active bullies. Passive adult bullies ignore bullying while it is happening, thereby implying that they approve of the behavior. A common example of this is coaches who allow hazing to happen on sports teams.[1] Active bullies participate in the negative behavior by calling teens names, disproportionately punishing them for misbehaving, humiliating them publicly, or even using physical violence such as hitting, pinching, or throwing things at them.[2] Both types of behavior are unacceptable.

Identifying adult bullying can be challenging and frightening. Teens may not recognize adult behavior as bullying because they believe that it is how adults are supposed to act. Furthermore, teens are often told that the first step in stopping violence is to speak to a trusted adult. But if adults are supposed to be trusted, how can they be bullies as well? Complicating the situation further, adults have power over teens, determining their grades, how much time they get on the playing field, and whether or not they get in trouble with their parents. When teens confront adults, they may be putting themselves at risk. For all of these reasons, adult bullying often goes unnoticed and unchecked.

In this chapter, you will learn why adults bully others. You will also learn strategies to identify and stop different types of adult bullying. By the end of this chapter, you should have a better understanding of how adults both purposely and inadvertently perpetuate teens bullying other teens.

What Adult Bullying Looks Like

Teachers, principals, assistant principals, secretaries, coaches, janitors, bus drivers, employers, and even family members can be bullies. There are four general categories of adult bullying that commonly occur in educational settings such as schools and colleges: verbal, physical, psychological, and professional abuse.[3]

Verbal abuse is one of the most common types of adult bullying.

Verbal abuse includes any hurtful behavior involving language. The most obvious examples of verbal bullying are calling students names, especially when those names are racist, classist, sexist, homophobic, or otherwise discriminatory.[4] It might also include questioning students' intelligence, abilities, or even physical appearance. If you have ever seen teachers, coaches, or other adults telling your peers they are worthless or mocking them in front of a class or team, then you have witnessed adults verbally bullying teens.

Physical abuse is any unwanted contact, including shaking students, pinching them, pushing them, hitting them with rulers or other objects, or otherwise inflicting pain.[5] Sometimes coaches push students to do extra athletic activities to the point that the teens collapse or otherwise suffer injury; this is also physical abuse. Some forms of sexual harassment can also be classified as physical abuse. Not all forms of contact are abusive: sometimes adults need to make unwanted contact with students for their own protection, such as holding back students who are fighting or restraining students with special needs when they are having a medical episode. This is not bullying, since the adult's intention is to stop harm, not to cause it.

Psychological abuse is manipulation designed to make another person feel powerless or ashamed. This might include publicly humiliating others or excluding them from activities, conversations, or groups. It could also be indirect, such as egging on abusive or destructive behavior.[6] Teachers who psychologically abuse students may scream at them unnecessarily, threaten physical harm, or make them feel embarrassed in front of a large group.

The last category is professional abuse, or behaviors that prevent students from being successful in school. Examples of professional abuse in classrooms include giving students unfair or inconsistent consequences for their actions, giving bad grades without justification, and denying access to resources such as tutoring or remediation.[7] When a student feels that a teacher "has it in for me" or is disproportionately harsh to him- or herself as an individual, the student may be experiencing professional abuse.

Adult-student bullying can be difficult to identify because there is such a strong power dynamic between adults such as teachers, coaches, and principals, and students. Sometimes adults are strict or harsh because they sincerely care for their students, but their students may feel they are going too far. Other times teens find themselves in hostile educational settings where they begin to accept bullying as normal, simply because it is so prevalent. If you ever have a question about whether you or someone you know are being bullied by an adult, talk to another trusted adult to get advice.

When trying to understand adult bullying, it is helpful to remember that, just like you, the adults in your life are not perfect. They may love and care about you, but, like teen bullies, they may have had past experiences that make them turn easily to violence, particularly in the face of conflict. In the next section, you will learn more about some of the personal and environmental situations that may lead adults to act like bullies.

Why Adults Bully Kids

Just like teens, adults act like bullies because of power and social expectations. For example, some adults see teen bullying as a natural part of masculinity. When they see it, they either do not intercede or, worse, they encourage it, thereby becoming bullies themselves. In one highly publicized case in 2012, substitute teacher John Rosi helped his students physically bully a thirteen-year-old: Rosi actually sat on the victim after his classmates dragged him around the classroom.[8] A student videotaped the incident and the victim's parents saw the footage. When asked why he acted the way he did, Rosi responded that he "viewed the interaction as a matter of boys will be boys and allowing the kids a diversion from the normal after a long period of intense studies."[9] Rosi saw bullying as an acceptable expression of masculinity. Therefore, he not only excused it, but he also joined in, even though he is an adult.

As we've learned, for teens, the consequences of being bullied are long-term and deeply felt. The same holds true for adults. Research shows that teachers are more likely to bully their students if they face bullying from their colleagues or other peers.[10] The same research suggests that teachers who were bullied as children are also more likely to identify colleagues who are treating students problematically.[11] However, these teachers may also have a tendency to be passive bystanders: since interventions did not help them, they may believe that bullying cannot be stopped, and that there is no point in interceding.[12] This research highlights the need for more effective prevention programs started earlier in life.

Sometimes adults become bullies because of their environment. In the next section, you will learn about how some schools inadvertently encourage adults to choose violence.

How Schools Can Create Adult Bullies

Just like teens, adults struggle to maintain control over their lives. Adults who work in schools where their colleagues use violence to manage their classrooms, sports teams, or other responsibilities may become bullies because they believe it is a normal way to interact with students. Likewise, adults who feel unsupported by supervisors may believe that they need to take extreme measures to gain the respect of their students and control over their jobs. In both of these cases, adults may genuinely want to embrace nonviolence but may not know how.

Research indicates that teachers are more likely to exhibit bullying behavior in schools that have zero tolerance policies that rely on punishment and aggression to maintain control. For example, teachers who work in schools where there are high rates of suspensions are more likely to bully students, see other teachers bully students, and be bullied themselves. In schools that have discipline issues, violence may be condoned as the only way to maintain a stable learning environment. In these contexts, teachers may receive positive feedback for being bullies: they may be told that their behavior is tough and masculine, rather than destructive.[13]

Similarly, some teachers bully students because they do not feel supported by principals, assistant principals, or other administrators who are supposed to help them learn how to be better educators. This can have numerous negative repercussions that lead to bullying. First, teachers may seek help from colleagues who are bullies because they have no other resources and falsely believe that violence is essential for good teaching. Teachers who feel unsupported may not know how else to manage their classrooms. Second, teachers may feel unsafe, perhaps because schools have high incidences of violence, or because they have been bullied by students in the past. These teachers may resort to bullying to try to make themselves feel powerful, a mentality that is similar to teen bully-victims, which you read about in chapter 3. Third, teachers may be overwhelmed by their jobs. When they are asked to teach huge classes, for example, they may feel that they do not have time to act humanely because they are struggling to serve all of the students. They may become impatient with one or two students because they are disruptive, and they may resort to bullying behavior to maintain order.[14]

Still other adults may bully students because they feel that they are under intense pressure. Examples of this include coaches who are told they must win certain games to keep their jobs, teachers whose evaluations depend on their students' test scores, and parents who feel they need to keep up with their neighbors (who may be bullies themselves) and live vicariously through their children.[15] They may take out their stress and frustration on teens who are unsuccessful because they cannot score goals or pass exams or win awards, and therefore put the adults' jobs or reputations at stake. In these cases, adults use intimidation and harassment to try to control circumstances that could negatively impact their futures by costing them their jobs, or worse.

Finally, some teachers may act like bullies because they believe that it is a natural part of teaching. This is particularly true of teachers who had negative educational experiences in which they, too, were bullied by adults. They may not even know that they are acting abusive: based on their worldview, they believe that they are acting like typical teachers. Teen Jared Swank experienced this when a teacher videotaped him and his transgender partner at prom and showed the footage to other classes. Swank's teacher thought that he was providing his students with a teachable moment, when actually he was embarrassing Swank. Read more about Swank's story below.

Prom Gone Wrong: Jared Swank's Story

Like many teenagers, eighteen-year-old Jared Swank was excited about his senior prom. Swank had decided to ask a transgender teen girl to be his date. Swank was confident in his choice, even though his classmates harassed him about his sexual orientation, calling him homophobic names and teasing him. On prom night, though, he was not bullied by a student: he was bullied by an adult.

One of Swank's teachers was chaperoning and asked if she could film Swank and his date so she could show her daughter. Swank agreed. Soon after, the teacher showed the video to one of her classes without Swank's permission. It is unlikely she would have done so if Swank's partner had not been transgender, or if Swank was straight. Showing the video violated Swank's privacy and drew unwanted attention to his personal choice, which should have been respected rather than highlighted as abnormal.

Students began to gossip about the video and Swank's choice of partner, which led to Swank experiencing bullying and harassment. The teacher's act made him angry. "She told me she wanted to show her daughter. Not the entire school,"[a] he said.

It is not clear whether Swank's teacher ridiculed Swank when she showed the video, or if she intended to bully Swank by making fun of him behind his back. In fact, Swank said he always had a positive relationship with the teacher before the incident. Swank and the press both reported it as bullying because—intentionally or unintentionally—it brought him unwanted attention that exposed him to verbal harassment from the student body, and therefore was a form of humiliation and psychological abuse. As an adult in the school, and therefore a person with power, the teacher should have thought about how using her power could affect her students. As Swank's mother put it, "This created a threatening and unwelcome environment."[b]

At the time of the incident, Swank was a senior who would be leaving the school. Like many teen activists, Swank used his experience to try to make change. With the help of his mother, he approached the school board about the incident and raised awareness about the school's homophobic environment.

Swank said he brought the act to the attention of the school board because he did not want future students to experience what he had experienced throughout his time as an openly gay student at the school. "I've been bullied constantly through high school with very little sympathy from school officials," he said. "My concern is for the next class and classes after that, who, if nothing happens, will have to deal with the bullying and torture I experienced, something that no kid growing up should go through."[c]

Passive Bullying

In the last section, we talked mostly about active bullying, where adults themselves perpetrated destructive behavior. In this section we will discuss passive bullying, which is the term for a pattern of behavior in which adults who are in positions of power watch bullying happen and do not intervene.

Some adults ignore bullying because they see it as a rite of passage, something that every child goes through: this is often the case with hazing on sports teams.[16]

Hazing is ritualized bullying that happens on a regular cycle, usually when new members are inducted into a club, team, or other organization. It is sometimes seen as a way to bring people together, since they all go through the same ordeal to be admitted. It is also a way for senior members of a club or team to exert power over new members. Coaches who ignore or encourage hazing may have gone through the process themselves in the past and may believe that it builds solidarity. Or they may see hazing happen every year and therefore do not believe that it is serious. In reality, as we've discussed throughout this book, violence can never be a tool for building healthy relationships. In fact, hazing and other forms of ritualized bullying can have dangerous consequences.

Sports teams should be places where students and adults build positive relationships. Unfortunately, sometimes coaches can be bullies.

Passively allowing bullying to occur may seem to be less serious than directly bullying students. In truth, passive bullying can be just as deadly as active bullying. This was true in the case of Teddy Molina, a teen who committed suicide because of the bullying he faced in school and on his sports team—bullying that his sister, Misa, thinks teachers and coaches could have stopped—became too much to bear. Read more about Teddy and Misa Molina below.

Teddy Molina's Story

In 2012, teen Teddy Molina committed suicide. His family says that he took his life because he was overwhelmed by a group of bullies, about twenty boys who called themselves "the wolf-pack."[d] The boys allegedly bullied Molina because he was biracial: he was half Latino and half Korean.[e]

Misa, Molina's eighteen-year-old sister and classmate in Corpus Christi, Texas, said her brother had been teased since he was young. However, things got worse when he joined the football team in junior high. Although Misa says that Molina joined the team to try to stop the bullying—perhaps by proving that he was tough, masculine, and athletic, or by trying to make more friends—it had the opposite effect.[f] Misa remembers protecting her younger brother at a taco stand when the group of boys verbally threatened to take his life and then tried to jump him.[g]

"They would pick on him and they didn't understand when enough is enough and I guess these kids don't understand how much pain he went through, how much of a toll it took on him," Misa said.[h]

Even though the bullying got so bad that Molina's mother withdrew him from school, Misa said that Molina's coach ignored the bullying, as did the administration. In response, Misa and her family organized an anti-bullying protest in front of the school on the day of Molina's funeral. During the rally, the school district insisted that they had a successful anti-bullying program that included teaching elementary school students about respect and asking students and parents to sign an anti-bullying pledge at the beginning of the year. At least one parent agreed, saying that the district had handled her son's complaints about bullying immediately and effectively. The superintendent claimed Molina's death was the first suicide in the district related to bullying.[i]

For Molina's sister, it did not matter whether or not other students had died. Losing her brother was one loss too many.

"We don't need any more people dying because kids can't stop being mean to each other," she said. "Hopefully, this will teach them a lesson that a life is very precious and we should hold onto that, we should keep that in our hearts to make . . . each and every one of us a better person."[j]

Misa wanted to see a change in the way students treated each other. She felt that this was the responsibility of everyone in the school, including adults.

"We need to come together and we need to stop this, and we need to do it peacefully," Misa said during the rally in front of her school.[k]

In 2013, Misa continued to be a vocal anti-bullying advocate. A key part of her message is that when bullying occurs, everyone in the community is responsible—including, and especially, adults.

Sometimes adults allow teen-on-teen bullying to occur because it is an avenue for them to abuse students psychologically without being directly implicated. They may believe that something about the teen's behavior invites abuse and punishment. Or they may actually believe that violence will make the victim stronger. Neither of these reasons is ever true: bullying has no positive effects on anyone involved, and no one ever deserves to experience violence.

Just as with teens, not every adult who chooses not to intervene is automatically siding with the bully. Sometimes adults do not intercede because they do not know how. Perhaps they are afraid that the violence will worsen if the bully sees an adult intervene on behalf of the victim or that bystanders will suffer the consequences. Perhaps they are frightened of the bully and his or her physical power. Or perhaps the bully is related to a powerful adult who can protect him or her. Indeed, in a recent report, a researcher noted that in one incident, teachers and students alike were afraid to confront a violent child about his behavior because he was related to the vice principal: the adults feared that by doing so, they would expose themselves to abuse at the hands of their administration.[17] Just like teens, adults need training and support to find thoughtful and effective ways to confront violence without endangering themselves or their students.

Coping with Adult Bullies at Your School

When a parent, teacher, counselor, professor, administrator, or coach bullies you, it can be difficult to know where to turn and how to act. After all, these are people who are directly responsible for your personal success and who are supposed to be on your side. In the school or campus setting, they may have more power than you, and you may feel like no one will believe your story. Plus, some experts say that often teacher bullies, in particular, are well established in their schools and have seniority, which means that they not only have power over you, but they also have power over other teachers and administrators.[18] Furthermore, since the majority of adult bullying that occurs in schools is not physical, many victims of abuse doubt whether what they are experiencing is actually bullying or just discipline.[19]

If you believe you are being bullied by an adult at your school, you should report it to the proper authorities. Try and report it with the help of a trusted adult who is outside of the school community and can be your advocate if anyone questions your claim. To further help your case, document every incident of bullying that you witness or experience, no matter how small. Make sure that you include details of who was present, what happened, when it happened, and where it happened. Keep a record not only for others, but also for yourself: often victims of adult-teen bullying start doubting whether they are actually experiencing bullying or not. Keeping track of what has happened will help you stay strong in your claim.

Besides reporting, there are some other immediate actions you may be able to take at your school. First, you may be able to remove yourself from the situation. For example, if a teacher is bullying you, a counselor could help you make a schedule change. If a coach is bullying you, you might make a decision to switch to a different sport or team. Still, remember that if the adult is in the wrong, you should not be forced to give up activities, classes, and friends you love. Instead, the adult should be asked to leave or to change his or her behavior.

If you feel that adult-student bullying is a widespread problem at your school, you may want to work with other students to address the problem. Remember that many times, teachers bully students because they themselves feel insecure, or they do not have sufficient tools for enforcing discipline or keeping classrooms under control. One thing that you can ask for on behalf of the adults in your school is the opportunity for them to receive training on alternative disciplinary techniques, such as the restorative justice models covered in chapter 2. As a student, you might also look into opportunities for you and your peers to engage in some kind of training that could help you bring these models to your community.

Adult bullying does not happen just on campus. In the next section, you will learn about adult bullying that occurs outside of educational settings.

Adult Bullies Outside of School

Adults who bully teens are not limited to school buildings. Unfortunately, you can also find them in work places, families, and even homes.

Some teens are bullied by their parents or other family members. They may be repeatedly called names or teased about personal or physical characteristics. This is particularly true of teens who are overweight. Family members may make hurtful comments about teens' physical appearance, the amount of food they eat, their bodies, or other characteristics, traits, or patterns. Although these individuals may believe that they are helping teens make better choices, in reality, they may be making teens feel ashamed, complicating their relationships with food, and embarrassing them. There are positive and constructive ways to talk to friends and family members about obesity, none of which involve bullying. These include helping obese teens make healthier food choices, involving them in athletic activities without being judgmental, and helping them value and love their bodies even if they want to lose some weight.

Extreme physical, verbal, or emotional abuse from parents or family members is often referred to as domestic violence. Adults who bully members of their families model poor behavior. They send the false message that physical and emotional violence are acceptable tools for navigating the world.[20] As discussed in the previous chapter, teens who are bullied at home sometimes believe that romantic relationships operate on blame, hurt, and anger. This can lead teens to either reproducing or accepting this treatment from their partners. The cycle is broken when teens are exposed to alternatives that make them realize that they can establish stronger relationships without violence. Domestic violence is a serious problem that requires professional interventions. If you or your friends believe that you are experiencing frequent, destructive bullying at the hands of family members, talk to a trusted adult or counselor to get help.

Violence can also happen in the workplace. Employers may bully teens professionally by asking them to do demeaning tasks, work overtime for free, or pay them exploitative wages. They may speak to teens rudely because they believe teens do not have the power to fight back or to find another job. A particularly common form of workplace bullying is sexual harassment. A study from 2009 shows that about 47 percent of young women experience sexual harassment where they work, which is about double the percentage of adult women who experience sexual harassment on the job.[21] Just as there are laws that protect your safety at school, there are laws that forbid employers from sexually harassing you at work. If you experience sexual harassment at your job, talk to a trusted adult or to a counselor at your school. He or she can help you understand your options.

Teens may also be bullied by adults at schools or campuses who are not educators, such as janitors, bus drivers, lunch aides, or counselors. These types of abuse often fit the patterns discussed already. The first step in addressing this is to document what happened and report it to the proper authorities.

Some Final Thoughts on Adults Who Bully Teens

Not much is known about how and why adults bully teens and what can be done about it. This area has received little attention, and many experts do not know how to cope with or address adult-teen bullying.

However, existing research makes a few things clear. First, adults, like teens, become bullies because of their exposure to violence in the past or in their daily lives. Adults who see friends, colleagues, and family members use violence to control their worlds are more likely to believe that this is the normal way to cope with anger, fear, and insecurity. Just like teens, adults need training and support to learn nonviolent ways of being.

Second, adult-teen bullying happens far more often than it is reported, which is part of the reason why little is done to prevent or address it. The more teens talk about this type of violence, the more attention the issue will get and the more likely we are to find solutions together. It takes a lot of courage to report being abused by someone who has power over you, but doing so could improve the lives of other students at your school, other members of your family, and the adult in question.

Finally, if you experience adult-teen bullying, you are not alone. Reach out to friends, family, and trusted adult mentors for support. You may find that they, too, have experienced or witnessed adults bullying teens. Adult-teen bullying is wrong, and if you think it may be happening to you or someone you love, it is well within your rights to do something about it.

Notes

1. Jessie Klein, *The Bully Society: School Shootings and the Crisis of Bullying in America's Schools* (New York: New York University Press, 2011), 137.
2. Teaching Tolerance, "Addressing Teacher Bullying," Teaching Tolerance: A Project of the Southern Poverty Law Center, http://www.tolerance.org/supplement/addressing-teacher-bullies (accessed January 10, 2013).
3. Teaching Tolerance, "Addressing Teacher Bullying."
4. Teaching Tolerance, "Addressing Teacher Bullying."
5. Teaching Tolerance, "Addressing Teacher Bullying."
6. Teaching Tolerance, "Addressing Teacher Bullying."
7. Teaching Tolerance, "Addressing Teacher Bullying."
8. Sunnivie Brydum, "Parents Seek Firing of Teacher Who Joined Students to Bully 13-Year-Old," *Advocate.com*, August 30, 2012, http://www.advocate.com/society/education/2012/08/30/parents-call-termination-teacher-who-bullied-student (accessed January 10, 2013).
9. Brydum, "Parents Seek Firing of Teacher."
10. Stuart W. Twemlow, Peter Fonagy, Frank C. Sacco, and John R. Brethour Jr., "Teachers Who Bully Students: A Hidden Trauma," *International Journal of Social Psychiatry* 52, no. 3 (2006): 193.

11. Twemlow et al., "Teachers Who Bully Students," 192.
12. Twemlow et al., "Teachers Who Bully Students," 193.
13. Twemlow et al., "Teachers Who Bully Students," 193.
14. Twemlow et al., "Teachers Who Bully Students," 195.
15. Klein, *The Bully Society*, 137–147.
16. Klein, *The Bully Society*, 137.
17. Twemlow et al., "Teachers Who Bully Students," 187.
18. Teaching Tolerance, "Addressing Teacher Bullying."
19. Teaching Tolerance, "Addressing Teacher Bullying."
20. Klein, *The Bully Society*, 132.
21. Susan Fineran and James E. Gruber, "Youth at Work: Adolescent Employment and Sexual Harassment," *Child Abuse and Neglect* 33 (2009): 550–559.

a. Bob Kalinowski and Bill Wellock, "Hanover Area Board to Probe Bullying Complaint," *Citizensvoice.com*, May 11, 2012, http://citizensvoice.com/news/hanover-area-board-to-probe-bullying-claim-1.1313673 (accessed April 13, 2012).
b. Kalinowski and Wellock, "Hanover Area Board to Probe Bullying Complaint."
c. Kalinowski and Wellock, "Hanover Area Board to Probe Bullying Complaint."
d. Miranda Leitsinger, "Family: Bullying by 'Wolf-Pack' Led to Texas Teen's Suicide," *U.S. News on NBCNews.com*, April 10, 2012, http://usnews.nbcnews.com/_news/2012/04/10/11118720-family-bullying-by-wolf-pack-led-to-texas-teens-suicide?lite (accessed June 18, 2013).
e. Leitsinger, "Family."
f. Daily Mail Reporter, "'We Don't Need Any More People Dying': Teen's Family Holds Anti-Bullying Protest after Boy, 16, Commits Suicide after Years of Threats," *MailOnline*, April 11, 2012, http://www.dailymail.co.uk/news/article-2128036/Teddy-Molina-Teens-family-holds-anti-bullying-protests-boy-16-commits-suicide-years-threats.html (accessed June 18, 2013).
g. Daily Mail Reporter, "'We Don't Need Any More People Dying.'"
h. Leitsinger, "Family."
i. Daily Mail Reporter, "'We Don't Need Any More People Dying.'"
j. Leitsinger, "Family."
k. Leitsinger, "Family."

CREATING EFFECTIVE ANTI-BULLYING POLICY

Young people are sick of violence. Some of them want their friends to stop being bullies or to stop being victims. Some of them want adults to be more responsive to teen concerns. All of them want the right to feel safe and to be themselves without fear of intimidation or harassment.

Teens across the country have taken action to stop bullying. When they see violence occurring, they intervene. They talk to teachers, parents, and administrators about bullies in their schools and neighborhoods. They work with their friends to educate others about conflict resolution, social inclusion, and peace.

But some teens believe that this struggle is more than just their responsibility. These young people are demanding more from their schools, communities, and governments. They believe that there should be systems to protect young people and both consequences and help for young people who choose to act abusively. They are asking policy makers to create rules about reporting, responding to, and preventing bullying in order to send a unified message that bullying will not be tolerated.

In this chapter, you will learn about anti-bullying laws and policies throughout the country and what makes them succeed. You will also learn how to take action in your own community to get organized and create change. By the end of the chapter, you will be knowledgeable about what it takes to prevent bullying in your community and beyond.

Anti-Bullying Laws and Policies

When young people work with their communities to create systematic approaches to preventing bullying, they often work with districts and legislative bodies to produce policies and laws. *Policies* are rules adopted by organizations or localities, such as individual schools or districts. In the United States, *laws* are passed by bodies of elected officials, like state assemblies, senates, or city councils, and are enforced by local, state, and federal governments.

International law is a bit different than American law. International law is passed by groups of countries that come together in an organized forum to discuss issues that affect human beings all over the world. This often happens through a group called the United Nations (UN). The UN has published an international law that outlines the rights of children, defined as any young person under the age of eighteen. The document is called the Convention on the Rights of the Child (CRC), and it passed in 1989 after years of lobbying from countries around the globe.[1] The CRC covers everything from children's right to food to health services to privacy to expressing their views and opinions without persecution. It also includes sections that are relevant to bullying. For example, the CRC guarantees all children the right to safety and protection, and the right to go to school without fear. Anything that interferes with these rights—including bullying—is a violation of the CRC.

Countries show that they recognize the CRC by signing onto it. After they sign on, countries must ratify the CRC, meaning that they agree to be legally bound to uphold the rights and responsibilities it sets out.[2] Unfortunately, as of 2013, the United States is one of three nations that has not ratified the CRC (the other

According to the Convention of the Rights of the Child, everyone under the age of eighteen has the right to learn in safety. Bullying violates this right.

two are South Sudan, which has just become a country, and Somalia, which does not have a stable government).[3] This means that groups within the United States cannot use the CRC to prove that American policies and laws violate the rights of children, and that the United States does not have to submit regular reports about the status of American children. Also, students in the United States who are fighting for their rights to go to school free of fear from violence may not have opportunities to work with like-minded teens in countries like India, Mexico, or South Africa, all of which have ratified the CRC. Some United States groups believe that signing on to the CRC is the first step to ending a number of struggles, including helping get all kids access to free and quality education, nutritious food, and safe living spaces. As of now, the fight for all of these things happens without the help of international law.

As of 2013, no national anti-bullying law has been passed. In 2011, the Safe Schools Improvement Act was introduced in the Senate, meaning that several senators worked together to draft it and present it for debate. Unfortunately, it did not pass. If it had, the bill would have amended the Elementary and Secondary Education Act, which governs how schools are run throughout the country. It would have required all school districts to conduct a needs assessment related to bullying, develop laws and policies that include clear procedures for responding to and reporting bullying, and conduct evaluations of how well the policy was working.[4] Additionally, the House of Representatives considered passing the Student Non-Discrimination Act (SNDA), which would have protected teens from harassment due to their sexual or gender identity, a historic piece of legislation discussed in chapter 5.[5] While President Obama endorsed both of these—meaning that he supported them and wanted them to pass—as of this writing, they have not yet become law.[6] Consequently, the United States still has no national school-based anti-bullying law. As a result, these laws must be designed and implemented by states and local school districts.

Knowing that there was no national law about bullying, President Obama and his staff decided to make sure that school districts had the tools they needed to design and enforce local anti-bullying laws and policies. In December 2010, the federal government issued guidance that includes draft language from existing, effective state laws.[7] Since then, forty-six of the fifty states have developed anti-bullying laws.[8] Forty-one states have also created model policies that contain components that school districts are required to adopt when they design their own anti-bullying policies relevant to their local communities.[9]

States tend to address bullying through two legal methods: education law and the criminal code.[10] These reflect two approaches to addressing and preventing bullying. Education laws take a youth development approach rooted in the belief that we can teach students not to be bullies. The criminal code uses punishment as a tool to both prevent bullying and send the message that it is a serious crime that will not be taken lightly. In some places, lawmakers combine both methods, which leads to debate about when it is necessary to treat bullying as a criminal activity. In New York, for example, there was heated debate about legislation that could require teens to serve jail time for cyberbullying.[11] In the end, New York State decided not to make it a criminal offense, which some New Yorkers were unhappy about. These critics felt that the current law does not properly protect victims, nor does it impose adequate consequences for cyberbullies.

With a few exceptions, most states have passed most of their laws against bullying in the last ten years. Policy makers are still learning what works and what does not, and gaps are beginning to emerge. For example, many states and districts are specific about how schools should respond to bullying, but they do not have plans about how students and staff can work together to prevent bullying.[12] Additionally, many districts may lack the funding they need to implement policies. Even though they may have excellent ideas about how to prevent bullying, some schools cannot afford to pay for staff, training, or curricula necessary to implement these ideas.

If you would like to create or strengthen an anti-bullying policy or law for your community, this chapter will help you think about what that policy or law should include.

Definitions

What exactly is bullying? At first, it seems like a simple question. But what kinds should be regulated? Should all types be treated equally? If bullying is defined as repeated violence, how many times count as repeated? These are the kinds of questions that state laws and district policies must answer before they mandate processes and procedures for responding to and preventing bullying.

As of 2013, forty-three states include definitions of "prohibited behavior."[13] This means that the laws explain what types of behavior count as bullying. Experts say that teasing becomes bullying or harassment when it happens repeatedly and when the bully and the person being bullied do not have the same amount of power.[14] While this may help teens frame what is happening in their own lives, the definition is too vague for a policy because it leaves many questions unanswered. How many times is repeatedly—twice a week, twice a month, or twice a year? What does it mean to have an imbalance of power? Does it mean that one teen is larger than the other, or has more friends than the other, or has more money or status? Consequently, the federal government recommends that laws and policies include specific criteria for determining whether behavior is direct or indirect, how long the behavior has been happening, and the "motivation or intent" of the behavior.[15]

Laws and policies are important because they hold people accountable for their actions and because they help individuals advocate for themselves. That is why addressing bias-based harassment has become a focus of many teen-led anti-bullying campaigns. Students who can claim that they are victims of bias-based harassment have access to numerous local, state, and national laws that can force their schools to deal with the violence rather than laughing it off as "harmless fun" or "kids being kids." Take the example of transgender teens: according to recent research, 90 percent of transgender teens experience homophobic verbal harassment at their schools at the hands of their peers, and one in three transgender teens experiences this same harassment from adults.[16] Yet, adults intervene to stop this behavior only about 16 percent of the time.[17] In places where bias-based harassment is clearly defined as a form of bullying, adults and peers are not allowed to dismiss the bullying behavior as something that teens deserve or that is just a natural part of growing up. Instead, transgender teens can demand that their issues be addressed.

Although including bias-based harassment as a key component in any definition of bullying may seem straightforward and, above all, right, it can become controversial. People have different definitions of what counts as having power and what does not. For example, in an area that is majority Black or Latino, can Blacks and Latinos still face bias-based harassment? What about students who have disabilities in a class designed for such students? Plus, some lawmakers believe that characteristics such as sexual orientation are actually a choice, rather than an identity, and therefore do not deserve protection. Consequently, only 31 percent of states actually have laws that include specific language about groups that could be victims of bias-based harassment, despite the fact that 71 percent of them recommend including bias-based harassment in the model policies they give to their districts.[18]

Another reason why defining bullying is important is because specifying different forms of violence helps schools track and classify incidents. They can use this information to develop comprehensive and targeted approaches to educating the school community and improving school climate. For example, if one school has a high number of sexual harassment cases, it may create an awareness program about gender. If another school has problems with racism, it may choose a different program. Just like defining bullying, though, tracking and reporting can be contentious.

Reporting

Schools and districts cannot address bullying if they do not know it is happening. Therefore, laws and policies must outline mechanisms for young people and adults to report bullying. This may seem simple at first, but in fact, reporting is complicated and—for some people—can be frightening.

Students do not report bullying for many reasons. Some fear that reporting will make the bully target them next. Others feel it will make them unpopular with their friends because they will be labeled a "rat" or a "snitch." One of the most common reasons why students do not report bullying to adults is because they see no reason for it: they think that the behavior will continue whether they report it or not.

Reporting is also complicated by the fact that it may not occur on school grounds. Bullying often happens on the walk home, on the bus, on the playground, or in the neighborhood. Although the bullying may be a result of something that happened in a classroom, the fact that it did not happen on school or campus grounds makes some teens feel unable to report it to faculty or administrators.

Teen Namit Satara was the victim of bias-based harassment when he was in middle school. For various reasons, he decided not to report the incident. Read his story below to find out why he made this choice.

Namit Satara's Story

When seventeen-year-old Namit Satara was in middle school, he experienced bias-based harassment. Even though the bullying incident was traumatic, he chose not to report it. Here is his story and his reasons why he did not bring it to the attention of adults that he trusted.

Mortified. I felt a tug on my turban, and realized a second later that it was off my head and in the hands of Robert, who was fleeing away, laughing hysterically. In front of my entire grade, I chased after him, with tears rolling down my cheeks.

As a practitioner of Sikhism, I don a turban, which is meant to cover my uncut hair at all times. It is more than a piece of cloth; it is my sacred crown, and it was now in possession of the grade bully. My classmates had never before seen my hair, and this was definitely not the way I wanted them to see it. Messy, tangled, and extending past my hips, my hair was exposed, leaving me feeling more vulnerable than ever. Why didn't anybody try to stop that bully as he made away with my turban?

Finally, I was just too upset and gave up. A few minutes later one of my classmates found me locked up in a bathroom stall. He returned my turban, which was now crumpled and maltreated. Even though my prized possession was in my hands, it felt as though a part of me had been ripped out.

This took place at a bar mitzvah, not on school grounds. Although it would've been possible to complain to the administration, I avoided this for two reasons. Firstly, as a 7th grader fairly new to the school, I didn't have the most friends, just because everyone already knew each other and I was new. This bully who took off my turban was unfortunately one of the most popular guys in the grade. There was this aspect of peer pressure on me, that if I had told on him, he would basically make my social life hell. Also, I had recently spoken to one of my teachers about another student who was giving me trouble because of my religion, and I didn't want the teachers to think I was just some kid who came running to them after every small incident even though this was one of the harsher experiences of bullying I've faced.[a]

After reading Satara's story, discuss the following with your friends:

1. Why did Satara choose not to report this bullying?
2. What would you have done if you were in Satara's position? Why?
3. What do you think Satara's school could do to make students more comfortable about reporting bullying?
4. What does this story make you think about your school and community? How could you implement the changes you think Satara's school should have implemented?

Excellent anti-bullying reporting procedures ensure that reporting is safe, anonymous, and effective. They include avenues for anonymous reporting, protect the reporter, gather important information about incidents, and provide information to the right people who have the authority both to address and stop the bullying and to keep the process confidential. Furthermore, the procedures designate key adults in the school who students like and trust to be in charge of collecting and addressing incident reports. This makes it easier for students to report bullying, even if it happens multiple times and even if students are new. In the rest of this section, we will discuss the characteristics of strong and effective reporting policies and procedures.

Anonymity

Many people are uncomfortable reporting bullying. Victims and witnesses may be afraid they will be targeted for telling others and may decide that it is not worth the risk. Parents may worry that reporting will worsen the violence their children experience. Teachers may be afraid that they will get into trouble for not being able to control the abuse. Principals may be afraid that students will think their school is unsafe if too many incidents are reported.

When developing anti-bullying policy, it's important to ensure that community members can report incidents without having to reveal their identities. Some districts have e-mail addresses that go to a central place, rather than the school. These districts can use the e-mails to contact the appropriate administrators and make sure that incidents are addressed without divulging who made the complaint. Other schools and districts have hotlines where complaints can be taken anonymously. Another option is to have a faculty or staff member who students deeply trust available to take reports. These adults should be skilled at addressing bullying without revealing the identity of the person who brought attention to the problem. Once community members see that an anonymous reporting mechanism works, they will be more likely to trust it and, by extension, to use it.

No matter how effective a reporting system is, the individual reporting always runs a risk that he or she will be found out. Additionally, some individuals may choose to report the bullying without wanting to be anonymous. In these cases, it is important that reporters are protected for their brave actions.

Protection

Sometimes, despite efforts to keep reporting anonymous, the reporter's identity is revealed. In these cases, the reporter might be victimized. Anti-bullying policies must state how reporters will be protected. This has several purposes. First, it clearly states the consequences of retaliating against a reporter. This discourages bullies from thinking they can intimidate others into keeping their bad behavior a secret. Second, it helps reporters feel safe, which in turn encourages witnesses to come forward. In both of these cases, having a protection plan in place ensures that those who choose to stand up are not punished for their decision.

Information

While the immediate goal of most anti-bullying policies is to establish a clear system for identifying and addressing bullying, the underlying objective is always to prevent it from happening in the first place. Before designing a prevention program, schools need to understand the nature and extent of the problem. One way to do this is to collect information about bullying incidents that can inform future actions. But for this information to be helpful, it must be relevant and accurate.

Schools can choose to collect a variety of information. One piece of data they may ask for is where the violence happened. In most schools, there are certain places where bullying is more common than others. For example, a recent study based on teen self-reporting shows that bullying occurs most often in the hallways, in the lunch room or cafeteria, online, and in classrooms.[19] The same study shows that the frequency of bullying can decrease by as much as 10 percent when teachers are present and able to intervene.[20] Furthermore, some districts collect information on the time of day when incidents happened. If schools can gather information on hot spots and dangerous times, they can implement strategies such as having staff available in these areas or at certain times of day to discourage violence or to intervene if necessary.

Another reason to collect data is to understand the types of bullying that must be dealt with. If, for example, reporting data shows that many incidents are classified as sexual harassment or target students of a certain religion or race, the school may choose to conduct training designed to raise awareness about these issues and to promote tolerance and respect. This kind of focused intervention can help all members of the school community—not just teens—become more sensitive to the impact that their actions have on others.

When collecting information, it is important to remember that a sudden rise in the number of reports does not necessarily mean that bullying has increased. In fact, this data could illustrate a positive trend, indicating that community members are feeling safer and more confident about reporting, and so are doing it more. When laws and policies are put in place, it is important for districts and governing bodies to avoid punishing schools and campuses for increased reporting rates. Instead, the information should be used to address the incidents themselves and to develop prevention strategies.

After a report has been made, the next step is for faculty and staff at a school or campus to respond to the incident immediately and effectively. This is a crucial part of any effective anti-bullying policy that also affects reporting rates.

Responding to Reports

Sixteen-year-old Dax Catalano nearly died in 2011 when a bully assaulted him in a parking lot in his home town of Lewiston, Maine.[21] The bully had sent Catalano violent messages on Facebook, threatening to beat him up because Catalano was dating the bully's ex-girlfriend. At first, Catalano did not talk about the problems he was having, mostly because he did not think the adults in his life could help him. "I thought I could handle it on my own," Catalano said.[22]

Catalano is not alone. Less than half of students who see bullying report it, and one in ten students who choose not to report bullying say that they feel that there is no point because schools will not respond effectively.[23] Similarly, only about one in five teens reports sexual harassment to an adult at his or her school, and almost a quarter of teens who do talk to adults about sexual harassment are told to forget about it or that they are overreacting.[24] Responses like these make many teens feel that reporting is futile and that they should just handle the problem on their own. This is why having a clear protocol for responding to bullying is essential: if teens have faith in the system and adults know what to do, then victims of bullying might be more likely to come forward.

The first step in responding to a bullying report is usually an investigation into what happened and who was involved. The investigation often requires notifying parents or guardians of the involved teens and, if necessary, involving local law enforcement officials, especially in assault cases. During this process—and, in particular, when adults are notifying family members—it is important to help teens maintain their rights to privacy. Victims of bullying who identify as LGBTQ (lesbian, gay, bisexual, transgender, or queer) may not have come out to their families and therefore may not want to involve their relatives. In these cases, schools must be prepared with procedures for providing adult guidance to students who believe that reporting the incident could compromise their safety at home.

Excellent laws and policies mandate that investigations must be completed "in a timely manner," which is defined differently in different places.[25] The purpose of rules like this is to ensure that school personnel react swiftly to stop the bullying as soon as possible and to send a message that bullying is a behavior that will not be tolerated.

Laws and policies about investigations also often have two additional components. The first specifies who is responsible for conducting the investigation. This could be an administrator, such as a principal or assistant principal, or it could be a teacher or counselor who is the point person for dealing with bullying in the school. The second specifies how the investigation should be documented, which usually includes who was involved, what happened, when the investigation took place, when the incident took place, and who received reports.

After the investigation has been completed, the next step is determining the consequences for the student who acted like a bully.

Consequences

As of 2013, forty-two out of fifty states had laws that clearly outlined the consequences of bullying.[26] The majority of these laws and policies take purely disciplinary approaches, in which the bully is punished for his or her actions. Sometimes the consequences can be severe. Georgia, for example, mandates that students who are involved in three or more bullying incidents must be transferred to an alternative school.[27] Fifteen states require that bullying policies include a clear procedure for "imposing criminal sanctions" on bullies, meaning that schools must have a system for getting the police involved in bullying incidents.[28] The individuals who drafted these ideas probably believe that harsh consequences—including potential criminal charges—communicate how serious bullying is and therefore discourage young people from making bad choices about their behavior. By bringing law enforcement into the picture, they are also involving their community and making bullying everyone's responsibility.

Not all schools, districts, and states believe in using harsh consequences as punishment. Some believe that teens act like bullies because of their histories, social pressures, or their inabilities to properly cope with strong emotions. These individuals believe that it is more productive to try to rehabilitate teens by finding out what underlying problems are making them behave violently. These law and policy makers often favor restoratives approaches like those discussed in chapter 2. Confronting individuals about their behavior is certainly a powerful strategy for breaking the cycle of violence—just ask teen Elizabeth Ditty, who confronted her bully about his behavior. Read more about Ditty below.

Elizabeth Ditty's Story

Teen Elizabeth Ditty spent years enduring teasing and harassment about her weight. Then, in her senior year of high school, it all became too much to bear.

"I had a simple, deadly, desperate plan to escape the social torment I'd been facing since fifth grade: leave school, lie in the street on my stomach, and wait until a speeding car came along. Then it would all be over," Ditty says.[b]

Luckily, Ditty sought help. She met with a counselor at her school and broke down hysterically in his office. For many days after, she stayed home. Ditty claims she was "wallowing in self-pity and depression"[c] and felt unable to face her classmates. She finally snapped out of it when she decided to reclaim her life and take action.

"I forced myself to get out of bed and write a letter. A letter to my bully. Three pages in red ink," she remembers.[d]

When she returned to school, Ditty set up a meeting with her bully in the dean's office. Then she read him what she had written. She found his reaction surprising, but also healing.

"He cried. Seriously, my bully cried. Then he apologized sincerely,"[e] Ditty says. After this emotional exchange, the violence stopped.

Ditty says that now she has reclaimed her life. In 2013, she was a freshman in college studying to become a counselor. Her goal was to use her experiences to help teen victims recover and move on with their lives. She credits her happiness to the second chance she gave herself—as well as the second chance she gave her tormentor. Thanks to Ditty's courage, both of them had the opportunity to change for the better.

If you enjoyed Ditty's story, check out the book *Bullying under Attack: True Stories Written by Teen Victims, Bullies, and Bystanders (Teen Ink)*, edited by Stephanie Meyer, John Meyer, Emily Sperber, and Heather Alexander. It's a volume of stories told by teen victims, witnesses, and bullies, and has many more stories like this one.

Another nonviolent way to respond to bullying is to implement Positive Behavior Intervention and Supports (PBIS), an approach that focuses on changing the whole school, as well as a small group of students that are identified as having a history of bullying or are at risk for becoming bullies.[29] In PBIS, the consequences for students who act like bullies are individualized and focus on how they can change themselves and stop the problem behavior. In some cases, though, PBIS can be both punitive and restorative: for example, in California, one district realized that most at-risk students ended up getting suspended, so they transformed their suspension rooms into places where students could reflect on and learn how to change their behavior, enabling students to both be served with a clear punishment and given an opportunity to improve how they act.[30]

Many policies embrace a mix of punitive and restorative approaches. Illinois, for example, gives schools the option of using a PBIS approach or a punitive approach, but recommends that schools consider both when drafting policies.[31] As we learn more about bullying, we will undoubtedly have more ideas about how to create consequences that both show how unacceptable bullying is and take real, effective steps for prevention.

Mental Health Services

As discussed in chapters 2, 3, and 4, victims, witnesses, and bullies all benefit from counseling. This could be provided at the school, or it could be from an outside organization or therapist who works with the community.

Although about half of states recommend that school districts include mental health services in their local laws and policies, only a quarter of districts actually do so.[32] Some simply require that organizations that support students who are involved in bullying communicate with the school regularly; they do not require any interventions.[33] Other policies say that the school must help connect families with services if they request them, but do not necessarily require it.[34] The strictest laws require local policies to include mental health and counseling services in any response to a bullying incident.[35] Different individuals have different opinions about these approaches. Some believe it is best to let the teens involved decide whether mental health services are appropriate. Others argue that many people who could benefit from counseling may hesitate to take advantage of it, fearing that it is a sign of weakness or that it is a waste of time. Mandating counseling could help these individuals overcome the taboos and stigmas associated with mental health

Mental health services can make a huge difference in the lives of victims, bullies, and witnesses.

services. Still others acknowledge that school systems and community-based organizations are short on resources, and therefore should spend their money on other priorities besides counseling.

One of the shortcomings common to all of these laws is that they focus almost exclusively on the victim: as we've seen throughout this book, witnesses and bullies can also benefit from mental health services.[36] Indeed, counseling can help a bully break a cycle of violence, thereby changing the climate of the school, benefiting numerous former and potential victims, and preventing future abuse. As laws develop and change, we may see a shift toward this mentality.

Training

Although it is important to address bullying when it occurs, anti-bullying laws and policies are supposed to prevent bullying from happening in the first place. A key component for prevention is education and training. Different states take different approaches. Some require annual training for adults in school buildings.[37] Others establish committees that are supposed to be resources in the school who can help implement curricula or provide one-on-one support for adults and students involved in bullying.[38] Still others require classes or units for students to help them appreciate diversity and learn how to deal with conflict without becoming bullies.[39]

Some schools hold annual celebrations that showcase what students have learned about diversity, tolerance, and conflict resolution. For example, every year New York City celebrates Respect for All week, in which schools hold special events and display student work on the anti-bullying curricula they have learned all year. Other districts raise awareness through events like the nationwide Mix It Up at Lunch Day, created by the group Teaching Tolerance, something you read about in a previous chapter.

Some of the most effective educational initiatives are designed and driven by teens. Teen Julia Kudler's experiences as a victim of bullying motivated her to use her story to try to teach others about tolerance, respect, and inclusion. Read more about Kudler's story on page 179.

The PBIS approach (described earlier) requires school districts to design educational interventions based on data they collect about students. For example, one district in Illinois noticed that the majority of bullying incidents were happening in ninth grade, so they created a new course for all ninth graders that helped them develop their communication and conflict resolution skills.[40]

In PBIS, interventions are not just for students; in fact, even teachers and principals are trained in how to change their behavior to create an environment where bullying is socially unacceptable.[41] In Escondido, California, an entire

Julia Kudler's Story

For years, teen Julia Kudler was the victim of bullying. Instead of letting her past weigh her down, she decided to use her story to create change. In 2013, she told her story in her own words:

Let's face it, I was never a popular kid. The other kids made fun of me, ignored me, and generally thought I was strange and stupid. I didn't really have many friends, and most of the friends I did have were in other grades. Let's just say I had a hard time.

It was after a long day at school and it was time to start my homework. I opened my bag to get my homework planner out. The first thing I saw in my backpack was a note from a girl in my class who I thought of as my only friend, and it said: "Julia, I don't want to be your friend anymore because I want to be popular."

Probably my worst moment in middle school was when I found that note. That hurt more than all the teasing or the general sense of dislike. That was a betrayal that I couldn't just shrug away.

My advice for others trying to start a program: The teens need to be the ones who take the initiative. It can't come from the adults. Teens need to be the ones fighting to end social isolation, because adults aren't close enough to the problem. Kids listen to other kids, because they can relate to them.

For the last two years (2011–2013), I have been a member of the Beyond Differences Teen Board. Beyond Differences works with Bay Area middle schools to help create a more inclusive social environment. Members of the Teen Board run middle school assemblies and start a conversation with the student body about social isolation. Giving the assemblies, especially at first, was difficult. Sharing your own story in front of a room filled with kids was challenging, especially as an 8th grader.

I ended up going to a different school about a year later [after I got the hurtful note]. I didn't see that girl again for four years. We recently met again because of a mutual friend. She turned out to be, actually, a very nice person. She shares a lot of the same interests as me, and we are now friends again. It's so strange how much a person can change.[f]

district trained their teachers to use the same disciplinary system in classrooms because students were transferring schools so often: doing so helped reduce the number of incidents because schools throughout the district consistently conveyed the message that violence would not be tolerated. Consequently, students knew what was expected of them no matter how many times they transferred.[42]

In fact, most anti-bullying laws require some kind of staff training. However, one of the limitations of some of these laws is they exclude nonteaching staff such as bus drivers, cafeteria workers, teacher assistants, and hall monitors who often are present when bullying takes place outside the classroom. Some districts concentrate on teachers, who are with students the majority of the time, because there is not enough funding to train everyone. Opponents of this approach say that bullying does not always happen in classrooms—indeed, as mentioned, many incidents occur in lunchrooms, cafeterias, or online, all spaces where teachers are not present.[43] As of 2013, advocates were still fighting for more comprehensive training and education methods for schools to address bullying that include every member of the community, including students.

Enforcement and Monitoring

Although many states may have excellent laws and policies in place, they mean nothing if they are not enforced. There are several common implementation barriers. One is financial. Sometimes legal requirements cost money, but the expenses may not be adequately covered in the budgets. For example, although thirty-nine states require some kind of training component, only three states earmark money for the training in the local budget.[44] This lack of clarity can make it especially difficult for districts to plan for preventative services, which are frequently sacrificed so schools can address more immediate issues.

Another reason why implementation may suffer is that districts may feel that they do not have the time or resources to take on yet another responsibility. This is particularly true in schools where teachers feel pressure to make sure their students get certain scores on standardized tests, or risk losing their jobs: they may feel that time spent helping teens deal with emotional issues will take away precious time from academic work.[45] These teachers may not see the connection between safety and academic outcomes, or they may feel overwhelmed with their existing job requirements and unable to take on the responsibility of stopping bullying.

Reporting is a key method for monitoring whether schools are actually following anti-bullying laws and policies.[46] This includes not only reporting incidents but also turning in documentation of how investigations are handled, how consequences are enforced, and who has participated in training programs. There are many reasons why schools may not comply with monitoring. Some may feel they will be punished if their rate of bullying incidents goes up, even if this signals that they have created an effective reporting mechanism. Others may not have time to do proper reporting or may decide that it is not a priority. In these cases, it is difficult to tell whether schools are actually following through on laws and policies, no matter how well they are designed.

In the next chapter, you will read about how teens like you have come together to demand that their schools and communities both create and implement effective anti-bullying laws and policies. Perhaps learning about what teens have done will inspire you to try to create change in your own school, with the help of a few strong allies.

Notes

1. Valerie Polakow, "A Question of Rights: Poverty and the Child Care Crisis," *New Educator* 4 (2008): 37.
2. "Why Won't America Ratify the UN Convention on Children's Rights?" *Economist.com*, October 6, 2013, www.economist.com/blogs/economist-explains/2013/10/economist-explains-2 (accessed October 8, 2013).
3. "Why Won't America Ratify the UN Convention on Children's Rights?"
4. "Bill Text 112th. Congress (2011–2012) S.506.IS," Library of Congress, 2011, http://thomas.loc.gov/cgi-bin/query/z?c112:S.506 (accessed January 19, 2013).
5. Valerie Jarrett, "Ending Bullying in Our Schools and Communities," *Winning the Future: President Obama and the LGBT Community* (blog), April 20, 2012, http://www.whitehouse.gov/blog/2012/04/20/ending-bullying-our-schools-communities (accessed January 19, 2013).
6. Jarrett, "Ending Bullying in Our Schools and Communities."
7. U.S. Department of Health and Human Services, "Key Components in State Anti-Bullying Laws," Stopbullying.gov, 2013, http://www.stopbullying.gov/laws/key-components/index.html (accessed January 19, 2013).
8. Victoria Stuart-Cassel, Ariana Bell, and J. Fred Springer, "Analysis of State Bullying Laws and Policies" (Washington, DC: U.S. Department of Education, 2011), 7.
9. Stuart-Cassel, Bell, and Springer, "Analysis of State Bullying Laws and Policies," xiv.
10. Stuart-Cassel, Bell, and Springer, "Analysis of State Bullying Laws and Policies," 7.
11. Karen DeWitt, "Cuomo Signs Anti-Cyberbullying Bill into Law," *WNYC*, July 9, 2012, http://www.wnyc.org/story/221550-cuomo-signs-anti-cyberbullying-bill-law/ (accessed October 8, 2013).
12. Stuart-Cassel, Bell, and Springer, "Analysis of State Bullying Laws and Policies," xiii.
13. Stuart-Cassel, Bell, and Springer, "Analysis of State Bullying Laws and Policies," xiii.
14. Dan Olweus, *Bullying at School* (Malden, MA: Blackwell Publishing), 9.
15. Stuart-Cassel, Bell, and Springer, "Analysis of State Bullying Laws and Policies," xiii.
16. Emily A. Greytak, Joseph G. Kosciw, and Elizabeth M. Diaz, *Harsh Realities: The Experience of Transgender Youth in Our Nation's Schools* (Washington, DC: Gay, Lesbian, and Straight Education Network, 2007), x.
17. Greytak, Kosciw, and Diaz, *Harsh Realities*, x.

18. Stuart-Cassel, Bell, and Springer, "Analysis of State Bullying Laws and Policies," xv.
19. DoSomething.org, *The Bully Report: Trends in Bullying Pulled from Student Facebook Interactions*, 2012, http://files.dosomething.org/files/campaigns/bullyreport/bully_report.pdf (accessed January 19, 2013), 6.
20. DoSomething.org, *The Bully Report*, 14.
21. Scott Taylor, "Facebook Threat behind Lewiston Mall Beating," *Lewiston-Auburn Sun Journal*, March 5, 2011, http://www.sunjournal.com/city/story/995695 (accessed October 8, 2013).
22. "Cyberbullied and Beaten Near Death, Lewiston Teen Speaks Out," *WCSH6 Portland*, August 7, 2012, http://www.wcsh6.com/news/article/209904/2/Cyber-bullied-and-beaten-near-death-Lewiston-teen-speaks-out (accessed October 8, 2013).
23. DoSomething.org, "11 Facts about Bullying," DoSomething.org 2012, http://www.dosomething.org/tipsandtools/11-facts-about-school-bullying (accessed January 19, 2013).
24. Catherine Hill and Holly Kearl, *Crossing the Line: Sexual Harassment at School* (Washington, DC: American Association of University Women, 2011), 26.
25. Stuart-Cassel, Bell, and Springer, "Analysis of State Bullying Laws and Policies," 38.
26. Stuart-Cassel, Bell, and Springer, "Analysis of State Bullying Laws and Policies," 38.
27. Stuart-Cassel, Bell, and Springer, "Analysis of State Bullying Laws and Policies," 39.
28. Stuart-Cassel, Bell, and Springer, "Analysis of State Bullying Laws and Policies," 39.
29. Laura Towvim, Kellie Anderson, Benjamin Thomas, and Amy Blaisdell, *Positive Behavioral Interventions and Supports: A Snapshot from Safe Schools/Healthy Students Initiative* (Waltham, MA: Education Development Center, 2012), 2.
30. Towvim et al., *Positive Behavioral Interventions and Supports*, 8.
31. Stuart-Cassel, Bell, and Springer, "Analysis of State Bullying Laws and Policies," 38.
32. Stuart-Cassel, Bell, and Springer, "Analysis of State Bullying Laws and Policies," xv.
33. Stuart-Cassel, Bell, and Springer, "Analysis of State Bullying Laws and Policies," 39.
34. Stuart-Cassel, Bell, and Springer, "Analysis of State Bullying Laws and Policies," 39.
35. Stuart-Cassel, Bell, and Springer, "Analysis of State Bullying Laws and Policies," 39.
36. Stuart-Cassel, Bell, and Springer, "Analysis of State Bullying Laws and Policies," 39.
37. Stuart-Cassel, Bell, and Springer, "Analysis of State Bullying Laws and Policies," 29.
38. Stuart-Cassel, Bell, and Springer, "Analysis of State Bullying Laws and Policies," 29.
39. Stuart-Cassel, Bell, and Springer, "Analysis of State Bullying Laws and Policies," 29.
40. Towvim et al., *Positive Behavioral Interventions and Supports*, 5.
41. Towvim et al., *Positive Behavioral Interventions and Supports*, 5.
42. Towvim et al., *Positive Behavioral Interventions and Supports*, 5.
43. DoSomething.org, *The Bully Report*, 6.
44. Stuart-Cassel, Bell, and Springer, "Analysis of State Bullying Laws and Policies," 30.
45. Jessie Klein, *The Bully Society: School Shootings and the Crisis of Bullying in America's Schools* (New York: New York University Press, 2011), 137–147.
46. Stuart-Cassel, Bell, and Springer, "Analysis of State Bullying Laws and Policies," 35.

a. Namit Satara has given Rowman & Littlefield permission to publish his story in his own words.
b. Elizabeth Ditty, "Never Again," in *Bullying under Attack: True Stories Written by Teen Victims, Bullies, and Bystanders (Teen Ink)*, ed. Stephanie Meyer, John Meyer, Emily Sperber, and Heather Alexander (Deerfield Beach, FL: HCI Teens, 2013), 5.
c. Ditty, "Never Again," 6.
d. Ditty, "Never Again," 6.
e. Ditty, "Never Again," 8.
f. Julia Kudler has given Rowman & Littlefield permission to publish her story in her own words.

COMBATING BULLYING TOGETHER

In the last chapter, you read about what great international, national, and local anti-bullying policies look like. You became familiar with debates that policy makers face when they create laws designed to send clear messages that violence is unacceptable, while giving teens a chance to learn from their mistakes. You learned about how solid laws and policies can be invaluable tools for moving personal behavior, educational institutions, and community attitudes toward tolerance, nonviolence, and acceptance.

Getting laws passed and policies enacted is not easy. Since the United States is a democracy, the power to legislate is spread among multiple individuals and organizations. Furthermore, any new idea must go through an intensive process before it is voted into law. This prevents any one person or body from wielding too much power, and it provides plenty of opportunities for anyone in the United States—including teens like you—to influence how government works, from the most local to the highest levels. However, it also means that the process can be long, slow, and complicated, requiring years of dedication and focus.

Organizers, activists, and politicians sometimes refer to avenues for changing laws and policies as "levers of change." Sometimes levers are people, such as council members who can author laws, school board members who can vote on policies, or teens who can rally information and support. Other times, levers are channels of information, such as editorials in newspapers that influence politicians, meetings that educate and inform communities, or academic reports presenting new data. Still other times, levers are methods of implementation, oversight, or reporting, such as requirements for schools to record bullying incidents, hearings by local governing bodies that oversee schools or school systems, or clear consequences for legal violations. What all of these levers have in common is that they establish rules or norms through laws, policies, popular opinion, or other forces that shape our society.

In this chapter, you will learn more about teens like you who use levers of change to create or improve local, state, and national anti-bullying policies. You will learn about tools you can use to create change in your community, and strategies that have worked in anti-bullying campaigns across the United States. By the end of this chapter, the biggest lesson you should learn is that with a little knowledge, dedication, and support, you and the people you know can create change.

Proving the Problem

The first step in any kind of political organizing is proving that the issue you choose is a serious problem that the general public should care about. This is sometimes called *building political will*. Political will is important because elected officials want to write, pass, and enforce laws and policies that they believe will both help their constituents, or the people who vote for them and make them popular enough to win reelection. If constituents show that they care about a problem deeply, politicians are more likely to believe that change will benefit both their chances of reelection and the people they serve.

An effective way to show that bullying is a problem in your community is to collect data that proves that the problem exists. To do this, you must figure out what data you want to find and how you want to communicate your findings. When people think of data, they often think of quantitative data, or information that can be expressed using numbers. Examples of quantitative data include percentages of populations or numbers of incidents. Many people believe that this is more reliable than qualitative data, which is data that is expressed using words. Examples of qualitative data include written survey responses or excerpts from interviews. Many people believe that numbers are objective, whereas words come from personal experience and are therefore subjective. Furthermore, they believe that words express opinions, rather than facts. Numbers, on the other hand, are fixed and unchangeable, and therefore are more reliable.

Measuring an Elephant

People often believe that numbers are objective because they are constant and unchangeable. However, numbers can be manipulated as well. Try this activity with your friends.

Your assignment is to measure an elephant to see if it will fit in an elevator. Write a plan (on a piece of paper other than this book) about how you will accomplish this task. Be as specific as possible.

When you are finished, compare what you have written with what your friends have written. Consider the following questions:

1. What measurement did you choose? Why? How is it different or similar to what your friends chose?
2. What tools would you use to measure your elephant? How are these different or similar to what your friends would use?
3. What was your biggest concern about getting the elephant into the elevator? How was this reflected in your choice of what measurements to collect? How does this compare with what your friends chose?
4. How did your measurement establish or address a concern? What concerns did your measurement ignore?

Perhaps you and your friend came up with exactly the same plan for measuring the elephant. Most likely, however, you did not. One of you may have wanted to measure the elephant from the tip of his trunk to the end of his tail using a ruler to see if it fit in the elevator lengthwise. Another may have wanted to measure her height in feet or meters to see if the elevator's ceiling was high enough. Still another may have wanted to weigh the elephant to make sure that the elevator would not collapse under the elephant's weight.

All of these approaches answer the question of whether our elephant will fit into the elevator. However, none of them provide the full story. Just because the elevator's ceiling is high enough does not mean that its doors are wide enough. Likewise, just because the elephant fits through the doors does not mean that the elevator can bear its weight. In the same way, researchers focus on specific questions that require specific kinds of data. Just because the data are numbers does not mean that they are more or less objective: just like words, numbers tell different stories, depending on which ones you choose.

This activity was adapted from a section in the book *Policy Paradox* by Deborah Stone.[a] If you found this activity interesting, check out Stone's book.

In reality, quantitative data, just like qualitative data, is not perfect. Just like words, numbers can be manipulated. For every topic, there are multiple ways to collect data. What you collect and how you collect it can influence the story that you tell, the problem that you establish, and the reaction that you get. Try the activity "Measuring an Elephant" on page 184 with your friends.

Once you have collected your data, you must analyze and then present it in a compelling way. This may seem counterintuitive because, as mentioned earlier, many people believe that numbers are objective and therefore tell one story: the truth. In reality, just like words, you can use numbers to tell multiple stories.[1] Counting, for example, creates categories that include and exclude certain individuals and define what a phenomenon looks like. In the case of bullying, counting people who are affected by bullying creates one category (victims) and counting people who engage in bullying creates another (bullies). In reality, these categories are blurry because many people fit into both. However, it can be useful to define these terms because it helps us visualize what bullying looks like by stating who is involved. This in turn helps us frame solutions by breaking the problem into smaller pieces; in this case, we define two individuals who are involved in most bullying incidents whose needs ought to be addressed.

Political stories are stories designed to make people take action.[2] If you are using your research for advocacy, this is a major goal of the story you plan to tell. Framing a political story requires considering what you are counting and why. It also requires thinking beyond the obvious—like, for example, just the people involved in bullying. You might also want to think about counting related statistics, such as the number of disciplinary incidents in your school every year or the number of teachers who have to break up fights. You could also consider phenomena that you suspect are related to violence, such as the number of teachers or other staff who look for jobs elsewhere, the number of students who pass state-mandated tests, or the number of parents who withdraw their children from school. All of these results can contribute to a story that establishes why bullying is a problem and how solving the problem can benefit the wider community.

There are many ways to tell stories about bullying using qualitative and quantitative data. You could gather information showing that the problem is widespread and that it affects the majority of students at your school. You could do this by conducting a school-wide survey where students answer questions about whether they have been bullied and how often it has happened to them. You could support this information by also interviewing parents, teachers, and school personnel about how much bullying they have witnessed.

You could show that the problem affects a specific population of students or is a specific type of bullying. For example, you could show that the majority of girls at your school say that they experience sexual harassment, or that LGBTQ students suffer from bias-based harassment, or that coaches are mistreating athletes. You could do this through a survey that collects the number of students in each of these categories, combined with stories about what the violence looks like and where and when it occurs.

You could show that the consequences of bullying are severe and impact both students and the school. You could prove that it affects students' grades,

Sometimes bullying affects just a few people, but the effect is severe enough to warrant a response.

attendance, participation in after-school activities, or other aspects of learning or safety. You could compare the grade point averages or attendance records of students who have and have not been victims, supplementing your evidence with stories of how students felt that it negatively affected their school performance.

Once you have done your research, you have the tools you need to convince others that the problem exists. Sometimes the data you collect supports your original predictions. Other times your data may surprise you, revealing trends that you did not know were there. You may find the problem is much deeper and more widespread than you originally believed. You may find an entirely new problem that you did not expect.

After you fully understand the scope of what you are facing, it is time to devise a strategic approach to addressing the issues you have identified. This is one of the most important steps in every campaign: identifying levers of change.

Levers of Change

When you meet with legislators or policy makers or any other officials who are capable of implementing the change you seek, you should prepare tools that will help you make your case. In this section, we will discuss a variety of these tools (sometimes called levers of change), which you can use to help make your community bully free.

Laws and Policies

Laws and policies are some of the most commonly utilized levers of change. As discussed in the last chapter, laws are rules passed by governing bodies, while policies are adopted by organizations of nonelected officials. When it comes to preventing bullying, laws and policies can serve numerous functions. Some incentivize positive behavior by establishing clear consequences.[3] Examples include laws that fine or otherwise punish teens for posting inappropriate content online, or school policies that inflict detention, suspension, or expulsion for violent behavior. Others promote transparency by requiring schools and campuses to create systems for reporting. An example of this is legislation that requires local schools to compile and publish reports about the number of bullying incidents at their school, broken down by category such as gender, race, or sexual orientation. This helps constituents hold educational institutions accountable and makes them more aware of their own behaviors and the need to personally avoid violence. Still others specify resources available for preventing bullying or caring for victims. These are often budgetary decisions, such as funding more mental health professionals in schools, or giving paid days off for teachers and administrators to attend training.

If you decide that passing a law is the best way to tackle the problems you have identified, begin by familiarizing yourself with what laws and policies already exist in your state or locality. Analyze these to decide what is missing or what could be improved. The federal government has created a page that includes both descriptions of existing laws and model policies that can guide you in your analysis. These resources can be found at www.stopbullying.gov/laws. You might also want to speak to local parents, teachers, administrators, school board members, and elected officials to understand the strengths and weaknesses of existing laws, as well as the process of enacting or changing what already exists.

Next, determine who to approach to help you get your legislation passed. First, you need to identify the appropriate level of government for your law or policy. Some levels only have powers over a city, whereas others have powers over states. The federal government has power over the entire country but allows states to make most educational policy, including budgetary decisions about schools. And while states make decisions about budgets and resources, they allow districts to make decisions about training, processes, and procedures.

After you determine what level of law or policy you need, you can target a politician or administrator who works at the appropriate department or legislature. Ideally, you should target someone you believe would be a vocal supporter of the work, either because he or she has a personal connection to the issue or because he or she has a group of voters who are affected and will therefore be supportive of the kind of change you seek. Be aware that you will have to work with this individual and his or her office over an extended period of time: laws must be drafted, revised, introduced, debated, voted on (sometimes in multiple legislatures), signed into law, budgeted, and then implemented. Laws may need to be introduced multiple times in multiple sessions, and so could take years to pass. Policies can take even longer, since they are not bound to legislative sessions that open and close on regular schedules.

Once you have found someone willing to sponsor your bill or author your policy, you must work with that person to draft it. Normally this happens with a lawyer who is a staff person for an elected official, agency, or department. A lawyer can guide you through what the particular level of government you are working with can and cannot legislate. He or she can also help you think about parts of the law that could be misinterpreted, ignored, or misused if drafted improperly.

Anticipating challenges or objections to the law or policy can help you anticipate challenges to implementation, or the process of carrying out the law or policy. Thinking ahead like this is a key element of lawmaking. After all, even if a law is perfectly written (which, incidentally, is impossible: no one can predict every issue that a law may face), it is useless if it is ignored or if its meaning is twisted. Implementation is so important that it can be considered a lever of change.

Implementation

During your research, you may find that your locality is bound by laws and policies that are comprehensive and well thought out. In this case, the problem may not be the legal framework but the way the law is being enforced (or, sometimes, the fact that it is *not* being enforced). In this case, it is time to consider how to improve a vital aspect of any law or policy: implementation.

Sometimes laws and policies are not implemented properly because of the way they are written. They may leave out information, be too general or too specific, or be outdated. For example, many schools and districts have had to rewrite their bullying policies to account for cyberbullying. Before the Internet existed, no one knew we would need tools to deal with bullying that occurred twenty-four hours a day on electronic devices that blurred the boundaries of physical space. School discipline codes did not include provisions for punishing cyberbullies, police departments did not have guidelines for investigating them, lawyers were ignorant about prosecuting them, and legislators were unclear about how best to punish them. Consequently, cyberbullies got away with negative behavior simply because no one knew how to approach the problem.

One lever of change is to try to rewrite or amend laws and policies so they specifically account for new situations or so they are general enough to be interpreted usefully as circumstances arise. The process of changing existing documents can be just as time-consuming as drafting a new one, but the patience required to do so might pay off if it effectively addresses new problems.

Another reason why laws and policies remain unenforced is because individuals in power—such as principals, legislators, or superintendents—communicate that the laws and policies are not a priority and can be ignored. These individuals may feel pressure to produce certain kinds of results, such as high test scores or graduation rates, and they may not realize the connection between making schools safer and higher academic achievement. This can be addressed in several ways. You can advocate for reporting requirements, such as asking schools to produce annual counts of how many bullying incidents took place, how quickly they were addressed, and who addressed them. Schools might be required to make these counts public and available to constituents and the press. You could also call for public hearings about the data once it is available so you and fellow advocates can ask questions about it. Imposing reporting requirements holds authorities accountable for results and gives them an incentive to ensure proper implementation. You can also meet with officials in power and persuade them to make your issue a priority by communicating to those who report to them that their responsibilities should be taken seriously and that they will be monitored in these areas.

Sometimes implementation fails because of a lack of resources: there may not be enough money to hire the proper personnel to handle the responsibilities outlined in the law or policy. An example of this may be a law that requires a minimum number of mental health professionals in schools, but does not have an accompanying budget. Schools may want to hire social workers and therapists, but their budgets may be too small to cover these additional salaries. Similarly, sometimes individuals asked to enforce laws and policies are already overwhelmed with other responsibilities, as with teachers who have a full course load and are asked to take on the additional task of monitoring and addressing bullying complaints. These individuals might be more effective if they were given paid time off to attend training or were able to dedicate one class period a day to responding to bullying. In this case, you may want to look at the budget as a lever of change.

Budgets

A budget is a plan a governing body makes about how much money it will spend on a set of priorities during a given time. Budgets are financial documents, but they are also political: the amount of money allocated to departments, programs, communities, and geographic locations is a reflection of a government's priorities. Not only does money represent resources that can be used to create real change, it also has a symbolic value in that it communicates who and what deserves spending. Usually state and local government bodies hold annual hearings where constituents and advocacy groups can testify about their financial priorities. These may be held by agency, such as the Department of Education, or area, such as a particular city or neighborhood. Attending hearings and advocating for funding for mental health services, hotlines, and other reporting mechanisms, or more staff to patrol the hallways, can be a great way to improve how consistently laws and policies are enforced.

Many advocates use budgets as a way to ask for more training. A common reason why laws and policies are not properly put into practice is that authorities lack the background or experience necessary to act. For example, school security guards may not be informed about adolescent and child development, conflict resolution, or nonviolent behavior management. Consequently, they may react overly harshly to bullying simply because they lack alternative tools and methods for addressing it, combating violence with violence and making the problem worse. Many may want to know about these approaches, but districts may not have the money to hire trainers, pay for space and curriculum, and give guards paid time off. In fact, training is a third lever of change, an extremely effective one.

Training

Education is one of the most powerful tools we have for creating change. The more we know about each other, the kinder and more empathetic we are. The more we know about ourselves, the better able we are to deal with conflict. The more we know about our rights, the more likely we are to ask for what we deserve.

There are several things to consider if you put together a plan to advocate for education and training. First, figure out who you are training. Think about whom bullying affects and the powers these individuals have to address or prevent it.

There are victims, bullies, teacher and student witnesses, principals who are responsible for school climate, parents, and school staff such as bus drivers, security guards, cafeteria workers, hall monitors, and others who could prevent bullying if they knew how.

Next, think about the content of your training, keeping your research in mind. Many organizations have anti-bullying curricula tailored to adults, students, or both. Often, this training is designed to promote empathy and understanding, and to change school climate. Certainly this approach can be beneficial, but it may not directly address the problems you've identified. For example, perhaps individuals in your community are not taking advantage of existing laws that could help prevent bullying. In this case, you might want to look into Know Your Rights training.

Know Your Rights training is designed to help people understand the resources available for their protection. The training usually covers things like what the laws say, what to do if you notice the law is not being enforced, who you can contact to help you make use of the law, and what you can do to let policy makers know that the law is important. For example, your district may have a law requiring every school to designate an adult responsible for addressing bullying complaints. However, the school may not have publicized the name of that person or his or her contact information. Know Your Rights training could inform students and parents who the point person is, how to get in touch with him or her, what the point person is supposed to do about a complaint, and what students and parents can do if they feel their complaint is not being responded to in a thorough and timely manner. The ideal outcome of Know Your Rights training is that attendees will have a better understanding of what they can ask for from their governments and communities, and will therefore put pressure on institutions that are not complying with existing laws. Know Your Rights training is often conducted by independent individuals or social justice–oriented organizations rather than governments and institutions themselves (although in some cases, teachers may also be interested in introducing these ideas to their classes). If you want to conduct this type of training, it may be useful to contact local legal advocacy groups or anti-bullying groups to see if they can help you organize Know Your Right events.

Once you have determined the content of your training, consider logistics. What are the best times and places to hold your training? Who are the best people to conduct it? How much will it cost to rent space, hire trainers, or purchase curricula designed by experts? What incentives can you provide to make people want to come to training and really learn, listen, and participate? How often should these individuals be trained? You do not have to have all of the answers to these questions, but if you have a rough idea it can help you have an informed conversation with elected officials and their staff.

Training can be implemented in a variety of ways. It can be mandated through laws or policies that specify who should be trained, how often training should occur, and what the training should contain. For example, some school districts have policies that require them to train teachers in anti-bullying curricula annually, while others require new employees to receive training only when they start their jobs. Another option is to work with educational institutions to include training about power, privilege, tolerance, inclusion, and acceptance in their curricula. You could ask your school district to adopt these topics in curricula for students in kindergarten through twelfth grade. You could also approach institutions that train adults who work with kids, such as teacher training colleges, counseling courses, and even principal training academies. Another option is to advocate for training through budget work. You could ask local politicians or donors to pay for training for your community. In these cases, you could find adults or teens you know to conduct the training.

It can be difficult to make training mandatory by building it into laws, policies, and procedures. Although it is certainly worth pursuing this goal, remember that it is also possible to raise money and hold voluntary training while you are working toward your broader objective of making it required. In fact, showing positive results from this work can help you demonstrate just how much potential your idea has. Furthermore, it can help you build confidence, community, and awareness. Take the example of Paige Rawl, an HIV-positive teen who chose to confront the bullying she faced by using her story to educate others. Read more about Rawl's activism below.

Paige Rawl's Story

At the age of three, Paige Rawl was diagnosed with Human Immunodeficiency Virus (HIV), a life threatening illness that affects the body's ability to fight diseases.[b] HIV is highly stigmatized, partly because it can be deadly and partly because of the way it is spread: although Rawl was born with HIV, it is also transmitted through sexual intercourse and intravenous drug use.

When Rawl revealed her status to a friend during a sleepover, the whole school found out and Rawl became the target of relentless bullying. "People thought I must have been . . . you know, a slut,"[c] she said, referring to the fact that some people contract HIV through unprotected sex. Her peers placed insulting notes on her locker, a group of boys started calling her "PAIDS," and even her soccer coach publicly spoke about her status inappropriately. Rawl remembers, "She [the coach] said we could use my HIV status to our advantage. That the players on the other team would be afraid to touch me and I could score goals."[d] The negative treatment became so severe that in eighth grade, Rawl became depressed and opted for homeschooling so she would not have to face her classmates daily.[e]

Then Rawl decided to tell her story in public for the first time. The experience transformed her. She remembers, "The first time I spoke, it was this huge relief . . . a big, huge weight was lifted off my shoulders."[f] She decided to become a certified American Red Cross HIV/AIDS educator and has gone on tour in her home state of Indiana teaching others about teens like her who have the disease.[g] She has used the power of her story to educate others about how people living with HIV and AIDS face discrimination and what can be done to end the false beliefs that lead to their mistreatment.

Although Rawl has come to terms with living with the disease, she believes that the world around her has not. "I tell people, 'HIV does not define who I am,'" Rawl says. "But I'm going to have to live with [HIV] for the rest of my life, and it's going to be something that not everyone is going to be OK with."[h]

Rawl's courageous decision to use her story to educate others shows the power of training to change the way people think, act, and behave. Most likely you also have a story to share. Perhaps you, like Rawl, could use your story to change the world.

Establishing Priorities

Governments run on limited time, money, and staff, and elected officials are highly sensitive to political will. These two factors make it unlikely that lawmakers will adopt sudden, drastic changes or immediately implement programs requiring significant resources or a shift in behavior. Although you should not be afraid to ask for all of the levers of change that you have identified, it is unlikely that you will get everything you want immediately. Consequently, it is wise to identify the most essential levers in your campaign, so that you know what your priorities are if you have limited time, resources, and support.

In determining your priorities, consider both how widespread a problem is and how severe. For example, you may prioritize a lever because it can help a wide variety of students with different identities and backgrounds. Or you may prioritize a lever because it addresses an extreme incident, such as a suicide or a massive, destructive fight: sometimes a single case is shocking enough that it warrants action.

Use your data to determine what you think needs to be addressed right away and what you are prepared to fight for long-term. For example, if your research has identified a number of students who are depressed because of bullying, an immediate solution might be to establish an emergency counseling hotline. In the months ahead, you may want to ask your school to increase access to mental health services by hiring more counselors and social workers, to train teachers to identify signs of depression so they can make referrals, and to create a class period where students have space during the day to talk about issues that affect them (schools that have this class often call it an advisory period).

After you have decided what your priorities are, it is time to start building support and political will. In the next section, we will discuss how to spread the word about your campaign.

Spread the Word

Policy makers are sensitive to the opinions of the general public: after all, their job security depends on ensuring that they maintain a positive reputation among their voters. This means that you have to convince policy makers that the change you are proposing will help constituents and will be popular. Some changes may be helpful but may not be popular. For example, some schools removed vending machines that sell junk food from their cafeterias. This is helpful because students make healthier eating choices. However, it is also unpopular with students

The Bully Project

Bully is a documentary film that follows the lives of teen victims and their families. The characters are targeted for a variety of reasons. One is bullied because he has an autism disorder called Asperger's syndrome, another because of her sexual orientation. Still another does not know why she is bullied, but her victimization drives her to violence against her classmates. The film also includes the stories of teens who have been driven to suicide because of harassment and how their families have used these tragedies to try to create change.

The filmmakers worked hard to publicize the movie because they wanted to raise awareness about how much more needs to be done to address and prevent bullying.[i] The director, Lee Hirsch, has traveled the country screening the film and speaking to audiences about his own experiences being bullied.[j] The film also received publicity it did not expect: the motion picture association gave it an R rating in 2012, which meant that teens under the age of eighteen could not go see the movie without adult supervision.[k] The directors objected, saying that the rating restricted access to teens under the age of eighteen who might be facing bullying issues and therefore might be uncomfortable attending screenings with an adult. They started a successful petition drive, collecting signatures from teens and parents who felt that the movie should be available to younger teens as well. The motion picture association eventually lowered the rating to PG-13.

Bully does more than just raise awareness. It's also a platform for activism. The film has spurred a website called The Bully Project (www.thebullyproject .com), which includes links to a virtual community committed to ending bullying. The site includes a viewing guide to the movie and a companion book and toolkits for educators, students, and teachers about preventing bullying. The film itself contains a reference to the website at the end and in its publicity material. It is an excellent example of using the arts to engage in activism: the makers of the film both cover the issue and give viewers tools to do something about it.

To find out more, check out www.thebullyproject.com. Check out the website for its resources and also to generate your own ideas about how you can use videos and films to raise awareness about bullying or any other issue that is important to you.

because they can no longer eat their favorite snacks and with candy companies because they lose profits.

Political will is key to creating change. To build political will, you need to build awareness. There are several avenues you can use to do this. One is through political methods, such as testifying at government hearings, holding rallies or protests, or scheduling meetings with politicians. Another is through the media, writing opinion articles, or producing radio or video news reports. Temitayo Fagbenle, for example, was a teen radio reporter who produced a piece about cyberbullying that was aired on public radio. To read more about Fagbenle, see page 100 in chapter 6.

Another way to spread awareness is through the arts. You can draw attention through creating visual arts exhibitions or murals, writing stories or poems, or making films. One example of a creative means of drawing attention to bullying is the film *Bully*, which is a documentary about the experiences of victims of bullying. It was designed to raise awareness and to encourage activism. Read more about the movie on page 195.

One of the best ways to raise awareness is to join forces with groups of individuals invested in the same cause. In the next section, you will learn about the importance of allies who can work with you toward a common cause.

Finding Allies

In chapter 3, we talked about allies, or people who may not be directly affected by a problem but who are motivated to support people who are. Allies can be vital

Allies can help you work toward a common cause by spreading the word and building political will about your issue.

influencers. Sometimes politicians hesitate to take stands on issues because they are afraid that they will alienate voters whose interests are directly tied to the issues. Allies who are supportive of issues that do not directly affect them can be essential in convincing politicians that voters approve of their actions. For example, many White allies fought alongside people of color in the civil rights movement, helping to end segregation in the United States and sending a clear message to politicians that racism is unacceptable. This has continued to be true in campaigns to legalize gay marriage, where before major votes on marriage equality, straight constituents call local leaders assuring them that they will support their reelection if they vote in favor of marriage equality.

Allies do not always have to be people who have power. They could also face oppression but belong to different identity categories than the ones you are working with. These allies can demonstrate how the problem that you are trying to solve affects a diverse range of people. An example of this was the passage of Respect for All, the New York City school district's anti-bullying policy, in 2008. Respect for All came about because the Asian American Legal Defense and Education Fund came together with the Sikh Coalition, the New York Civil Liberties Union, and LGBTQ rights groups such as the Gay, Lesbian, and Straight Education Network, Hetrick-Martin, and Parents and Friends of Lesbians and Gays to demand its implementation. When politicians saw that a race-based group, a faith-based group, a freedom-of-speech-based group, and a series of sexual-orientation-based groups had united for the cause, they realized how strongly public opinion favored bullying prevention. For more on how teens were essential in passing Respect for All, see below.

The Respect for All Story

In 2008, years before New York State passed an anti-bullying law, New York City schools adopted Chancellor's Regulation A-832, known as Respect for All (RFA). The regulation requires schools to train students and teachers about tolerance and respect, establish an anonymous reporting system, designate an adult in the building to be in charge of responding to complaints in a timely manner, and draft and implement annual school safety plans.[1]

This policy was drafted because a variety of groups came together to demand action. There was the Sikh Coalition, an organization dedicated to protecting the rights of followers of the Sikh religion. Sikh men traditionally wear turbans, a practice that made many young people the target of bias-based harassment. There was the Asian American Legal Defense and Education Fund (AALDEF), an organization that provided legal defense to Asian Americans suffering from discrimination. There was the New York Civil Liberties Union (NYCLU), a group dedicated to protecting the freedom of expression. And there was a network of organizations supporting LGBTQ youth, including the Hetrick-Martin Institute; Parents, Families, and Friends of Lesbians and Gays of New York City; and the Gay, Lesbian, and Straight Education Network. As the word spread, groups representing immigrants, other faiths (such as Islam and Judaism), and women (such as Girls for Gender Equity, discussed in this book) also joined the coalition.

The groups behind RFA mobilized and testified at hearings held by the city council about the status of bullying in schools. They worked together to survey teachers and students and to write and publish reports proving that bullying is pervasive and severe. They met with local politicians to recruit allies and with the Department of Education to express their concerns. They held rallies to raise awareness among the general public.

Getting the regulation passed was not easy. The city council passed the first anti-bullying law with the help of these student groups in 2004, but Mayor Michael Bloomberg refused to enforce it. After four more years of struggling and negotiations, the groups came together with the city government to draft Chancellor's Regulation A-832 in 2008. A Chancellor's Regulation is a rule issued by the chancellor, or head, of the school system that all principals have to follow. It is up to the Department of Education to enforce it.

The passage of A-832 was a major victory, but it was just the first step. The group of allies continued to fight to expand the policy and to hold the government accountable for its implementation. For example, in 2010, just one academic year after A-832 was implemented, they came together to publish a "report card" for the policy, surveying students and teachers about their awareness of A-832 and its enforcement.[m] As of this writing (in 2013), they continued to meet regularly with the city council and the Department of Education to press for their demands.

Although this political work is challenging, it is helped along by the fact that so many diverse groups have a stake in it. This means that politicians from all over the city feel that they can benefit from supporting anti-bullying laws, given that all of them have some constituents who are invested in addressing and preventing bullying. It also means that groups can rely on each other to stand together in the face of opposition, and that they can share resources and ideas. Plus, teens and adults working together on the issue developed strong positive relationships with individuals who they might never have met otherwise. While creating change is never easy, having allies can make it a little bit easier—and a lot more fun.

Sometimes, celebrities and politicians become allies. Lady Gaga, for example, has publicly put her fame behind ending bullying through founding the Born This Way foundation (bornthiswayfoundation.org) in 2012, which is dedicated to building a movement of young people willing to combat bullying. Born This Way Foundation has developed creative ways to get teens involved in the fight against bullying. For example, they've established a massively multiplayer online social game called PlayBrave that invites players to become secret agents assigned to undertake missions promoting tolerance, kindness, social inclusion, and individuality. To find out more about PlayBrave, read about it below.

Politicians and administrators are also essential allies in any attempt to change laws and policies. If you are trying to get a new law passed or an existing law amended, you should talk to local politicians who can sponsor a bill or an amend-

PlayBrave

Even celebrities can't end bullying alone. That's why Lady Gaga's Born This Way Foundation has built a nationwide network of allies against bullying. For these allies, fighting bullying can be fun: that's because they can participate in the foundation's online game, PlayBrave.

According to the website, the PlayBrave is "about playing together to build a kinder, braver world."[n] Players sign up to be secret agents who undertake missions using social media such as Twitter, YouTube, Instagram, and Tumblr. They get points for successfully completing each mission and for getting "likes" from other players.

The missions encourage teens to be both creative and kind. Past missions include writing positive affirmations on Post-it notes and hanging them in public places, sharing a photo of yourself wearing a brave outfit in a public place, sharing a link to a video that makes you laugh and feel good about yourself, and making a new friend. Participants must confirm that they have completed the mission by sharing their work on social media outlets such as Tumblr and YouTube. Past entries, which are available on the site, include a picture of a yellow Post-it note saying, "Show your true colors, I bet they are beautiful," a YouTube video of a girl singing, a photograph of a Tinker Bell statue, and quotes about being kind to others.° Each of these fulfilled a mission created to help participants appreciate others as well as themselves. The site also contains a ticking clock that counts down the minutes remaining to complete each mission.

The game has thousands of players from all over the nation. According to the website, the players "believe that to play is to be free from fear. Through play we can remake the world into a place where we are all kinder and braver."ᴾ

If this mission speaks to you, join the game at www.playbrave.org. Or, start your own game with your own missions. To do so, discuss the following with a group of friends:

1. What social media do you use? Tumblr? YouTube? Twitter? Make a list.
2. What are your favorite creative activities? Drawing? Singing? Writing? Taking photographs? Make a list.
3. What are some messages you want to send about bullying? Make a list.
4. How can you use your artwork to get these messages out to the world in fun, creative, and affirming ways?
5. How can you use the social media available to you to promote your message beyond your group of friends?

After you have answered these questions, try designing some missions yourself. Do them with your friends and start a movement in your school or community.

ment. If you are more interested in working with your school system or your individual school, you should consider finding a superintendent or principal or administrator who sets district policy and may be able to implement a local policy without going through a legislative process. One of the best ways to find these kinds of allies is to make contact with staff members who work with these politicians and administrators. Staff members can help you schedule meetings, take advantage of opportunities like hearings and public forums, and advise you on how to position yourself so that your agenda will be attractive to politicians. They can help you gauge how hard to push people who are being unresponsive and make contact with media outlets that may be willing to take up your cause.

Political change takes time. Passing laws is not easy, and even when laws are passed, it can be a struggle to make sure they are enforced. You may have to keep working for months or even years before you see even the smallest progress. In addition to being patient, you must be persistent: the challenges of addressing policy cannot be an excuse for inaction. This means that you must keep meeting with your allies, publicizing your issue, and pushing policy makers to listen to you even if they are resistant, and even if you are feeling frustrated. This is another reason why when it comes to change, community matters so much. When you are ready to give up, it can be helpful to have friends and community who will support and encourage you. Likewise, when they are frustrated, encouraging and supporting them can make you feel powerful and strong.

Another challenge you may initially face is building a community of like-minded people. Finding friends and allies can feel especially overwhelming if you are currently being bullied, an experience that leaves many of us feeling hopeless, afraid, and alone. However, as you have read throughout this book, bullying negatively affects a huge number of teens, and many want to work together to stop it. One way to start building a community like this is to participate in groups in your area that are committed to stopping bullying. If you don't know of any and don't yet feel confident enough to start one yourself, you can look through this book for examples of online groups that could get you started. For example, the Bully Project (www.thebullyproject.org) connects teens through social media, as does PlayBrave (playbrave.org). When seeking online friends, it is best to try to go through organizations like these that screen individuals and moderate content, so as to avoid being a victim of cyberbullying or invasion of privacy.

Stopping Bullying Together

As you have seen throughout this book, change is not easy, but it is possible. Teens like you have made significant impact on anti-bullying policies throughout the nation. You have the power to improve your school, community, and world. All you need is a little bit of patience and persistence, a strong community, and a lot of hope.

But remember, no matter how many laws or policies you pass, how much training you receive, or allies you make, you hold the power to stop bullying with your everyday actions. Sometimes, the smallest act of kindness can make the biggest difference. Just by including someone in a conversation, discouraging a friend from teasing someone else, or smiling at someone across the cafeteria, you can promote a friendlier, gentler world.

You are powerful. Your actions make a difference. Stopping bullying starts with you.

Notes

1. Deborah Stone, *Policy Paradox*, 3rd ed. (New York: W. W. Norton and Company, 2001), 172.
2. Stone, *Policy Paradox*, 138.
3. Stone, *Policy Paradox*, 261.

---

a. Deborah Stone, *Policy Paradox*, 3rd ed. (New York: W. W. Norton and Company, 2001), 163–164.
b. Clara Ritger, "Teen Hopes Her Story of Living with HIV Helps Others," *Indianapolis Star*, June 22, 2013, http://www.usatoday.com/story/news/nation/2013/06/22/teen-hopes-her -story-of-living-with-hiv-helps-others/2449457/ (accessed July 9, 2013).
c. Ritger, "Teen Hopes."
d. Ritger, "Teen Hopes."
e. Ritger, "Teen Hopes."
f. Ritger, "Teen Hopes."
g. Ritger, "Teen Hopes."
h. Ritger, "Teen Hopes."
i. Julia Rappaport, "Interview with Director Lee Hirsch: 'Bullying Impacts Who We Are as a Nation,'" Facing History and Ourselves: Creating Safe Schools, March 19, 2013, http:// safeschools.facinghistory.org/content/interview-director-lee-hirsch-bullying-impacts-who -we-are-nation (accessed July 9, 2013).
j. Rappaport, "Interview with Director Lee Hirsch."
k. A. O. Scott, "Behind Every Harassed Child? A Whole Lot of Clueless Adults. 'Bully,' a documentary by Lee Hirsch." *New York Times*, March 29, 2012, http://movies.nytimes .com/2012/03/30/movies/bully-a-documentary-by-lee-hirsch.html?pagewanted=all&_r=0 (accessed July 9, 2013).
l. New York City Department of Education, *Regulation of the Chancellor A-832: Student-to-Student Bias-Based Harassment, Intimidation, and/or Bullying*, New York City Department of Education, October 12, 2011.
m. The Sikh Coalition, AALDEF, NYCLU, *Bullying in New York City Schools: Educators Speak Out, 2009–2010* (New York: The Sikh Coalition, AALDEF & NYCLU, 2010).

n. Born This Way Foundation, "About," PlayBrave, 2013, http://www.playbrave.org/about/ (accessed July 3, 2013).

o. Born This Way Foundation, "Gallery," PlayBrave, 2013, http://www.playbrave.org/gallery/ (accessed July 4, 2013).

p. Born This Way Foundation, "Gallery."

Recommended Reading

Alexie, Sherman. *The Absolutely True Diary of a Part Time Indian.* New York: Little, Brown Books for Young Readers, 2009.

American Association of University Women. *Hostile Hallways: Bullying, Teasing, and Sexual Harassment in Schools.* Washington, DC: American Association of University Women, 2001.

Anderson, Laurie Halse. *Twisted.* New York: Penguin Books, 2007.

Asher, Jay. *Thirteen Reasons Why.* New York: Razorbill, 2007.

Bajaj, Monisha, Ameena Ghaffar-Kucher, and Karishma Desai. *In the Face of Xenophobia: Lessons to Address the Bullying of South Asian Youth.* Washington, DC: South Asian Americans Leading Together, 2013.

Beam, Cris. *I Am J.* New York: Little, Brown and Company, 2011.

Brown, Jennifer. *Hate List.* New York: Little, Brown Books for Young Readers, 2010.

Budhos, Marina. *Tell Us We're Home.* New York: Atheneum Books for Young Readers, 2011.

Costello, Bob, Joshua Wachtel, and Ted Wachtel. *The Restorative Practices Handbook for Teachers, Disciplinarians, and Administrators.* Bethlehem, PA: International Institute for Restorative Practices, 2009.

DoSomething.org. *The Bully Report: Trends in Bullying Pulled from Student Facebook Interactions.* 2012. http://www.dosomething.org/bullyreport.

Estes, Eleanor. *The Hundred Dresses.* Orlando, FL: Harcourt, 2004.

Greytak, Emily, Joseph G. Kosciw, and Elizabeth M. Diaz. *Harsh Realities: The Experiences of Transgender Youth in Our Nation's Schools.* Washington, DC: Gay, Lesbian and Straight Education Network, 2009.

Hall, Megan Kelley and Carrie Jones, eds. *Dear Bully: 70 Authors Tell Their Stories.* New York: HarperTeen, 2011.

Hill, Catherine and Holly Kearl. *Crossing the Line: Sexual Harassment at School.* Washington, DC: American Association of University Women, 2011. http://www.aauw.org/research/crossing-the-line/.

Hyde, Catherine Ryan. *Diary of a Witness.* New York: Alfred A. Knopf, 2009.

Kevorkian, Meline and Robin D'Antona. *101 Facts about Bullying That Everyone Should Know.* Lanham, MD: Rowman & Littlefield Education, 2008.

Meminger, Neesha. *Shine, Coconut Moon.* New York: Margaret K. McElderry Books, 2009.

Meyer, Stephanie, John Meyer, Emily Sperber, and Heather Alexander, eds. *Bullying under Attack: True Stories Written by Teen Victims, Bullies and Bystanders (Teen Ink)*. Deerfield, FL: HCI Press, 2013.

Olweus, Dan. *Bullying at School*. Malden, MA: Blackwell Publishing, 1993.

Palacio, R. J. *Wonder*. New York: Knopf Books for Young Readers, 2012.

Preller, James. *Bystander*. New York: Macmillan, 2009.

Satyal, Rakesh. *Blue Boy*. New York: Kensington, 2009.

Shapiro, Ouisie. *Bullying and Me: Schoolyard Stories*. Chicago, IL: Albert Whitman and Company, 2010.

Smith, Joanne, Mandy Van Deven, and Meghan Huppuch. *Hey Shorty! A Guide to Combating Sexual Harassment in Schools and On the Streets*. New York: Feminist Press, 2011.

Stone, Deborah. *Policy Paradox: The Art of Political Decision Making*. Revised Edition. New York: W.W. Norton and Company, 2002.

Swearer, Susan M. *Bullying Prevention and Intervention: Realistic Strategies for Schools*. New York: Guilford Press, 2009.

Thompson, Holly. *Orchards*. New York: Ember, 2011.

Williams-Garcia, Rita. *Jumped*. New York: Amistad Press, 2009.

Winfield, Cynthia. *Gender Identity: The Ultimate Teen Guide*. Lanham, MD: Scarecrow Press, 2007.

Youth Communication and Hope Vanderberg, eds. *Vicious: True Stories by Teens about Bullying (Real Teen Voices Series)*. Minneapolis, MN: Free Spirit Publishing, 2012.

Glossary

bully: an individual who uses violence to intimidate, harass, or otherwise inflict harm upon another person

bully-victim: an individual who simultaneously experiences violence and inflicts violence upon others

bystander: an individual who sees bullying happening; also called a witness

cisgender: an individual who identifies with the same gender as his or her biological sex

cultural violence: any idea, belief, or attitude that creates an atmosphere where hurtful actions become socially acceptable

cyberbullying: bullying that takes place in virtual spaces or online, including bullying that occurs through websites, text messages, or e-mail

direct violence: harmful behavior that prevents us from being who we are and living our lives in the way we choose; can be physical, verbal, psychological, sexual, or emotional

gender: our society's ideas of what it means to be male or female

gender nonconforming: used to describe individuals or behavior that challenge traditional ideas about masculinity and femininity

identity: personal characteristics that affect the way people treat us and how much power we have in society

implementation: the process of putting a law or policy into practice

law: a rule passed by bodies of elected officials, such as state assemblies, senates, or city councils, and enforced by local, state, and national governments

lever of change: a tool for changing the way a community responds to an issue such as bullying

oppressed group: a group of individuals who share an identity that does not traditionally have power within our social structure and that has suffered a history of discrimination

policy: a rule adopted by organizations or localities, such as individual schools or districts

restorative justice: an approach to discipline that requires those convicted of wrongdoing to work with the community to make up for their mistakes

sex: biological characteristics that are unique to males and females

structural violence: the process by which certain groups of individuals who have power grant themselves access to more resources than those who are less powerful, which can result in harm and discrimination against those with fewer assets

transgender: an individual who is born with an ambiguous sex or who chooses a gender identity that is different than his or her biological sex characteristics

victim: an individual who experiences bullying

violence: any act that harms us emotionally, physically, or psychologically and that prevents us from feeling comfortable being who we are and expressing ourselves

witness: an individual who sees bullying happening; also called a bystander

Index

Stone, Deborah, 184–185

street harassment. *See* sexual harassment

Student Non-Discrimination Act (SNDA),
83, 88, 167

suicide, xii, xiii–xiv, 35, 45, 56, 81, 88, 99,
101, 102–103, 104, 137, 158–159, 195;
resources, 45

Swank, Jared, 155–156

Teaching Tolerance, 50, 76, 178

Teen Dating Violence Awareness Month,
147

Title IX, 80, 83, 88, 119, 121–124;
coordinator, 121–123, 126; history,
121–122; sports, 80, 121, 122

To, Wilson, 2–3

training, 76, 90, 123, 125, 126, 147, 159,
160, 162, 168, 173, 178–180, 188,
191–194, 203; Know Your Rights,
191–192

Tran, Loan, 86–87

transgender, xiii, 2, 21, 39, 40, 79, 80–81,
95, 99, 155–156, 169; resources, 89,
135; sexual harassment, 115–116, 118

Twitter, 62, 63, 95, 102–103, 104, 105,
107–108, 128, 201

U-Visa, 145–146

Van Zanten, Sarah, 141

victim, xi–xii, 4, 7–8, 12, 15, 16, 20–21,
24, 27, 35–53, 55, 59, 71, 159, 160,
168, 172, 174, 186, 195–196; age,
42; arts, 47; bias-based harassment,
73, 83–84, 169; books about, 43–44;
characteristics, 36–38, 83–84;
cyberbullying, 98–102, 105; dating
violence, 136–139, 143; definition, 7;
effects of being a victim, xi–xii, 44–45,

118–121, 136; healing, 27, 28, 46–49,
60, 64, 177–178, 188; identity, 38–42,
47; power, 38–42, 66–67; prevention,
49–51; sexual harassment, 113, 117–
121, 123, 125. *See also* bully-victims;
witness

violence, xi, xii, 1–3, 5, 11, 12–14, 20–23,
25–27, 35, 37, 47, 57, 71, 73, 116,
126, 131–133, 139, 143, 153–154, 157,
159, 161, 165, 167–169, 173, 175,
180, 183, 186, 191, 195–196; bullies,
12–14; bully-victims, 45–46; cultural,
1–2, 5, 39, 90–91; cyberbullying, 59,
102, 104; direct, 1, 12, 77, 84, 132,
151; emotional, 131–132; masculinity,
20–22; resources, 15, 134–135; sexual,
132–133; structural, 2, 5, 82, 83

Violence Against Women Act (VAWA),
145

wealth. *See* economic class

weight, 161, 175–176

witness, xi, 2, 3, 4, 7, 8, 55–70, 99, 101,
105, 123, 126, 140, 142, 144–145,
160, 172, 177, 178, 186, 192; adults,
39; cyberbullying, 61, 62, 63, 99, 101;
dating violence, 140, 142, 144–145;
defender, 57–58, 60–69; definition, xii,
7, 55; effects of being a witness, 55–57;
frequency, 55; sexual harassment, 113,
120, 123, 126; types, 57–59

Young, Sheryl, 85–86

Youth Communication, 13, 61, 175–176

Youth Empowered to Act, 81–82

YouTube, xiii–xiv, 85, 90, 104, 110, 201;
reporting abuse, 63

zero tolerance, 154

About the Author

Dr. Mathangi Subramanian, EdD, has over a decade of experience in the field of education. A former public school teacher and community educator, she served as a senior policy analyst for New York city council speaker Christine Quinn, where she helped strengthen anti-bullying policies, organized a community forum on cyberbullying, and successfully advocated for including restorative approaches in the citywide school discipline code. As an adjunct professor at Columbia University Teachers College, she taught Human and Social Dimensions of Peace and Television and the Development of Youth to preservice teachers and future international development professionals. Her children's stories about nonviolence, activism, and social justice have appeared in *Kahani*, *Skipping Stones*, and the *Hindu's Young World*. She is also the co-editor of *US Education in a World of Migration: Implications for Policy and Practice*, published in 2014.